Sons of the Buddha

SONS
of the BUDDHA

❧

THE EARLY LIVES OF THREE
EXTRAORDINARY THAI MASTERS

Kamala Tiyavanich

WISDOM PUBLICATIONS • BOSTON

Wisdom Publications
199 Elm Street
Somerville MA 02144 USA
www.wisdompubs.org

Library of Congress Cataloging-in-Publication Data
Tiyavanich, Kamala, 1948–
 Sons of the Buddha : the early lives of three extraordinary Thai masters / Kamala Tiyavanich.
    p. cm.
 Includes bibliographical references and index.
 ISBN 0-86171-536-5 (pbk. : alk. paper)
 1. Phra Thepwisutthimethi (Nguam), 1906–1993. 2. Phra Thepwisut-thimethi (Pan), 1911– 3. Jumnien, Ajahn, 1936– 4. Buddhist monks—Thailand—Biography. 5. Buddhism—Thailand—History—20th century. I. Title.
 BQ556.T585 2007
 294.3092'2593—dc22
 [B]
                                    2007021081

11 10 09 08 07
5 4 3 2 1

Cover and interior design by Gopa & Ted2, Inc. Set in Sabon 10.25/15. Cover: Temple Boy in Siam, circa 1908. Author photo: Dylan Litchman

For the younger generation

CONTENTS

PART I. AJAHN BUDDHADASA
(BOYHOOD NAME: NGUAM)

PART II. AJAHN PANYA
(BOYHOOD NAME: PAN)

PART III. AJAHN JUMNIEN
(BOYHOOD NAME: JUMNIEN)

Maps and Illustrations

FIG. 1. MAP OF THAILAND.

Map labels (from north to south, west to east):

Chiang Rai
Maehongson
Phayao
Nan
Chiang Mai
Lampang
Lamphun
Phrae
Nongkhai
Uttaradit
Loei
Sukhothai
Udonthani
Sakon Nakhon
Nakhon Phanom
Tak
Phitsanulok
Khonkaen
Kalasin
Mukdahan
Kamphaeng-phet
Phetchabun
Phichit
Mahasa-rakham
Nakhon Sawan
Chaiyaphum
Roi-et
Yasothon
Uthaithani
Nakhon Ratchasima
Ubon-ratchathani
Chainat
Suphan-buri
Buriram
Surin
Sisaket
Kanchanaburi
Nakhon Nayok
Prachinburi
Nakhon Pathom
Ratburi
Chachoengsao
Phetburi
Chonburi
Rayong
Chanthaburi
Trat
Prachuapkhirikhan
Chumphon
Ranong
Suratthani
Phangnga
Nakhon Si-thammarat
Krabi
Phuket
Phatthalung
Trang
Satun
Songkhla
Pattani
Yala
Narathiwat

Gulf of Thailand

Andaman Sea

Malaysia

1 Singburi
2 Lopburi
3 Ang Thong
4 Saraburi
5 Ayutthaya
6 Pathumthani
7 Nonthaburi
8 Bangkik
9 Samut Prakan
10 Samut Sakhon
11 Samut Songkhram

I N *Sons of the Buddha* three extraordinary Thai monks reimagine their formative years in Peninsular Thailand, before the enormous shifts in the economy and the intellectual order that began with the modernizing reforms of the late nineteenth century. This book recreates a lost world with great concreteness and immediacy.

On a map, Peninsular Thailand depends from the Asian mainland, an improbably thin ribbon of land wedged between the Andaman Sea and the Gulf of Siam. At its narrow waist, you could probably ride a bicycle across in a day or two. Flying over its compressed precincts, you see beaches, rice plains, forests, and low mountains jumbled together, so one is never far from either the sea or the forest haunt of wild animals. Growing up here meant learning to navigate around crocodiles or finding out that the family buffalo had been taken in the night by tigers.

Archeological evidence reveals layers of diverse Hindu and Buddhist religious influences dating from as early as the fifth century C.E. and culminating in the overwhelming presence today of Theravada Buddhism, at least among the Thai speakers. Much of this is dramatically visible in the clay votive tablets that litter caves in the limestone mountains rising from the plains.

We may imagine that a place is just a physical fact, an arrangement of forms located in space, but these vivid memories offer a profound challenge to that view. What steers the ordinary course of life and shapes the appearing and arising of things, people, and actions is the pervasive presence of Dharma. But it is equally the case that the kind of remarkable persons these monks became was also inextricably tied to the places with which they were engaged.

This is a beautiful, life-enhancing book. It is full of wonderful stories and adventures. You are swept up into an unfamiliar world made tangible and massively present.

STANLEY O'CONNOR
Emeritus professor, history of art,
Cornell University

AJAHN BUDDHADASA, the most famous name in socially engaged Buddhist philosophy and practice in modern Thailand, was an inspired cook from the age of eight. Taught to cook as a child, Buddhadasa throughout his life cultivated the culinary arts and discussed food, with the assumption that it was a vital concern worthy of thought and attention. This image of Buddhadasa is an indispensable supplement to the philosophical and political depictions of Buddhist monks in other books.

What is the relationship between cooking and Buddhism? The importance of the cook and the kitchen in Japanese Zen monasteries has been noticed, and there are books detailing various Zen instructions for cooking in which the preparation of food and the spiritual paths of Buddhist practice are understood to be intimately related. Introductory books on Buddhism, such as Rupert Gethin's *Foundations of Buddhism*, contain observations on dietary matters in different Buddhist cultures that often center on the question of whether monks should be vegetarians (Tibetans: no; Chinese monks: yes; Theravada monks: it all depends on what goes into the alms bowl). But generally speaking, the discussion of Buddhism on the one hand and, on the other, observations about that most concretely cultural of human practices—the transformation of the raw into the cooked—take place in different regions of our contemporary culture, different aisles of the bookstore. Buddhism is philosophical, meditatively spiritual, universalizing, and inward, whereas cooking is materially and ethnographically concrete, of the body, and refracted through the varieties of human cultures.

Sons of the Buddha is the third book by Kamala Tiyavanich which refuses this separation between spirit and matter, between Buddhism and the most concrete and particular aspects of a specific Buddhist culture, that of Siam (now Thailand). Kamala's works present Buddhism in Siam as immersed in the concrete details of a particular culture at a historically specific time—the era during which many regional traditions and local forms of Buddhist culture were gradually transformed by the centralizing modernity of Bangkok. In her writings Kamala both preserves and transmits a strongly atmospheric sense of the Siamese past while also illuminating the differences between that past and the modern present. She understands the interdependence of religion, culture, and psyche and shows that there is really no such thing as "Buddhism" separate from innumerable cultural factors. The image of Theravada Buddhism in Thailand as text based, for instance, itself is a consequence of the historical forces at play in the transition to modernity, particularly the pressure from the state for monks to study textbooks rather than to learn the oral tradition from local teachers. Buddhist monks who were once healers, carpenters, and cooks—as well as meditators and tellers of tales—have in the modern period become primarily scholars and teachers of written texts.

Kamala's work subverts a sense of the naturalness of this historical change and performs a kind of dialectical overcoming of the modern period. By this I mean that she has written books that are based on and transmit a fundamentally oral tradition. Recognizing that the particulars of cultural life as well as their historical changes are most vividly conveyed through narrative, Kamala records in writing the tales of the past, transcribing and weaving together a tapestry of stories from sources both textual and oral. These books are antidotes to our ingrained tendencies to separate aspects of human life and to assume the universality of our own quite particular forms of experience.

Sons of the Buddha, like Kamala's *The Buddha in the Jungle*, is a pleasure to read. It is full of adventure stories—some amusing, others scary or sad, all of them compelling. But it is also a serious contribution to the study of Buddhism in the contemporary world, calling us back to thickly described cultural particulars and reminding us that learning how to meditate and learning to cook may be more closely related than we think.

BRIAN KARAFIN

Professor of religious studies, Ithaca College

I AM DELIGHTED to offer this foreword to Kamala Tiyavanich's third book on the lives and cultural backgrounds of Thai monks. Kamala's work gives us an important view behind the surface of modern Theravada Buddhism. We hear stories of popular American teachers practicing in places like Burma and Thailand, but what of their teachers? Where did they come from? And the teachers of those teachers? What shaped them? How did they grow up? What cultures nurtured them? Kamala has made a life's work of charting these resources. In the process, she helps to clear up assumptions, biases, and other distortions created by Western ignorance and fantasy. This is crucial in both the West and in Asia, though for differing reasons.

Given the shallow roots of our own culture (America), we can appreciate the richness of ancestry, local cultures, and traditions that Kamala documents. It is unfortunate that the historical record between the early centuries recorded in the classic Pali texts and quite recent times is vague and sparse, with large lacunae. The period in which Kamala specializes (late nineteenth and early twentieth centuries) requires difficult, ingenious hunting through obscure sources. The standard sources, often royal, have other agendas that provide only limited history. In the biographies of monks, the accounts of early Western visitors and missionaries, and obscure temple publications, she finds telling details that lead us into another time and place. She is also skillful in contextualizing these details so that we can better understand them in their own terms. I know of no better way to understand the soil that has nurtured modern Buddhism. A visit to Southeast Asia today cannot reveal so much of a past that has been largely displaced by development imported from the West.

Once influential monks become old and venerable, stories about them accrue that often enough serve the wishes of devotees more than the Dhamma or history of real-life human struggles. As a direct personal student of two of these monks, I was continually abashed by the fantasies told about them, no matter how much the monks disavowed such stories—"He's so humble" being a common rationale. How refreshing, here, to have stories of the monks' childhoods and early monastic experiences that don't extol their saintliness. In his oral memoirs, portions of which are included here, Ajahn Buddhadasa Bhikkhu took pains to portray himself as an ordinary human being who, for example, misbehaved and was punished by his mother, and took interest in "worldly pursuits" like cooking, music, and photography. Nonetheless, an exceptionally bright, inquisitive, precocious child comes through. Foundations of his genius, of his striving to understand, of his creativity, are visible here, as is the real-life child. These are complemented by the different backgrounds and styles of two other important Southern Thai monks, one his younger brother in Dhamma, and the other practically a neighbor, though of a subsequent generation.

For us Western students of Buddhism and practitioners of "Vipassana," who blithely incorporate aspects of Buddhism into our attitudes, values, assumptions, and uncritical beliefs, and thereby recreate Buddhism in our own cultural image, Kamala's work gives us an opportunity to question and examine what we are doing. How do cultures like Siam, shaped by a millennium or more of interaction with Buddhism, compare with our modern, capitalistic, Christian-influenced consumer culture and our secular liberalism? It seems to me that the differences are important and profound, not to be shrugged off as "just the past." A task of history is to keep the past meaningful; ignoring it leads to needless suffering. I hope that Kamala's work inspires us to make the most of this opportunity. To honor and understand our Asian elders, we must know where they came from, the environments and experiences that shaped them. Only then can we shape equally valid cultural expressions of Buddhism today. To those who wonder what this has to do with practice, I suggest they reflect on how their own culture—or lack thereof—generates this very question.

SANTIKARO
Liberation Park

PREFACE

T HIS WORK has a long history. During the fall semester of 1993 I taught a course at Cornell University titled "Buddhism Exemplified: The Lives of Asian Masters in Various Traditions." Using the life stories of a number of Buddhist masters as texts, this course introduced the students to the human face of Buddhist traditions and helped them understand how a religion could flourish by accommodating local customs, beliefs, and practices. It was the first time that the Asian Studies Department and the Religious Studies Program offered a course about Buddhism as a lived tradition. The students who enrolled in this course took it as an elective. They were majoring in various disciplines that usually had very little to do with religion.

For their final assignment I asked the students to write an essay describing what they had learned from the Buddhist masters. It was evident that what the students learned depended on their own life experiences. A junior in engineering admitted, "I took this course to learn about Buddhism and Buddhist experiences, but little did I know that what I would actually learn, through the life stories of monks and nuns, was a means to overcome obstacles in my life." A freshman in biology wrote, "These Buddhist masters and mystics demonstrated the universal qualities of Buddhism in crossing cultural lines, while at the same time revealing a set of valuable lessons to be applied to everyday life." A junior in psychology wrote, "If I remember one thing from the monks' life stories, I hope that it is this: not to try to own my emotions. If I can let go of some of my feelings of self-importance, I think I will be a better person for it."

In 1993 few published biographies or autobiographies of Buddhist masters in Southeast Asia or in Sri Lanka were available in English, and in these only a few pages were devoted to the early lives of the masters. My students were curious about the monks' lives before they were ordained. What time did children get up in the morning before schools reached their villages? What daily chores were they expected to do? Did boys and girls do the same work? Before radios, televisions, and movies, what did youngsters do for fun? When these masters were children, were they naughty or well behaved? As adolescents, did they rebel against their parents? Did they smoke or drink? Did they have girlfriends?

Teaching this course confirmed my decision to write a series of books about Buddhist masters and village life in Siam. *Sons of the Buddha* tells the early life stories of three well-known Thai preachers: Ajahn Buddhadasa (1906–93), Ajahn Panya (b. 1911), and Ajahn Jumnien (b. 1936). Their stories have been drawn both from my own interviews and from the monks' recollections as recorded and written by their monastic disciples. Of the three monks, information about Buddhadasa's childhood is the most fragmented. In their Dhamma teachings Ajahn Panya and Ajahn Jumnien often spoke about their childhood experiences, and these recollections have been recorded.

All three masters grew up during the period that Thai environmentalists call the Jungle-Village era, which ended in 1957, the beginning of the Forest-Invasion period. During this era most of the land beyond the river valleys was covered by forest. People back then procured a great deal of their food from the natural environment: from farmland, forests, rivers, and the sea. Siam (as Thailand was called before 1939) was mostly rural and blessed with what appeared to be unlimited natural resources. Villagers then were deeply connected with nature and spent a lot of time outdoors, walking barefoot. Boys and girls knew how to cook, clean house, tend gardens, take care of livestock, haul water, and help their parents obtain food.

The *wat* (temple and monastery) was still the social and religious center of the community. Even after modern education was introduced, parents, schoolteachers, and monks shared similar values concerning child rearing. "Spare the rod, spoil the child" was a guiding principle in Siam. Early on, parents established their expectations. The child knew what the consequences would be for willful violation of the rules, especially if the offense was repeated. Parents assigned chores suitable to a child's age. Even toddlers were taught to swim. As they became older, children learned to be self-reliant, working outdoors on their own. When they were away from their villages, youngsters were expected to take safety precautions. If a problem occurred when a child was not under parental supervision, that child had to solve it alone.

Growing up in a village or small town, each of the three monks featured here had plenty of opportunities to learn from adversity. They helped their parents earn a living and did not shrink from work. A well-known line from Wordsworth, "The child is father of the man," captures the gist of this book. Childhood formed the character of these Buddhist masters; it led to their fearlessness and strength as monks and teachers of Dhamma.

According to an old Thai expression, when a young man turns twenty and is ordained, he becomes a son of the Buddha. His parents usually expect him to become a monk for only a short time: a single rains retreat of three months. Some well-known masters in the twentieth century intended to ordain temporarily, but after they found the renouncer's life suited them well, they remained sons of the Buddha for life.

NOTE ON ROMANIZATION
AND TRANSLATION

IN TRANSLATING monks' recollections I have followed the romanization system of the Royal Institute of Thailand. One exception is the word *ajahn* (teacher or master). Instead of *achan*, the institute's spelling, I write *ajahn*, because it reflects both local pronunciation and English usage more faithfully. Names of Thai monks, such as "Nguam" and "Panya," conform to the Royal Institute's spelling, unless the name has a preferred English spelling: "Buddhadasa" instead of "Phutthathat," and "Jumnien" instead of "Chumnian." The first time a Pali or Thai term is mentioned, it appears in italics; after that, it is in plain type.

Besides the title "Ajahn" (teacher), laypeople, young monks, and novices generally call elder monks "Luang Pho" (Venerable Father) or "Luang Pu" (Venerable Grandfather) or "Luang Ta" (also Venerable Grandfather). I try to keep these Thai terms of address.

In order not to confuse the general reader, all the place names in the passages quoted from Western travelers' accounts have been romanized according to the Royal Institute system used today.

In this book I use the Pali words *Dhamma*, *nibbana*, *Tipitaka*, and *arahant* instead of their Sanskrit equivalents, *Dharma*, *nirvana*, *Tripitaka*, and *arhat*. Sources of quotations and information have been grouped at the end of the book. Works mentioned are by no means the only books or articles on a given subject; I list only those from which I drew material.

I am indebted to Santikaro for providing a partial translation of

Ajahn Buddhadasa's *Lao wai mua wai sonthaya*, since the complete work has yet to be translated into English. In the case of works for which no translator is given and that have not yet been published in English, the translations are my own. When translating the monks' recollections I have attempted to capture both the essence of their ideas and the tone and color of their expressions. In quoting from interviews I have tried to translate the monks' recollections literally. Sometimes, however, I omit repetitions or switch the order of sentences within paragraphs to produce a natural flow in English.

The country called Siam was renamed "Thailand" by Prime Minister Phibun in 1939. The words "Thailand" and "Thai" are used in post-1939 contexts. As a result of the nationalist policies of the Phibun government, the word "Thai" came to encompass all ethnic groups in Thailand, not just the Siamese.

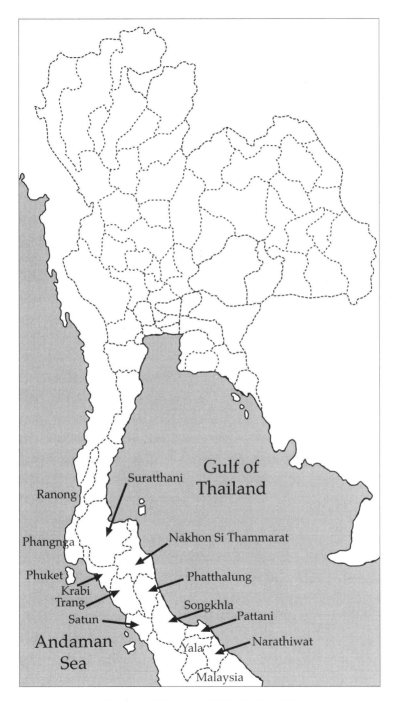

FIG. 2. PROVINCES OF SOUTHERN THAILAND.

SONS OF THE BUDDHA tells the early life stories of three well-known master preachers from southern Thailand. Ajahn Buddhadasa (1906–93), the founder of Suan Mokkh (Garden of Liberation), lived in Chaiya; Ajahn Panya (b. 1911), the first abbot of Wat Chonprathan, was born in Phatthalung; Ajahn Jumnien (b. 1936), the founder of Tiger Cave Monastery, grew up in Nakhon Si Thammarat.

Buddhist customs and practices in the South had always been very different from those in other regions of Thailand. Chaiya, Phatthalung, and Nakhon Si Thammarat were once ancient kingdoms, each with its own religious traditions. Before Theravada Buddhism arrived, sometime between the twelfth and fourteenth centuries (depending on the kingdom), a wide range of religious traditions were already thriving in the region, known today as Peninsular Thailand. These traditions were either observed in different kingdoms during the same period or practiced in the same kingdom at different times. Hinduism along with Mahayana, Vajrayana, and Hinayana Buddhism (especially the Mulasarvastivada sect) flourished at various times and places before the arrival of Theravada Buddhism. When, centuries later, in 1972, Ajahn Buddhadasa invited His Holiness the Dalai Lama of Tibet to visit Suan Mokkh at Chaiya, the Dalai Lama taught the Prajnaparamita Sutra to the Theravada monks in residence there. But in a historical sense, the Dalai Lama was visiting a land that had once been a center of Vajrayana Buddhism.

FIG. 3. THE DALAI LAMA AND AJAHN BUDDHADASA AT SUAN MOKKH, 1972.

In ancient times one of the important religious practices in Peninsular Thailand was the making of votive tablets, called *phra phim* in Thai and *tsha tsha* in Tibetan. An art historian who has studied religious traditions in southern Thailand describes votive tablets as "small Buddhist icons, usually made out of baked or unbaked clay by a press-mould technique, a process that has been used for many hundreds of years to produce religious objects.... The stamping was repeated over and over as a method to gain merit and as a meditative devotional exercise similar to counting the rosary." Monks also left behind tablets they stamped as they traveled. Votive tablets showing buddhas and various bodhisattvas, such as Avalokitesvara and Amitabha, can still be found scattered in the high caves of Chaiya, Nakhon Si Thammarat, Phatthalung, and other southern provinces.

In local traditions Buddhist masters used votive tablets or amulets as vehicles through which to teach *Dhamma* (dharma). Local masters understood that ordinary people needed to possess something sacred for their psychological security. The making and use of amulets, castigated as magic or superstition by rationalists, was actually guided by the practice of moral virtues (*sila-dhamma*). State Buddhism, which has its roots in Prince Mongkut's reforms, opposes superstition. Phra Paisal, a Buddhist thinker inspired by Ajahn Buddhadasa's teachings, wrote that the reformers did not "get rid of" superstitions, they merely "expelled them from the wats." Consequently, the making of once-sacred objects fell into the hands of moneymakers who were outside the influence of Buddhist masters. By the second half of the twentieth century, amulets had become products of commerce. Once made by hand, amulets are now cranked out in huge numbers by machines. Anyone who has money can buy "sacred" amulets without making any moral commitment, without any need to practice sila-dhamma. Amulets that were once simply given away by local masters, as reminders of the teachings and the protections offered to practitioners of the Dhamma, are now sold as commodities or collectors' items.

Buddhadasa was born during a time of great change. The monastic community in Bangkok was well aware of the criticisms that Western visitors leveled against Buddhist practices in Siam, which, in the Christians' view, lacked unity, a fixed hierarchy, and devotion to scholarship. They thought Buddhist meditation was unimportant. The Sangha Act of 1902 brought monks of various lineages under the umbrella of a national Sangha centered in Bangkok. To foster a national consciousness, the monarchy introduced modern secular education throughout the land and authorized significant changes in religious instruction that required monks to study new Dhamma textbooks rather than learn through oral transmission and ancient palm-leaf manuscripts under the tutelage of revered local masters. Buddhist sermons were standardized in style as well as form, and all monks had to preach according to the guidelines set by the established Sangha. As the Sangha was transformed into an extension of the state, monks became less responsive to their own communities. Though these changes did not occur overnight, local and regional differences with respect to custom, teaching, and practice were gradually eroded or eradicated.

The bureaucratization of the Sangha and the standardization of Buddhist teachings and practices have over time had a stifling effect on Thai Buddhism. State Buddhism encouraged monks to study academic texts, pass examinations, do administrative work, raise money for repairs or construction of monastic buildings, and perform rituals and ceremonies according to prescribed guidelines. The practice of meditation and the art of preaching were not promoted. Master preachers became increasingly rare.

One senior monk, Venerable Rattana-thatchamuni (Baen), the Sangha head of Nakhon Si Thammarat, understood what it took to be a preacher. According to Venerable Rattana (1884–1978), a preacher must have a pleasant appearance, a strong voice, quick wit, great courage, and the ability to take criticism well. A preacher must have "a skin as tough as that of a rhinoceros." And "he must have common sense, know how to turn everyday life experience into Dhamma lessons, an ability to judge his audience and never go over their heads."

All three masters, Ajahn Buddhadasa, Ajahn Panya, and Ajahn Jumnien, were endowed with these essential qualities. It took tremendous discipline, stamina, psychological insight, and long training for each of these monks to mature into a master preacher. In their younger days, the three monks trained themselves to preach at local monasteries in southern Thailand. They were skilled not only in the art of solo preaching but also in double-pulpit preaching, when two debating preachers occupied adjacent pulpits. People liked to hear a local monk engage in a Dhamma debate with a monk from another town or, better yet, from Bangkok. Double-pulpit preaching usually drew huge crowds.

In May 1932 the young Buddhadasa left his studies at Wat Pathum in Bangkok and returned to his hometown in Chaiya, now a district in Suratthani province. He moved to an abandoned monastery and spent the rains retreat alone, studying the Tipitaka (canonical Buddhist texts). Soon he began extracting "gems" of Dhamma principles from the Pali texts. Over the years Ajahn Buddhadasa's interpretation of Dhamma, which included the noble truths (*ariya-sacca*), non-self (*anatta*), and dependent origination (*paticca-samuppada*), came to differ radically from the orthodox interpretation taught in Bangkok.

By this time the young monk Panya had been studying at Wat Mahathat (locally known as Wat Boromthat) in Nakhon Si Thammarat. It was here that Panya began training himself to preach (see chapter 26).

In June 1932, shortly after a coup in Bangkok led by military officials and their allies in the civilian bureaucracy brought an end to the absolute monarchy, a Buddhist monk named Lokanatha came to visit Bangkok. Born in Italy in 1897, his original name was Salvatore Cioffi. He had received a bachelor's degree in science from Columbia University in New York City, but at twenty-eight he was ordained as a Buddhist monk in Burma and went to practice meditation in the Himalayas and in Sri Lanka. In a lecture he gave in Bangkok, Venerable Lokanatha announced his plan to propagate Buddhism in Europe and the United States and to recruit "lionhearted monks and novices" to go with him to study in India so that they could preach in English. In those days in Siam it was a rare sight to see a Buddhist monk who was a Westerner. King Prachatipok (Rama VII), the first constitutional monarch, was confident enough in Ven. Lokanatha's project to donate his own money to pay the passport fees of one hundred monks and novices who wished to go with Lokanatha. Quite a few members of the People's Party were also supportive of Lokanatha's project. Followers of Lokanatha were required to observe ascetic (*thudong*) practices; they had to be vegetarians and travel on foot unless they were offered the use of a vehicle.

When Panya heard the news about Ven. Lokanatha's recruiting "lionhearted monks," he traveled to Bangkok to join the Italian monk. Of the hundred monks who answered Lokanatha's call, ten were from the southern region. All the Thai monks traveled with Lokanatha from Bangkok to Nakhon Sawan, where they stopped to rest, and the Italian monk gave Dhamma talks to local people. Lokanatha's sermons were delivered in English and translated by Khru Liam, a Thai teacher who had studied in England on a King's Scholarship. Khru Liam was the only layman allowed to travel with Lokanatha's party. In Nakhon Sawan more young monks and novices joined Lokanatha. The youngest novice ordained by Lokanatha was a thirteen-year-old boy named Karuna, a native of Paknampho.

When the monks arrived in Sukhothai, Panya suggested that the ten southern monks travel together in a small group, explaining that they would be able to travel faster by themselves. The ten monks then walked through forests and crossed over hills until they reached the district of Mae Sot, from which they crossed the Moei River into Burma. Having no *klot* (an umbrella tent with mosquito net), they slept under trees.

When the ten monks arrived in Rangoon, they learned that one hundred more monks from Chiang Mai had joined Ven. Lokanatha. These were newly ordained monks. Although their journey was beset with hardship, Panya and his fellow monks were moved by the generosity of the Burmese people, who provided the Thai monks with food, shelter, robes, and medicine. After five months of traveling, however, Panya and a number of his fellow monks realized that they no longer wished to continue their trip to India, so they turned back. By the time they got back to Bangkok, they had been wandering for eight months.

Panya then went to visit his parents in Phatthalung, only to discover that his father had died while he was on his way to Burma. When he went to spend the 1934 rains retreat at Wat Uthai, a small monastery in Songkhla, a province south of Phatthalung, Panya had more opportunities to train himself to preach. At this monastery most of the monks were between seventy and eighty years old. Ajahn Panya was one of just a few young monks, and he was invited to give a sermon every night. Instead of following standardized sermons recited from texts, he always expounded the Dhamma extemporaneously in the local dialect. He used anecdotes from people's daily lives to teach the Dhamma. When there were conflicts or misguided decisions being made in the local community, he pointed them out to the audience. The locals who often came to listen to his sermons were pedicab drivers, workers from the nearby brickyard, and vendors who lived at the market near the wat. Since Panya had endured hardships of his own, working people found what he preached believable. During the two years that he stayed in

Songkhla, Ajahn Panya's reputation as a talented preacher, able to engage in solo, two-pulpit, three-pulpit, or even five-pulpit preaching, spread far and wide.

Ajahn Panya received invitations from people all over Songkhla to preach at funerals, weddings, and wat ceremonies. His experiences serve as a reminder that a preacher needed to have physical strength and stamina. If the villagers who invited him lived on a river or a canal, Ajahn Panya went there by boat. If the village was not by a river, Ajahn Panya got there on foot, walking all day alongside paddy fields and through forests. On one occasion Ajahn Panya arrived at a village around 9 P.M. after a six-hour hike. The young preacher immediately took a quick bath to refresh himself and went straight to the pulpit to deliver his sermon.

Before he met Ajahn Buddhadasa in person, Ajahn Panya had read Buddhadasa's Dhamma teachings, which had been published in a journal issued from Suan Mokkh. In 1936 Ajahn Panya went to spend the rains retreat at Suan Mokkh. From then on the two southern monks became Dhamma brothers and vowed to work together for the Buddha. Decades later, Ajahn Panya's disciples described the first meeting of the two monks with the Thai expression "The tiger met the lion." It was the beginning of a spiritual friendship that lasted until Ajahn Buddhadasa's death in 1993.

By the middle of the twentieth century, the Sangha was playing an increasingly peripheral role in the lives of urban people. The "modern" form of Buddhism had come to be regarded as traditional. Under the control of the state for decades, the institutionalized Sangha lost its role in providing intellectual and spiritual leaders. By changing the way Dhamma was usually taught, Ajahn Buddhadasa and Ajahn Panya were able to capture the attention of urban elites. Although Buddhadasa had been living at Suan Mokkh, a center for study, practice, and Dhamma teaching, he had been invited to speak at other wats. The quarterly journal *Buddhasasana* (Buddhist Religion), which he and his brother Dhammadasa published, had been well received by urban readers. Buddhadasa's innovative interpretations of the Dhamma influenced judges, educators, doctors, and other members of the urban elite. In 1940 the Buddhist Association of Thailand invited Ajahn Buddhadasa to give a sermon in Bangkok.[1] After that first visit, Buddhadasa was invited to give a series of lectures in Bangkok almost every year. His presentations—delivered in plain language, rational and clear—drew very large crowds. At Chulalongkorn University as many as three thousand people came to hear him speak.

About a year after Buddhadasa gave his talk to the Buddhist Association, the Thai government under Prime Minister Phibun passed the 1941 Sangha Act to replace the 1902 Sangha Act. The new act, which shifted authority away from the Sangharaja to councils of elders, broadened the governing body of the Sangha. Under this act, monks were encouraged to travel around to preach.

In 1944 Ajahn Buddhadasa moved Suan Mokkh to a new location in Chaiya, which became its permanent site. Having gained a reputation as a good preacher of Dhamma, the Ajahn was appointed Sangha chief of the Dhamma propagation unit for the southern region in 1949. In the following year the governor of the southern region, at the request of the Minister of the Interior, asked Buddhadasa to join him and his secretary on their official tour of the southern provinces. The monk's duty was to give Dhamma talks to the civil servants and local people in every district that they visited. For Buddhadasa, then forty-four years old, this was to be his first marathon preaching effort, requiring trips to fourteen provinces in thirty-five days.

At a time when travel was still a very difficult undertaking in Thailand, the regional governor and the monk were required to do a great deal of walking, although they also traveled by boat or train. If there was no vacant seat for the monk in the passenger coach, Ajahn Buddhadasa recalled, he traveled with the freight. "Our schedules had been mapped out in advance and the arrival dates had already been fixed. I ate my small meals in a boxcar with the animals. At every place we stopped, I was scheduled to give a sermon. Sometimes I gave as many as five sermons a day. I gave a talk in the morning. After I had the one meal of the day, I delivered another talk to subdistrict chiefs and village headmen. In the afternoon I gave another Dhamma talk to a group of civil servants. In the evening I preached to prisoners in the jail. Around nine o'clock at night I gave another sermon to village folk." The Ajahn remarked, with a chuckle, "I almost died! But I was strong then, and I didn't lose my voice. At every place we stopped, I spent the night at a local wat." The regional governor either stayed at the residence of a provincial governor or a district officer.

FIG. 4. AJAHN BUDDHADASA AT SUAN MOKKH, 1947.

During this time a lay follower asked Ajahn Buddhadasa to send a monk to teach in Chiang Mai in the North. Buddhadasa wrote Panya and asked him to go to Chiang Mai. To create a new Dhamma center, Ajahn Panya and his followers transformed a deserted monastery, Wat Umong, into a wat along the lines of Suan Mokkh and called it the Garden of Buddha-dhamma. From his residence at this branch of Suan Mokkh in Chiang Mai, Ajahn Panya left to preach in other provinces in northern Thailand. By mentioning the day's news and referring to local happenings, and by relying on his own experiences and observations, Ajahn Panya kept his Dhamma talks fluid and spontaneous. His lively lectures captured the imagination of the younger generation, particularly schoolchildren. He was able to draw young audiences away from the theaters in town. When the Ajahn first arrived in Chiang Mai, he was unknown, but after nine years in Chiang Mai his reputation as an outspoken preacher had spread far and wide. He was often invited to give Dhamma talks in Bangkok.

Ajahn Buddhadasa and Ajahn Panya revolutionized both the form of the sermon and the manner of delivery. They gave Dhamma talks while standing up instead of sitting on a Dhamma seat. The audience sat on chairs. Ajahn Buddhadasa referred to his talks as Dhamma lectures rather than sermons. Sulak Sivarak, a founder of the International Network of Engaged Buddhists, recalled that before he went to study in England he thought Ajahn Buddhadasa's teachings were too advanced and too radical for him. "I had been brought up conservatively and my temple was conservative. Buddhadasa was very pro-democracy. He wanted to rewrite the story of the Buddha without using royal language. That was very progressive for the time, and for me. He shocked a lot of people. He was the first monk to stand up at a podium and use his hands when he lectured." According to established rules, when preaching a monk was required to sit at a pulpit and preach quietly. Today the sight of a monk standing up to talk is not unusual, but back in the 1940s it shocked many laypeople and most senior monks. Young people, however, felt comfortable with this new style of teaching because it was informal and spontaneous. They did not have to sit on the floor with their palms pressed together and their legs going to sleep while they listened to the sermons.

In the early 1950s there were nine radio stations in Thailand, but except for the king's station all the broadcast facilities were owned, operated, and controlled by the government. Among the departments operating radio stations were the five defense services (army, navy, air force, police, and border patrol police), the Post and Telegraph Department, the Ministry of Education, and the Public Relations Department. On one occasion General Phin, leader of the Interim National Administrative Council, was in the audience when Ajahn Panya gave an impromptu talk at Wat Sam Phraya in Bangkok. The military commander so liked the monk's straightforward style of preaching that he

invited Ajahn Panya to give a sermon at the radio station owned by
the Public Relations Department. According to government rules, the
monk was supposed to submit his written sermon ahead of time so
that his message could be censored by the officials who ran the radio
station. But Ajahn Panya never wrote down his sermons. He told the
officials that he always spoke extemporaneously. Thus, when Ajahn
Panya arrived on the scheduled day, the station officials had to let him
speak. At the time it was a well-known fact that a large number of
high-ranking bureaucrats received huge kickbacks from commissions
they authorized for construction projects and the purchase of equipment. Ajahn Panya used his airtime to criticize these government officials, particularly members of the army and police. Ajahn Panya was
particularly good at wordplay and quick to come up with impromptu
satirical verses about corrupt government officials.

Since it was rare for the military government to allow a preacher
to be heard on the air, millions of people tuned in to listen to Ajahn
Panya's sermon. When they heard the monk's criticism, the high-ranking bureaucrats were furious. The radio station staff received so much
heat from the government that they never forgot that day. Journalists
were elated and wondered how in the world this monk had the courage
to say what he did. They, too, never forgot the day they heard the southern preacher using a state-run mouthpiece to criticize official wrong-
doing. From then on, Thai journalists began calling Ajahn Panya "the
Dhamma warrior." His style of preaching was characterized as
"straight arrow," "right on target," and "no beating around the bush."

In 1957 an army general, Sarit, staged a coup and became the prime
minister of Thailand. Under Field Marshall Sarit, in 1961 the government promoted economic growth and coined the slogan "Work is
money. Money is work. This brings happiness." The slogan was posted
on huge billboards along the streets in Bangkok and in provincial
towns. So Ajahn Panya countered the government slogan with a motto
of his own: "Work is life. Life is work. Enjoy your work. There is pleasure in work."

In his sermons Ajahn Panya often told stories from his early years as a way of teaching Dhamma. The audience could see that all those things that seemed terrible at the time of his youth ultimately led to positive outcomes. When speaking to young monks who were studying at Mahachula Buddhist University in Bangkok, Ajahn Panya urged them to take on the social responsibilities of their vocation—the way monks had prior to the Sangha centralization of 1902. "After graduation we should set out to work. Urban monks often complain that we are not told what to do. Why wait for work to be assigned?... Look around. There are lots of things that need to be done.... We don't have to wait for anyone's orders. We monks take orders directly from the Buddha."

In Ajahn Buddhadasa's opinion, the government slogan about money bringing happiness simply encouraged greed and more desire. "The reason a person is incapable of doing his job perfectly, faultlessly," he tell us, "is that he is always far too concerned with getting something and being something, always motivated entirely by his own desires. As a result, he is not the master of himself and cannot be consistently good, honest, and fair. In every case of failure and ruin, the root cause is slavery to desire."

Ajahn Buddhadasa pointed out that a person equipped with right knowledge and right understanding is actually in a far better position to carry out any task than the person who is subject to strong desires. "In becoming involved in things, we must do so mindfully; our reactions must not be motivated by craving. The result will follow accordingly. The Buddha and all the other arahants were completely free of desire, yet succeeded in doing many things far more useful than what any of us is capable of. If we look at accounts of how the Buddha spent his days, we find that he slept for only four hours and spent the rest of the time working. We spend more than four hours a day just amusing ourselves."[2]

In his lectures and writings Buddhadasa attempted to raise the consciousness of educated groups who could effect change in society. The government, however, looked upon monks like him as radicals and banned them from broadcasting their sermons. Nonetheless, the more vehemently the government officials condemned the preachers, the more the youth were drawn to them.

To understand why Ajahn Panya was able to capture the attention of the younger generation, one must understand the influence that American popular culture was exerting. By the mid-1960s young teenagers in urban areas were hooked on Westerns written and produced for television. Among the most popular Westerns shown weekly on television were *Gunsmoke, Wanted Dead or Alive, Lawman, Colt .45, Bat Masterson,* and *Have Gun, Will Travel.* In these serials the frontier marshal, the lawman, and the bounty hunter are good guys. These heroes adhere to a code of moral principles that lead them to oppose corrupt forces. The heroes in Westerns never get drunk; they always are clearheaded and act decisively. In contrast, the bad guy does not play by the rules. Although in many of the weekly episodes there is a great deal of violence, most of it comes from the bad guys. What appealed to the Thai youth was that the good guys always came out ahead.

But when the young viewers looked at the situation in their own country, the image that they had of the Thai police was very different. The police, as they saw them, adhered to no code of ethics. The younger generation believed that many policemen were engaged in corrupt activities and had no social conscience. During the Cold War, as young people in Thailand saw it, the corrupt and the greedy got away with bad conduct and received promotions while the good guys became destitute or ended up in jail. Some young television viewers wished they could hire Steve McQueen, who played the bounty hunter in *Wanted Dead or Alive,* to capture the corrupt officials. Others were determined to enter the police force when they grew up so there would always be good police officers to defend the weak against the unjust. Although there were of course some good police officials, they were far outnumbered by the corrupt ones.

As a preacher, Ajahn Panya has never been afraid to criticize army or police officials for setting bad examples for the younger generation. Thus, young people looked up to Ajahn Panya for daring to cross swords with members of the armed forces. Feeling frustrated and restless under the military regime, the youth were inspired by Ajahn Panya's moral courage.

State Buddhism had already lost the younger generation to Western science and to American popular culture, but Ajahn Buddhadasa was able to recapture the attention of young people by elevating Thai Buddhism beyond the worldly realm of science. As Phra Paisal put it, Buddhadasa's "scientific" Buddhism was the science of timeless ultimate truth, with meditation as an integral "technology." Thai university students in the 1960s considered Ajahn Buddhadasa the greatest Thai Buddhist thinker of our time. His Dhamma teachings reenergized the younger generation exposed to Western educational concepts and to realms of information and knowledge unknown to most older Thai.

In local forms of Buddhism, the term "practice" had far wider meaning than just the act of meditation alone. Under state Buddhism, "practice" came to be associated with sitting meditation, walking meditation, or going on a meditation retreat. Ajahn Buddhadasa showed the younger generation how to practice in their daily lives and how to respond to the demands, complexities, and expectations of the modern world. In a talk given to Thammasat University students in January 1966, he summed up the essence of the Buddha's teaching as *anatta* (non-self), *cit wang* (nonattachment), and *suññata* (emptiness, voidness, freedom). Back then there were six universities in Thailand, all government run, and only a small number of high school graduates passed the entrance examinations that would enable them to study at a university. Without a bachelor's degree, it was difficult to find good employment. Some students who flunked exams committed suicide because they felt that they had no future and did not want to work in a factory or a tin mine.

Knowing that students felt anxiety whenever they took an examination, Ajahn Buddhadasa gave them this advice: "When you are sitting for an examination, you should forget about yourself. When starting to write an answer to a question, you should forget about being yourself. Forget about the 'me' who is being examined and who will pass or fail.... A mind free of any 'me' or 'mine' who will pass or fail immediately comes up agile and clean. It remembers immediately and thinks keenly.... This is how to apply *cit wang* (a mind free of the illusion of self), or Buddhist non-grasping and non-clinging, when sitting for examinations. In this way you will get good results."

In teaching general audiences, Buddhadasa also addressed a prominent feature of local Buddhism in the southern peninsula: the tradition of lay renouncers who lead a life very different from that of ordinary laypeople. These religious figures included hermits (*rishi*), holy men, and male and female ascetics known as white-robes. In ancient times a holy man was a respected founder of a settlement or a community adviser. Local monks as well as lay renouncers were the most important leaders of a community, and lay renouncers were prominent figures in the local histories of southern villages. Before modern education prevailed, village elders were men who had spent several years in the monkhood and women who knew Dhamma teachings by heart. The centralization of the Sangha, which focused on monastics, eliminated the holy man tradition. Bangkok authorities found it difficult to control these religious figures. According to the authorities, one is either a monastic or a layperson, not someone in between.

In his teachings, Ajahn Buddhadasa has brought the ultimate goal, *nibbana*, back to its central place in Thai Buddhism. He tells us that it is not always necessary to renounce the worldly life in order to cultivate spiritual progress. Laypersons as well as monks can attain the first stage of enlightenment and within a lifetime the individual can progress to the last stage, which is arahantship.

In 1960 the government employees who worked for the Department of Irrigation in Nonthaburi, a province about twenty kilometers north of Bangkok, established a new monastery called Wat Chonprathan (literally, Irrigation Monastery). The department officials invited their favorite preacher, Ajahn Panya, to become the abbot. He accepted the invitation because this was a new monastery outside Bangkok, which meant that he could set up a completely new system and select his own monks. During the first year ten monks came to join Ajahn Panya from the southern provinces of Phatthalung and Songkhla. The new monastery became a center for study as well as meditation practice. By 1983 there were between 140 and 180 monks in residence.

One of the most important Buddhist traditions in old Siam was temporary *bhikkhu* ordination, when young men became monks for awhile before getting married and becoming householders. Having young men live as monks for a year or so helped make them mentally fit to take on the responsibilities of family life. Temporary ordination also served as a way for young men to show gratitude to their mothers.

But by the middle of the twentieth century, the number of young men who were ordained temporarily for one rains retreat had declined significantly. Young men who had a college education were not interested in temporary ordination either to show gratitude to their mothers or to obtain useful mental discipline. It took a reformist preacher like Ajahn Panya to change their attitude. Over the years Ajahn Panya has ordained thousands of young men and trained them during the short time they spent in the robes. Some of these university students then went to the South to study under Ajahn Buddhadasa at Suan Mokkh.

FIG. 5. AJAHN PANYA, ABBOT OF WAT CHONPRATHAN.

As a preacher, Ajahn Panya is the most widely traveled monk of his generation. In 1954 he was invited to teach in Europe. He went from Bangkok to Burma, then on to Karachi, Baghdad, Cairo, Rome, and Switzerland. The trip took six months. He was the first Thai monk to go around the world preaching. By the early 1980s Ajahn Panya had been to all the provinces in Thailand. He had given Dhamma talks at temples, associations, universities, teachers' colleges, government agencies, and other institutions that regularly invited him to teach. During the year 1982, for example, Ajahn Panya gave 546 Dhamma talks in forty-four provinces. When asked by a journalist in 1983 what topics his sermons cover, Ajahn Panya replied, "Most of the time I speak on current topics. For instance, before the elections I spoke on radio and television about a citizen's responsibility to select the right candidate." On Labor Day, May 1, Ajahn Panya said he would talk about the labor force in Thailand. In response to the question whether or not his sermons were too worldly, the Ajahn replied, "We all belong to this world, so why shouldn't I adapt my sermons for the layman? Since people can identify directly with their environment and the current goings-on, I use anecdotes from their daily lives to teach the Dhamma. When there are errors in society, there is nothing wrong in pointing them out. If a monk doesn't remind the people, who will?" In a historical sense, Ajahn Panya has simply revived the role that was long played by Buddhist masters of local traditions.

Ajahn Jumnien, a generation younger than Ajahn Buddhadasa and Ajahn Panya, is completely rooted in southern culture. When he was a young monk he did not go to Bangkok to study; he trained instead under meditation masters in the southern provinces and studied a variety of meditation methods. Today Jumnien is a meditation master, a skilled preacher, and a traditional healer. His deep connection with the physical world and his understanding of people have given him an unusual resourcefulness.

Ajahn Jumnien's teachings, couched in simple language laced with local humor, appeal to village folk and townspeople. In the southern region Ajahn Jumnien was even able to compete successfully with shadow puppet masters who were known for their skillful wordplay. On one occasion Ajahn Jumnien was giving a Dhamma talk in a wat compound in Suratthani while a shadow theater performance was being given nearby. Hearing much laughter from the monk's audience, the shadow puppet master became so intrigued that he asked his assistant to take over the show while he went to listen to the Ajahn's sermon. Upon hearing Ajahn Jumnien's wordplay, the puppet master is said to have laughed so hard that his sides ached.

The Ajahn recalls that as government officials became increasingly corrupt and exploitative, more and more locals turned against the government. In southern Thailand a large number of people fled into the jungle to join the rebel groups or to escape danger. The forested and mountainous areas of the South were the sites of prolonged violence between government forces and insurgents. Village folk experienced considerable hardship when their villages were situated in areas of conflict. Soon after Ajahn Jumnien began teaching meditation at Wat Sukhon-thawat in Nasan district in Suratthani in 1967, he was told to leave the area or risk being shot. The police thought Jumnien was a communist sympathizer; the insurgents thought he was a government spy. But Ajahn Jumnien refused to leave the wat.

Each side thereupon offered to "protect" his wat against the other. Ajahn Jumnien replied to both sides that living in harmony with the true Dhamma was all the protection he needed. "The Dhamma is above politics. Our temple is a refuge from the battleground of desires. I share my teaching equally with all who come, and when I go out to teach, I teach to all people who ask…. True peace, true happiness, will not come from a change in the social order. Both sides in these fights may have legitimate complaints, but true inner peace can only come through the Dhamma. For monks and laypeople alike, security comes from the Dhamma, from the wisdom that sees the impermanence of all things in the world."

Eventually Ajahn Jumnien was able to teach Dhamma both to the government soldiers in the town and to the rebels in the mountains. The monk usually walked alone to the forested mountains to visit the insurgents. He told the soldiers not to shoot the insurgents and told the insurgents not to shoot the soldiers. Both the soldiers and the insurgents informed the monk that because they were afraid of getting killed, they had to shoot first. Knowing that protective amulets were a safeguard for many people, Ajahn Jumnien came up with a skillful means to stop the killings. When the Ajahn was with the soldiers, he gave each soldier an amulet that he called "No Death," telling them, "I have blessed this protective amulet. As long as you wear my amulet you won't be killed. Now you don't need to shoot first." When Ajahn Jumnien was with the insurgents in the jungle, he also gave them amulets with the same instructions.

During the nine years that he lived at Wat Sukhon, Ajahn Jumnien was able to save many lives. He acted as a trusted intermediary in getting insurgents and villagers to take advantage of the government's offer of amnesty. According to Ajahn Jumnien, by the middle of the 1970s tens of thousands of people had been reintegrated into village life.

FIG. 6. AJAHN JUMNIEN, FOUNDER OF TIGER CAVE MONASTERY.

In 1975 Ajahn Jumnien, inspired by a vision during his meditation, began to search for a new Dhamma center. He and his assistant found a suitable location west of the provincial town of Krabi on a densely forested mountain with several caves. In the forest, Ajahn Jumnien tells us, were a thousand kinds of trees, "huge trees that survived because guardian spirits protected them." After Ajahn Jumnien took up residence at Tiger Cave Monastery, fifty-three monks and fifty-six nuns came to stay there. Although the majority of the inhabitants in the area are Muslims, they have lived peacefully with the local Buddhists. When the Buddhist monks began construction of a twelve-hundred-step stairway to the summit of the mountain, local Muslim artisans were hired to help build it.

As a meditation master and traditional healer, Ajahn Jumnien is often called on to provide herbal and spiritual remedies to people suffering from illness and fear. Large numbers of Chinese from Singapore and Malaysia have come to visit his monastery, and each year Ajahn Jumnien is invited to teach in Malaysia. He is always accompanied by a Thai monk who interprets his Dhamma talks for the Chinese followers. For over ten years Ajahn Jumnien has been teaching Dhamma and leading meditation retreats at Spirit Rock Meditation Center in California and elsewhere in the United States. Although Ajahn Jumnien does not speak English and his Dhamma talks require an interpreter, he has a large American following. His lighthearted yet illuminating style of teaching appeals to both the young and the old.

Of the three masters, Ajahn Buddhadasa has left the largest body of innovative work and is the most widely known in the West. On May 27, 2006, the hundredth anniversary of Buddhadasa's birth was celebrated at monasteries and meditation centers in the United States: Wat Thai, in Washington, D.C.; Atamayatarama Buddhist Monastery, near Seattle; Insight Meditation Center, in Redwood City, California; Wat Buddha Dharma Meditation Center, outside Chicago; and Liberation Park, also outside Chicago (now in Norwalk, Wisconsin).

All three masters attempted to effect changes in moral attitudes and Dhamma practices, restore the social dimension of Buddhism, and bridge the divide separating laypeople and monastics. They have opened doors to monks and laypeople throughout the world community. Several Westerners ordained by Ajahn Panya went to Suan Mokkh to study with Ajahn Buddhadasa, whose teachings have inspired social and environmental movements in Thailand as well as in other countries. Many Dhamma teachers in the West today have been Dhamma students of Ajahn Buddhadasa, Ajahn Panya, and Ajahn Jumnien.

True to the spirits of their ancestors, Ajahn Buddhadasa, Ajahn Panya, and Ajahn Jumnien have been among Thailand's most vocal proponents of open-mindedness toward other religions. In light of the violent conflicts in southern Thailand and elsewhere in the world today, we would do well to heed the advice of these masters who have led by example. The chapters that follow may help us understand how the first twenty years of each monk's life shaped his development and led to his becoming a fearless preacher.

PART I

AJAHN BUDDHADASA
(BOYHOOD NAME: NGUAM)

A MERCHANT-POET FATHER

URING THE REIGN of King Chulalongkorn (1868–1910) European experts in various fields were hired by his government to assist in the modernization of Siam. By the end of his reign the number of foreigners employed by the king had increased to over three hundred. H. Warrington Smyth was a British geologist serving as the director of Siam's Department of Mines. In June 1896 Smyth and a number of local men set sail from Bangkok along the coast of southern Siam. About a month later they arrived in Phum Riang, the principal town of Chaiya, and anchored the ship alongside the governor's house. Smyth wrote in his journal, "We remained a week in Chaiya, a week of rains and watery gales, while we obtained the information we required, and the skipper [who had fallen ill] was made fit for sea again. Of all the places we were ever in, this is one which claims the kindliest memories. The aspect of neatness and good order in the trim grass lawns and the rows of palms which greeted us here was in striking contrast to that of most other governors' residences in Siam. The welcome we received was of the heartiest, and we were ensconced in a charmingly built wooden bungalow where everything was as clean as in a coastguard cottage."

The governor of Chaiya was away attending to business with the governor of Ban Don. Smyth, who visited Ban Don sometime later, commented in his journal, "The Malay elements seem to have been comparatively small in Ban Don, and of its population of 22,000 an unusually large part are Chinamen from Hainan, Hokien, and Kwantung, who are engaged in the export of timber, rattans, and skins, and the other jungle produce in which the densely wooded province abounds; and quite a fleet of Chinese-owned junks is engaged in this trade."

FIG. 7. SURATTHANI PROVINCE SHOWING DISTRICTS.

The governor, whose official title was Lord of Chaiya, arrived two days later. Smyth was impressed with him. "He is a remarkable man, and is one of the few Siamese I have met who can talk for hours in an interesting manner and give you a stream of information worth having the whole time. He is a good carpenter and mechanic, and as a lad went to sea, whence it comes that he is the best of Siamese sailors. He has a fine *rua pet* [a locally made boat] as his yacht, and manages her so well that they say she can beat anything in the gulf, and no other man knows the islands and shoals as he does. He has in like manner acquired his experience ashore, and as a youngster has hunted elephants, like a jungle man—not to shoot them down like the barbarous African, or the savage Christian, but [to] catch and tame and utilise them, as it was meant they should be used by man. This is a sportsmanlike pursuit, and calls for far more skill and daring than shooting them dead as you might a hungry wolf."

The men of Phum Riang built their own boats. Smyth, who was a keen observer of local craftsmanship, wrote that these boats were "long narrow flat-bottomed craft with Malay clipper stems built entirely of *mai takian*, brought from Ban Don, and are rigged with the horizontally matted lug sail of the *orange-laut* type, which they declare is the only thing strong enough to stand the squalls of the bight. We saw some boats in course of construction in a shed used for the purpose. A large crowd stood round criticising, and one nearly finished was being polished till she shone again."

Among the Phum Riang locals was a young Chinese merchant named Xiang who owned the only general store in town. Xiang's ancestors had migrated to Phum Riang from China in the early nineteenth century. Xiang married a Siamese woman named Khleuan. According to Chinese custom, the wife moved into the husband's household. They settled into living quarters above Xiang's shop. Their first child died when he was still an infant, but in 1906 another son was born. At the request of Xiang and his wife, a respected monk chose a name for their son, Nguam, which means a cave high up on a mountain. Three years later another boy, Yikoei, was born, followed by a daughter, Kimsoi.

In 1926 Nguam became a monk. Years later he established a forest monastery he called Suan Mokkh (The Garden of Liberation) and took the Pali name Buddhadasa, meaning Servant of the Buddha. Yikoei took the name Dhammadasa (Servant of the Dhamma) and became a firm supporter of his elder brother's work. Kimsoi, his sister, got married and set up a stationery store in Ban Don, which had become the provincial seat of Suratthani province.

Like all children who were part Chinese, Nguam, Yikoei, and Kimsoi addressed their father as "Tia" (father, in Chinese) and their mother as "Mae" (mother, in Thai). The Chinese in southern Siam had been calling their fathers "Tia" for generations. As Ajahn Buddhadasa later wrote, "The children of the Chinese called their fathers 'Tia,' as did the grandchildren and great grandchildren.... At that time children weren't ashamed of their Chinese ancestry; they didn't feel that it was any kind of blemish."

FIG. 8. XIANG, BUDDHADASA'S FATHER.

Buddhadasa's father had two younger brothers, Siang and An, both of whom were also merchants. Their family name was Kho. In 1913 King Vajiravudh issued a proclamation ordering his subjects to attach surnames to their personal names. Unlike the Chinese, who have family names, surnames were unknown to the Siamese and the Lao; so the people of Siam had to come up with them. The three Chinese brothers adopted "Panich" as their Thai surname (*panich* means merchant). Xiang called his store "Chaiya Panich."

As Buddhadasa recalled, "Uncle Siang was not home much. First he went to Bangkok as a monk. Before long, he was the secretary of the abbot of Wat Pathum Kongkha." Then, after twelve years as a monk, Uncle Siang disrobed and became the manager of a passenger ship.

Xiang's youngest brother, An, was an artist. Ajahn Buddhadasa recalled that Uncle An "died when he was still rather young. He had a trading ship that brought goods from Bangkok to sell. On one trip he died after having caught a fever. The captain of the ship said they buried him on the shore of Chumphon. An uncle went to dig up the body in order to cremate it, and having done so brought back the remains for ceremonies here in Phum Riang."

Although Uncle An's life was short, "from what I've heard, he liked to sing, although he never had any formal training. He could sing ancient Thai songs quite easily and could perform the 'Phra Malai before the Corpse' chant." Phra Malai, around whom many popular stories revolved, was a monk who visited all the realms of heaven and hell, then came back to tell people where their karma would land them. This tale, which could be recited by monks or laymen, was considered a fitting topic for funeral rites. From the story of Phra Malai, local people learned about the *bodhisatta* (future Buddha) Metteyya, living in Tusita Heaven, who they believe will be reborn in the human realm as the next Buddha, the Buddha of Loving Kindness.

Like most young men of his generation who grew up before modern schooling, Buddhadasa's father learned to read and write Thai at a local monastery. "Father only spoke a little Chinese, just a few words," Ajahn Buddhadasa recalled. "Uncle Siang could speak more, because he had business with the Chinese."

Ajahn Buddhadasa tells us how his love of poetry was influenced by his father. "Something else that stuck with me was that Father liked to write stanzas, verses, and poetry. He had a poet's spirit, which led me to enjoy that sort of thing." When the Ajahn was still a child he used to see his father writing poetry in the *sala*, the small shelter that he had built on the cremation grounds. The latrines Xiang built as offerings to the wat also had verses written on them.

Buddhadasa's father "liked to write medicinal formulae in verse," the Ajahn tells us. "I saw these in his notebooks, and so I liked poetry also. He wrote them properly in the classic style but did not have much time for them because his business constrained him...He learned to write poetry by studying examples. He didn't learn it at school. Perhaps he got it from Uncle Siang, his younger brother, who had a chance to go to school and knew something about poetry. They shared knowledge when they met and were always in contact by letter. If there was anything strange, new, or modern, Uncle Siang—who was in Bangkok

—would write about it in a letter to Father. This was a kind of education in itself about all kinds of matters, including medicine."

In addition to his gift of poetry, "Father had a carpenter's mind, which I liked. If I had received such a training myself, it would have been very nice; that is, I liked that kind of work. There are many things at Suan Mokkh that I made myself, using my own skills. Father had carpentry skills, and boatbuilding was what you could call his hobby. He earned his living mainly as a petty merchant, but his hobby livelihood was that of boatbuilder. The last boat he built he never finished—it rested on the support blocks where he was making it until it rotted and crumbled.... Father did not finish the last boat because his business constrained him. At the end, he wanted to plant a coconut grove but wasn't able to finish the planting. He got sick and then was chronically ill until he died."

FIG. 9. THE SHOP-HOUSE IN WHICH NGUAM AND HIS FAMILY LIVED AND WORKED.

2

THE ART OF COOKING

WILLIAM A.R. WOOD arrived in Bangkok during the reign of King Chulalongkorn. During the course of his thirty-five years of service with the British government (1896–1931), Wood was stationed in various major northern and southern cities. He held several high-ranking consular positions before retiring. Wherever he worked, Wood employed local men for domestic tasks, and in the process he came to admire their adaptability. "As a matter of fact," Wood tells us, "a great many Siamese and Lao men really can do a large variety of different things, and may be called rather versatile as compared with their English or American opposite numbers. For instance, almost everybody can do some gardening, sewing or cooking. In England or America, if you were to request the average chauffeur or gardener to cook, say, a four-course dinner, he would probably phone for the nearest mental specialist to come and have a look at you. In Siam he would quietly get three bricks and a bundle of twigs, and would set to work to cook the dinner. Quite possibly the result would be hardly equal to the fare provided at the Cecil or the Ritz, but would be more or less eatable."

It was not unusual for Siamese and Lao men to know how to cook. From an early age, boys as well as girls were expected to help their mothers with chores, including cooking. Nguam, the future Ajahn Buddhadasa, was an excellent cook before he was even ten years old. Nguam lived with his parents on the second floor of their shop in Phum

Riang. Although his father wasn't at home much, Ajahn Buddhadasa remembered, his mother was there all the time. "I was much closer to Mother, and because I had to help her in the kitchen. I learned to do everything there just the way she did. Father was also a good cook; his mother was really talented and sold many kinds of sweets, so Father learned how to make these things too. My father could cook like a woman because his mother made him. Preparing good food is an art."

FIG. 10. NGUAM ABOUT FIVE YEARS OLD.

Not only Nguam but his younger brother, Yikoei, too, had to help their mother in the kitchen. Since ready-made curry pastes and canned coconut products were not then available, all dishes had to be made from scratch. This took patience. To obtain coconut cream, both boys learned to scrape coconut meat carefully. "I ground the ingredients for the curry. I scraped coconuts too, but those coconut scrapings of mine never pleased Mother. She preferred Yikoei's scrapings. His were soft to the touch, which produced more cream. Mine were coarse," Ajahn Buddhadasa continued with a chuckle, "and made something more like meal than cream. Yikoei scraped like someone without any strength, so his came out fine and yielded cream easily with hardly any squeezing at all."

Since Nguam's father was Chinese, his parents regularly performed the ceremonies of the Chinese New Year and Autumn Festival. After his father died, Ajahn Buddhadasa recalled, "Mother didn't really care about the ceremonies, but she still observed them in his memory. She still made the customary sweetmeats to give to the monks, share with neighbors, and for us to eat—especially steamed sweets with pork. I feel that nobody made them better than Mother, and I know why they were the best—because she prepared them differently from everyone else, using leaves from the *paan* tree." As the Ajahn recalls, he was sent to pick leaves from a paan tree near their house. "Mother then told me to pound, pound, pound them and then squeeze out their green juice. This liquid was mixed with the flour used for making Chinese sweets. After they were steamed, the smell was different and the flavor was especially distinct because of the paan leaves. I never found anyone else who made sweets this way. Among many dozens of households, only one or two used anything more than the flour. If you add paan-leaf juice, the color turns a dark green that is easy to identify." Decades after he was ordained, Buddhadasa still remembered the taste of his mother's desserts: "I've never eaten this kind of sweet made by anyone who made it more deliciously. Mother followed the recipe of her ancestors. Others were probably lazy. The old way was difficult and thus unpopular."

When a young monk at Suan Mokkh once asked him about cooking, Ajahn Buddhadasa replied that three basic steps are involved. "First, you need meat, fish, or vegetables. Second, you need the spices and herbs to prepare the curry that will make the meat, fish, or vegetables delicious. Finally, you need oil—preferably coconut cream—in which to dissolve the curry powders and get them to blend into the food that is being curried. In our home we got oil from coconuts. People who didn't reject meat used animal fat. See for yourself. Whatever kind of curry you decide to make, you will always need these three ingredients.... Whether you're making a soup, a boiled dish, or dry food, there's no avoiding the three basic ingredients, except for incomplete dishes like sour curry, and even then, some people add coconut cream."

By the time Nguam's parents took him to stay at Wat Phum Riang he already knew how to cook well. The monks could scarcely believe that an eight-year-old boy had mastered such recipes as fish casserole and buffalo curry. "I was the leader in the kitchen," Ajahn Buddhadasa recalled. "None of the other temple boys believed I could make fish casserole. Neither did the monks or novices. We bet on it! I showed my stuff. There wasn't anything I couldn't make, even the hard stuff like fish casserole or buffalo curry, which were the standard measures of a good cook. I had a little cooking school going at the wat. Hardly any of the other temple boys could cook." Making these curries involves a lot of chopping and pounding of ingredients in mortars. Nguam and other temple boys had to chop cilantro roots, stems, and leaves; chop galingale and shallots; slice the lemongrass and peel the lime rinds finely; and grind the coriander, cumin, black pepper, turmeric.

Although many village boys knew how to cook meat, making desserts was not so easy for them, but Nguam had learned to make these from his father and mother. "Even sweets," he said, "need three basic ingredients: flour, sugar, and oil. The flour is the main ingredient; sugar makes the dessert sweet, and the oil—coconut cream—makes it rich. Most sweets have these ingredients in them. One can add other things to improve the flavor as one likes."

Thai cuisine, including sweets that are sometimes served as desserts, owes much to Indian cooking. As the Ajahn tells us, "In India, which is the source of many things for us, they use cow's milk. Even now, that's how they do it. Sweets made of the three basic ingredients of flour, sugar, and oil are still used in caramels, which around here are called the lord of all sweets. I believe that we have carried on the original recipe from India." After he became a monk, Buddhadasa visited India. On one occasion, while walking in a market, Buddhadasa saw local people making caramels just like women in southern Thailand do. "I asked the owner of the shop when this sweet originated. He didn't know but said it was ancient."[3]

After Ajahn Buddhadasa was ordained as a monk in 1926 he continued to teach youngsters in Phum Riang how to cook. "Sometimes I
had to teach the novices and temple boys how to cook properly. They
didn't know how. While I was overseeing the cooking, villagers passing the wat would catch a whiff of the curries and sometimes couldn't
help but stop by to ask for a taste," the Ajahn laughed.

FIG. 11. KHLEUAN, BUDDHADASA'S MOTHER,
KEY FINANCIAL SUPPORTER OF SUAN MOKKH.

TEACHERS OF FRUGALITY

NGUAM AND YIKOEI were born three years apart. Like other young boys, they often argued and got into fights. Ajahn Buddhadasa recalled with humor, "I was beaten fairly often, according to custom, mostly by Mother. Father hardly ever hit me. Mother used a small branch from a *mayom* tree as a switch, never anything heavy or strong. When I argued with my brother, we both got hit. Both of us had to take responsibility." Even if, after punishing her sons, their mother found out it was the younger son Yikoei, not Nguam, who started the argument, it would make no difference to her. She told Nguam to keep in mind that "older siblings should give preference to their juniors."

When asked if the beating was enough to make Nguam cry, the Ajahn chuckled, "Of course. That was normal. If we didn't, they wouldn't stop. If we cried, they had to stop. Mother wasn't an angry person; she didn't hit us out of anger. What got us into trouble most often was our making too much noise or fighting. It felt to me that a punishment such as a beating was just local custom to keep things orderly, to keep us in line. Mother's teaching didn't include sermons and explanations. She just said we were wrong and hit us. She didn't teach with sermons or reason like monks."

Nguam's parents never showed favoritism or extended more love to one child than to the other two. As Ajahn Buddhadasa recalled, "I never felt that kind of thing. As far as I could tell, there weren't any preferences. All three of us wanted to make our parents happy and contented.

Any praise or compliment gave us great joy. Father was the kind of person who gave compliments freely if you did something that pleased him. But Mother hardly ever did that, as if nothing quite pleased her."

When asked how his mother influenced him the most, Ajahn Buddhadasa replied, "Frugality. We were taught to be thrifty. Even with water for washing our feet, we were forbidden to use a lot. If we wanted a drink of water, we weren't allowed to take just one sip from the dipper and throw the rest away. And we had to use the appropriate amount of firewood. If wood didn't burn up completely, we had to quench the fire and save that wood for later. Everything that could be conserved had to be conserved. We were frugal in every way, so it became a habit. I consider this all the time: useful ways to save and how to do it."

The Ajahn picked up his mother's frugality while helping in the kitchen. "An example of her frugality is how she made coconut cream. Usually, people would squeeze the coconut meat twice. We had to do it three times, taking what was left from the second pressing and pounding it more finely, so that much more cream could be squeezed out. People are generally lazy. They throw out the remains from the second pressing. We had to pound, pound, pound and then squeeze again. If the cream was thick, we had to squeeze a fourth time. That's how frugal she was. No other household was nearly as thrifty.

"Mother saved time, too; time had to be used beneficially. When resting, she didn't waste time doing nothing. She had to have something useful to do." As for his father, he was less frugal. "He usually just did things in the usual ways.

Recalling his youth, the Ajahn said, "I picked up the habit of using things without waste, but I also adopted frugal habits in order to boast. There's a kind of boastfulness in showing off one's knowledge of how to save. It turns into having a kind of superior knowledge. Even when it isn't necessary to be frugal, one is so, just to show that one can be."

In his seventies Ajahn Buddhadasa confessed, "Later in life I haven't been so careful. I've become rather lazy about frugality. In my younger days, I preferred to do things myself. I didn't like hiring people and paying them." In the early years of Suan Mokkh, the Ajahn always told his monks, "If something breaks, we should try to fix it, not just throw it away. Some of the things that other people just threw away, we didn't. Old nails, for instance. Others might toss them; we straightened them for reuse."

FIG. 12. NGUAM WITH HIS FATHER AND BROTHER AWAIT THE VISITING SANGHARAJA.

Nguam was about five years old when, in 1912, he and his family went to see Prince Wachirayan, the Sangharaja of Siam. The prince had come to Phum Riang while on an inspection tour of southern monasteries. Before he became ordained, the young prince loved to dress in the latest European fashion. After spending three months as a novice at a royal monastery, Wachirayan received a gift of four hundred *baht* from his elder brother, King Chulalongkorn. "I had never received such an amount before, and I was very excited. It delighted me to buy things. It made me feel grown up, since I was really spending the money myself, but actually I was still very much a child about handling money."

Wachirayan became a spendthrift, confessing, "I was unable to be frugal with my assets." When he ran out of cash, Wachirayan discovered that European merchants in Bangkok were willing to extend credit to him. "When the debt grew large, they would periodically send a bill requesting payment.... Since I was given credit it was as if I received the thing for free." When, eventually, the bills came in, Wachirayan was rescued by his maternal grandmother. "My grandmother loved me very much. Whenever I asked for money I could have it, and she did not even complain."

The man who came to influence Wachirayan the most during his adolescent years was Dr. Peter Gowan (1847–1902), a Scotsman who served as a royal physician. The young prince was impressed with Gowan, a bachelor whose moral conduct was exemplary. Twelve years older than Wachirayan, Gowan, according to the prince, "lived alone ... like an ... ascetic. He had no love for a good time the way gamblers did. I liked him because he was a European, and I attached myself to him to learn something of his character and conduct and to receive advice from him. I wanted to follow his example. I observed those excesses which disturbed Dr. Gowan the most." These "progressively diminished to the point where I became an ascetic like Dr. Gowan," who "was the cause of my reform."

4

FIGHTING FISH

IN 1908 Arnold Wright wrote an article about sports in Siam. Among the sports that the Englishman singled out were Siamese boxing, fish fights, and kite fights. The fighting fish of Siam, Wright told his European readers, "are a species of stickleback, the male members of which ... are endowed with extraordinary pugnacity.... [U]pon becoming enraged they display a marvellous range of iridescent colouring which shifts about in kaleidoscope fashion. They are fed with the larvae of mosquitoes, for the sale of which there are regular shops in the Sampeng district of Bangkok. Large sums are wagered on the fighting powers of the finny warriors, and in many cases their owners refuse to sell them for hundreds of [baht]."

Quite a few European men who lived in Siam mentioned that they had witnessed Siamese fish fights. In 1896 William A.R. Wood arrived from Britain to work as an interpreter at the British consular office in Bangkok. In the course of his travels in the southern region, Wood noticed that the Siamese of Peninsular Siam were very fond of bullfights, cockfights, and fish fights. One day he decided to go see Siamese fighting fish. "They are very beautiful little creatures," he observed, "with long, lacy fins, and their scales show all the colours of a sunset sky. Their pugnacity is remarkable; not infrequently both combatants succumb to their injuries, their fins being so torn that they cannot swim. A great deal of money is often staked on fish fights, but to foreigners they are more or less slow and unexciting performances. Sometimes the two

fishes will hold on to one another's mouths for almost an hour; the spec-
tators wait in a state of rapt attention, but I must admit that I have often
longed to poke the performers with a stick to liven them up a bit."

In Phum Riang, Buddhadasa's father also enjoyed raising Siamese
fighting fish. As the Ajahn recalled, "Father liked them just to look at,
never to get them to fight. He kept them on the counter of his shop in
widemouthed jars. When I was little my job was to swat mosquitoes
and feed them to the fish. I liked this the most, feeding mosquitoes to
the fighting fish. Those fish were spirited. If one looked at them too
closely they would try to bite."

Nguam began raising his own fighting fish before he was eight. "I
enjoyed raising them and playing with them, but never had them fight,"
Ajahn Buddhadasa tells us. "I was more interested in breeding them,
and I liked to watch them. Watching them gave me an extraordinary
feeling; they made a big impression on me and stuck in my mind." Not
only did the fighting fish give Nguam pleasure, they helped take the
fear of ghosts off his mind. "When I went to the outhouse beside the
canal, I had to pass a bodhi tree that everyone believed was haunted.
I closed my eyes and saw only fighting fish. Didn't need to fear any
ghosts whether going or returning."

The Ajahn says he kept his fish "in a big earthenware basin that had
edible greens growing around the edge. I'd tie string to some bait, like
raw shrimp, and lower it into the middle of the basin. The fighting fish
would pounce on it from all sides. It was the most beautiful sight, very
hard to describe."

Recognizing Nguam's passion, his parents let him raise the fish at
home for fun but forbade him to let them fight. "In spite of this pro-
hibition, I found a way to make them fight so well that no others could
have matched them. I would choose the best-looking male, a strong and
sturdy one, and put it into a round pond. Then I would place a female,
suspended in a glass bottle from a string, into the middle of the pond.
As soon as the male saw her, he would fly all over the place. He swam
around and around, more than for mere exercise. After three or four
days, the male would become stout, ornery, and thick-finned and would
bite my hand if I tried to catch it. If I had been able to take it to fight,

it would definitely have won." Apparently another fighting fish aficionado stole Nguam's prize fish and left a different one in its place. "When I asked who had stopped by, Mother gave the name of a professional fish fighter. He stole my fish and took it to fight, and it really won. I had a lot of fun doing this and breeding them. In the end, some were stolen, and others I gave away."

Decades later, Ajahn Buddhadasa's early passion for Siamese fighting fish would develop into the practice of raising exotic fish at Suan Mokkh. His study of animals and plants provided him with insights for his Dhamma teaching.

In one of his poems, "Chatting with the Fish," Ajahn Buddhadasa wrote:

> In chatting with the fish I came to know something strange;
> They segregate into two styles well worth studying:
>
> The fighting fish, gourami, oscars, and the like
> cling to self, attach to mates, and protect their nests.
> Honor crazed and fierce, they are instinctual fighters,
> snapping and biting their fish friends most insanely.
>
> The other kind, like Tilapia, are curiously different:
> they make no effort to dominate a mate as their own;
> they wander like ascetics, hearts like monks,
> leaving their eggs behind without a care.
>
> They are just like homeless wanderers,
> rather than those stuck on Ego till they die.

TEACHING TEMPLE BOYS

WHEN NGUAM was eight years old his parents took him to be a temple boy at Wat Phum Riang in his hometown. In 1914 it was still customary for boys to live at a local temple where they did chores for their teachers and learned to read and write. Ajahn Buddhadasa recalled a ritual that every temple boy performed. To become a temple boy at the wat, "one made an offering of flowers, incense, and a candle to present oneself as a student or apprentice of the monks. The wat appointed one or two monks to look after us: to see to our food and behavior while eating, make sure we studied, and train us in things like bowing and chanting and serving the monks."

Temple boys learned to read and write Thai. When they were not studying, temple boys did chores. "We took turns hauling water, which couldn't be skipped, and growing vegetables next to the pond. We did everything." The boys did a lot of hard work, so they were fed well. Parents whose sons were temple boys usually cooked extra food for the wat. "Rice came from the monks' alms round. The curries and soups were sent by various households in pots. Whoever's house it was from, that boy went to fetch it. So there were plenty of pots of curry and always enough rice. In Phum Riang food was plentiful." The reciprocal relationship between laypeople and monastics was deeply rooted in the local culture. Monks taught the children and disciplined them free of charge, the boys served their teachers to the best of their abilities, and the laypeople supported the monks by providing all the basic necessities.

Living at the wat, temple boys got to hear plenty of Jataka stories, which local monks used for teaching. Jataka stories recount events in over five hundred of Gotama's (Sakyamuni Buddha's) previous existences as a bodhisatta. "Back then," Ajahn Buddhadasa recalled, "monks would preach on the benefits of giving alms for the construction of various buildings, describe how much merit one would get for building an ordination hall, casting a bell, building a sala, and so on." Among the meritorious deeds was the practice of offering toilet facilities to the wat. According to the Buddha's teaching, for example, whoever contributed by building latrines for the wat would have good health, free from all kinds of disease. At death such a person is on the path that leads to the ultimate goal, nibbana. In the last decades of the twentieth century, during their Dhamma talks some abbots had to remind people of this practice and convince lay supporters to finance the construction of dozens of toilets to accommodate the large numbers of visitors to the wats.

In the Phum Riang of his youth, Buddhadasa said, each year "the monks would preach the Vessantara Jataka, the story of the Great Birth, which was always popular.⁴ It brought in money and was great fun." Although older people had heard the story many times, there were different layers and levels of Dhamma teachings that they could always appreciate. The wat usually received the largest donations for repairs or the construction of buildings during the Great Birth festival. It was said that when the monks recited the beautiful verses of the Vessantara Jataka, the performance could deeply move even the most stingy person or the worst bandit in the audience.

From the practice of giving, whether by donating labor, materials, or money or by observing precepts, one could gain merit and dedicate this merit to the welfare of relatives and all sentient beings. The monks' teachings had a significant impact on the way local people lived their lives. When he was young, Ajahn Buddhadasa remarks, "the village people kept the sila-dhamma well enough, better than people do today. There were some who didn't, of course, but those with homes and property upheld the precepts because they risked embarrassment if they failed to do so. Still, there were quite a few who didn't follow the basic precepts, especially the one about not killing animals, such as fish and crabs, for food." Old people tended to refrain from killing animals. "At our home Mother was very strict, herself, about not killing living crabs and fish. So it was the duty of us kids to cook them in boiling water. Fear of *papa* (evil, trespass) back then was much more pronounced than today. There weren't many people who stole or drank whiskey. Those who drank didn't drink much." Buddhadasa's grandfather was a licensed distiller who held the distillation rights in Chaiya township, but his father neither drank nor smoked. For relaxation he played Thai chess.

In 1915 the Nak-dham, an academic course of Dhamma study, had not yet been introduced to the monks of Phum Riang. "In those days," Buddhadasa recalled, "the monastics did a lot of physical work. They didn't have the Nak-dham. Most learned the various chants, and that's how they meditated. I never saw them meditating at other times. The rest of the time they worked with wood a lot. They were carpenters and built *kuti* (huts), cottages, cabins, and small houses. If any wat lacked a main shrine hall, monks from other nearby monasteries would go to help build one."

Before the modern school system spread into the countryside, education was the product of the boys' close relationship with the monastic community. Living at the wat, they received moral as well as mental training. "In those days before we had schools, if parents didn't need you to work at home, you could live at the wat until being ordained as a novice or monk. You could stay in robes for three or four years, then disrobe and start a family. There was a special reason why parents were happy to have their boys live at the wat. It was because they learned how to do all kinds of practical things, such as weaving nipa palm leaves, used for baskets. And there was very little bullying, because we were afraid of the abbot's displeasure."

6

TRAINING STORYTELLERS

NGUAM was a temple boy from the age of eight to ten. A key component of temple education in Phum Riang was learning to tell stories, not just for entertainment but "to train the temple boys to be clever and intelligent, or as we would say in the local dialect, to have a 'lawyer's head.'" This sharpening of the intelligence often took the form of a game played by temple boys and novices. "No one organized it; we arranged it ourselves. As soon as we sat together, whoever was a bit of a leader would choose a topic," the Ajahn recalled.

Nguam and his fellow temple boys trained each other in the craft of storytelling. Topics covered such important matters as doing household chores, tending water buffaloes, and trapping fish. For example, the leader might suggest a topic related to the first chore of their daily life. "Today," the leader might say, "we will speak about steaming rice. Who wants to go first?" In Ajahn Buddhadasa's words, "Usually, those who volunteered to speak first were somewhat less clever than the others. So somebody would describe how to steam rice, and the rest would listen. If the first speaker was rather foolish, he might start off by saying, 'I put the rice in a pot and place it on the fire.' The rest would object immediately, pointing out, for example, 'You haven't gotten into the kitchen yet, how can you do that?' Or somebody might interject, 'You haven't even made the fire.' If the speaker left too many holes for others to question and raise objections, somebody else would take over. Every successful objection caused immediate laughter and glee. These sometimes got as detailed as 'You didn't open the door, how could you enter the kitchen?' or 'You haven't picked up the dipper, how can you scoop up the water?' Eventually every little step had to be mentioned until no irregularities or mistakes remained. These were like the lectures of the most detailed scholars. Because there were many objectors, we objected a lot. This was training in subtlety and in the use of logic. The smarter kids usually waited until the end, when they could narrate in detail without anybody finding an objection."

Usually these sessions took place at night after the temple boys had finished their studies and chores. This was how boys amused themselves in the days when there was no electricity and thus no radio or television. (Today, if one walks into a town wat at night, one might see a group of temple boys watching a soccer match on television in the quarters where they sleep.) From detailed descriptions of everyday tasks, the boys would proceed to topics that had to do with concrete experiences in their natural environment. Learning to tell stories by themselves, temple boys gained not just speaking and communication tools but confidence and life skills. "The subjects chosen as topics came in many forms: culture, customs, humor, lies," Ajahn Buddhadasa tells us. "Whoever could speak well was considered clever. Although these sessions weren't about book learning, they were a highly effective way to develop intelligence. For kids like us, who had spent our lives in the rice fields, the subjects were things we knew about, things like plowing the fields and herding buffaloes. Or a boy could talk about something he heard from others; but he had to take responsibility for not leaving any openings for objections. So we kids were all expert storytellers. Only at the wat did we have the opportunity for this, during the short time before we went to sleep."

The monks encouraged temple boys to play this game, which developed presentation and speaking skills. As Ajahn Buddhadasa recalled, "Sometimes the abbot would moderate, but not very often" because the abbot "didn't have the time. He had a lot of work to do."

Some of the stories that temple boys enjoyed telling involved dirty jokes or double meanings. Compared to what children see on TV and in movies today, however, these stories may seem rather tame; yet they were often filled with subtleties. "The fable of Grandpa Then and Grandma Chi," the Ajahn tell us, referring to a story about two ascetic laypeople, "had dozens of scenes and parts to play. Some parts were dirty, some were humorous, and some were put in so someone could show off his wit. The wat was a school for making a boy clever without his knowing it. There were hardly any topics about women or anything that might provoke our sexual feelings. It was all about being skilled, clever, and admired for these qualities."

In the early 1980s—by which time children were attending state schools and the number of temple boys in Thailand was steadily declining—the Ajahn observed that "none of this activity continues today because kids don't stay at the wat any more. The custom has been broken." In his youth the wat was like a public school, but one in which boys received moral training. "Kids couldn't play truant and had to be responsible for their duties. Certain things could be done at home but not at the wat. For example, we weren't allowed to sleep late. If anyone failed to get up in the morning, he'd be doused. We had the right to pour water all over the unfortunate snoozer if he overslept. 'Oversleeping' meant not being up by the time the chickens came down from their roosts."

Buddhadasa remembered a trick the older boys pulled on him and other young boys during their first months at the wat. "Now, if you wanted to get someone, one way was to wake up early and chase a few chickens down to the ground. Then you could douse your friends early. Temple boys received a multifaceted training in intelligence, work, and fun."

7

CHAIYA BOXERS

AJAHN BUDDHADASA once said of his hometown that
"Phum Riang was an ancient boxing city with a good reputation." Phum Riang was then the provincial seat of
Chaiya, and Chaiya's boxers had been famous for a
long time. The art of boxing that became known as *muai chaiya* was
brought to Chaiya by Ajahn Ma in the mid-nineteenth century. Originally from Bangkok, Ma came to Phum Riang and was ordained as a
monk there. He was a very learned man who had somewhere acquired
knowledge of the martial art of boxing. He might have been a boxing
master before his ordination. Eventually Ajahn Ma became abbot of
Wat Thung Chap Chang, whose name means "the monastery of the
field where elephants are captured." Here at this monastery in Chaiya,
Ajahn Ma taught young men how to box.

Boxing in Chaiya flourished. Governor Kham, who ruled Chaiya
during the reign of King Chulalongkorn (Rama V), was also a boxing
instructor. At the end of the nineteenth century, Governor Kham was
invited to bring his best student, a young man called Plong, to participate in a boxing match that was to be performed before the king. As
a result of that match, the king created an official governmental rank,
Master of Boxing Fame, which he conferred upon Plong, the champion boxer from Chaiya.

In Chaiya the governor ordered the construction of a new pavilion, to be called the Nine Room Hall, within the vast monastic compound of Wat Boromthat, famous for its ancient stupa. Adjacent to the

sala was a grass-covered area which was to serve as the site of an outdoor boxing arena. From that time on, local people referred to the years when the art of boxing flourished in Chaiya as the era of the Nine Room Hall.

The boxing arena, constructed on the grass in front of the Nine Room Hall, consisted of four posts driven into the ground, with ropes stretched tight around them. The audience gathered around all four sides of the arena; the governor of Chaiya and his officials sat inside the pavilion. Boxers wore shorts and were bare-chested. Since at that time there were no rigid groin protectors, they strapped on a rolled piece of cloth called a *lobo*. The boxers did not wear gloves; instead, their hands were wrapped in unbleached cotton strips to form what were known as "braided hands." Their heads were covered with a ritual headpiece that they kept on even while fighting. In addition to using their fists, boxers were permitted to kick, knee, elbow, and head butt their opponents.

In time a Boxing Department was incorporated into the government of Chaiya. This department consisted of four important boxing divisions representing the four townships of Chaiya: Ban Paktho, Phum Riang, Ban Wieng, and Ban Thung. Each division was led by a boxing master. Under Rama V, the master and the boxers in each division received special privileges. For example, twenty-five boxers and their instructor, Master Plong, were exempt from the poll tax and from corvée labor.[5]

Since temple boys were encouraged to practice the art of self-defense, "boxing was a special activity for them," Ajahn Buddhadasa said, recalling his youth at Wat Phum Riang. "I was made to practice even though I didn't like it. It was a tradition; my friends pressured me to practice. Sometimes even the monks wanted me to train and gave advice. Mostly, though, we kids taught each other." But Nguam was not very robust. As the Ajahn later remarked, "I was rather weak. I wasn't stout or sturdy, but I wasn't skinny either." After he was ordained as a monk, however, he said he "gradually grew stronger."

In Buddhadasa's youth, boxing masters and good boxers were held in high regard, and the country supported them. The boxing masters were virtuous men who demanded honesty and integrity in their students. Boxers who cheated in any way were immediately expelled and lost their rights and privileges. "Wat boxing was civil boxing that followed rules," the Ajahn tells us. "Nobody hurt anyone else so much as to draw blood. In the season after the rains retreat, when the Buddha images were displayed on boats in the villages, there was boxing."

Every year in October or November each temple celebrated the Festival of Hae Phra with a procession of Buddha images. Hae Phra was a most entertaining festival for the young as well as the old. Years later, grandparents often told the youngsters how much fun they had had in the old days on these occasions.

Buddhadasa's brother, Dhammadasa, recalled the annual Hae Phra festival in Phum Riang as among the most enjoyable times of his youth. The day before their wat's Buddha image was carried out in procession, everybody took part in the ceremony of pouring fragrant water over it and wiping it sparkling clean. The event was regarded as a sacred ceremony in which people made merit collectively, thus binding the community together. Friends poured sacred water over one another.

Every year children looked forward to making and eating a special sticky rice desert during this festival. In the morning the children and young men and women woke up before dawn, put on their new clothes, and wore all the jewelry they had. The children then offered the sticky rice treat to the monks. For young men and women it was a special day, as they got to meet young people from other villages, spend time together, and have fun. Around 8:30 A.M. the Buddha image left the wat on a boat accompanied by musicians playing rousing music to encourage people to march. Everybody in the procession took part in bringing the Buddha image all the way to the Nine Room Hall on the monastic grounds of Wat Boromthat. Several temporary pavilions were built to accommodate the large number of people. In the afternoon there were boxing matches.

Governor Chuen, a son of Governor Kham, recalled that at Wat Prasop the Buddha image was carried out onto a boat which proceeded along the Chaiya Canal until it reached a sala in Tha Chang. At midday the monks were offered food at the pavilion. In the afternoon if the governor of Chaiya or the district officer was attending the festival and put up prize money, there were boxing matches. In years when the governor or district officer could not attend, there were no boxing matches, since the officials were the only ones who could afford to put up the purses. There were no tickets to buy; everybody watched the matches free of charge. While adults watched the boxing matches, children jumped into a nearby pond and had fun swimming.

During the Hae Phra festival the governor sponsored many matches in the Nine Room Hall at Wat Boromthat. Whoever wanted to box found an opponent; there were referees to supervise. Many pairs were able to box before the boats returned to their monasteries. The boxers always got a free lunch, for there was plenty of food offered to the monks. They would stop for the monks' lunch at the Nine Room Hall, which was located between the site of Suan Mokkh and the village of Lamyai, where there is a long stretch of swamp. At two in the afternoon, they would begin to box.

"At the boxing match," Dhammadasa recalled, "the parents, brothers, sisters, and other relatives who had come to the festival cheered the boxers on. The winners received prize money of four to ten baht. The boxers spent their money buying drinks for their friends and relatives. These men were not professional boxers. They were sons and grandsons of boxers who had entered the matches out of love of boxing and to bring fame to their villages." Back then professional boxing as an occupation was unknown; the village boxers supported themselves through other occupations.

In the past there was a boxing camp in every village of Chaiya. Buddhadasa recalled that virtually all boys knew how to box. In those days Chaiya boxing was famous far and wide.

The changes that Thai boxing underwent over the decades reflect the process of modernization in Siam and the abolition of local Buddhist traditions under the newly centralized Sangha hierarchy. Originally, Thai boxing was found all over the small principalities which today comprise the nation-state of Thailand. Training in the monastic compound, boxers were imbued with religious sentiment and moral imperatives. Instruction was passed along the lineages of boxing masters, comparable to the lineages of Buddhist masters. After the centralization of the Sangha in 1902, boxing was forced out of the wat as the Dhammayut authorities viewed it as inappropriate and belonging to the secular realm. This was what happened to Chaiya boxing. Thawi Chuaiam, the author of "Chaiya Boxing," writes that by mid-century "the boxing environment of Chaiya had become very dispirited. The boxing camps are not as united and stable as they were in the past.... For future generations the saying 'Chaiya is a boxing city' will simply be another Chaiya legend."

8

FOLK REMEDIES

M OST CHILDREN in Siam learned how to care for themselves when they were out in the woods with no adults around. When young Nguam was living at Wat Phum Riang as a temple boy, he collected medicinal plants for the abbot. He learned to identify a great many plants and knew their healing properties. Ajahn Buddhadasa retained this knowledge throughout his life, used it personally, and occasionally advised others. "This understanding of herbal medicine and ancient healing I learned both from home and from the wat. I can say that every temple boy knew about herbal medicines. For instance, if told to fetch a certain plant commonly used as a strengthener, we could all recognize it because we had been sent to gather it regularly. I had lived at the wat as a child and can still remember that the *ya gratung* I was sent to gather was mixed with betel palm root, coconut root, *maprang* root, and *yor* root. Sometimes something different was added, like *neem* root. That's how it was made by the teacher who taught me the Thai alphabet."

Temple boys learned about ancient healing by becoming apprentices to the monks. "Anyone could ask the monks for medicines," Ajahn Buddhadasa recalled. "Some medicines had been prepared already, some had to be made on the spot, some had been written down as a recipe." The most common medicine for the sick was ya gratung. "For fevers, ya gratung worked as a cooling herb. It worked by forcing or pushing [the literal meaning of *gratung*] the fever to its end point quickly. We temple boys helped each other to prepare, pulverize, and mix the herbs."

Children of Nguam's generation had taken an all-purpose green medicine. If one of the temple boys did something wrong, the abbot would send him "to collect a bunch of green leaves, any green leaves except those that caused itching or were poisonous. These, then, were spread out all over the porch to dry. When they were crispy we pulverized them and filled up jars. Whenever people had fevers, they would take some. This was correct because 'green medicine' has the cooling effect of the chlorophyll. Green medicines cool heat and fever. I still believe this. Just eat green leaves, and they will cool down any heat or fever. They also reduce gas in the intestines. Even better, dissolve the pulverized leaves in water and then spray or paint the solution all over the body until it's completely green. Green medicine wasn't very bitter, because there were many kinds of leaves in it, only some of which were bitter. Little children could take it; they either drank it dissolved in water or it was dissolved and sprayed on them."

"Many medicines were difficult to make," the Ajahn recalled, "each required particular techniques. One had to be careful with measurements, even using a scale. There were at least four or five herbal preparations for which we had to collect ingredients immediately if a sick villager was in need. In the case of ya gratung, we temple boys would collect the herb for the abbot to boil, then we would take the pot of boiled medicine to the house of the sick person. For children, the first pot of medicine was usually enough to cure them. If the patient didn't improve after the first day, the abbot would go see for himself and prepare other pots of medicine as needed. He would try different things until the person was cured. If patients were not cured, they would die. That's how it was in the old days. There wasn't anything magical. If one made mistakes or the illness was stronger than the medicine, the patient would die. But most of them got better."

Buddhadasa recommends simple medicines made with readily available ingredients. "Every temple boy knew what to do if touched by a *bung*, a caterpillar with long yellow hair. If a bung touched us, there wasn't any need to ask what to do; we just pulled some mucus out of our nose and rubbed it onto the sting till it went away. Much better than the balms they sell nowadays. This makes me think: the law of nature created these things in pairs; it's only that we don't know enough. Everything we need is here, but we only know ten percent. Unbelievable? Sounds silly? Pull out some snot—earwax would probably work too— and rub it where the insect stung you. Funny!" the Ajahn laughed.

Children of Nguam's generation learned to be competent enough to treat themselves. "There are some things that children had to know. I often ate things that made my mouth itch; palm sugar solved it right away. Or take the sting of a wasp. It's like a bee sting but much worse, like being knocked over with a club. As soon as you paint the sting with papaya sap, it goes away immediately. There's a reason for this. Papaya sap contains a protein that is an antidote to certain poisons."

Another treatment, maybe the most primitive, "is to cover a wound with spiderwebs and the soot from above a stove. It works. It's antiseptic. It prevents germs from getting in. Even better is to use the tips of *marang*, both sap and new leaves, to cover the wound. This is better than tincture of mercury. For hot water scalds, use the yellow gum you get from slicing open a *tava* plant. It will heal scalds and burns." Both marang and tava are edible tubers that exude a gum that produces itching.

Recalling the domestic medicines of his youth, Ajahn Buddhadasa says, "For a child with breathing problems and asthma, they roasted a centipede until crispy, pulverized it, then dissolved it in rice whiskey. For emaciated children with swollen bellies, and also for cataracts, they coated monitor lizard meat with turmeric and salt, then roasted it till tasty. Eat one monitor, and you're cured. I had to do this." Some children considered monitor lizards ugly. Nguam's younger brother, Yikoei, "couldn't keep monitor meat down; he threw it up every time. Funny, I never had trouble keeping it down. I don't know why he couldn't. Maybe he hated monitors too much to eat them. Even when monitor meat was prepared to look like chicken meat, he could tell from the smell it wasn't chicken. He couldn't eat stingray bones either. I told him they were delicious, but he didn't feel that way. Actually, ray bones weren't all that delicious, but I could eat them."

With regard to his upbringing, the Ajahn says, "Strangely frugal—that was the home that gave birth to me. They didn't have the medicines we have today, yet people lived and survived, giving birth to us. These are examples of the knowledge I received from the village and wat of those days. The wat was like a university for the villagers."

When local people got sick, whether they were Muslims or Buddhists, they went to the monks for help. In the early decades of the twentieth century, the Ajahn recalled, "all the local abbots in Phum Riang had to know about herbal medicine. No matter how late at night, if someone arrived to tell the abbot that somebody had this or that, he had to go, even if it was pitch black outside. Back then, local teachers were like that. Late at night they would go to help people until they could trust that the danger was over; only then would they return to the wat. Sometimes they didn't get back till after dawn. They had cultivated the character of first thinking of others. They were patient and tolerant, not hateful or spiteful, never thinking of their own rest and comfort. Naturally, people loved and respected them. If there was work to do at the wat, people helped without questioning."

Buddhadasa had many relatives who were monks. The oldest relative was his great-uncle, his maternal grandmother's older brother, who became abbot of Wat Mai Phum Riang until he died in the late nineteenth century. Buddhadasa recalled, "This great-uncle was interested in traditional medicines and passed his knowledge along to my father." Xiang in turn passed on medical knowledge, as well as everything he knew about the trade he plied, to his son Nguam. "Father enjoyed making traditional medicine. Whenever a book was published about traditional medicine, he was interested in buying and studying it. This added to the knowledge he gained while a temple boy. Consequently, he was able to make medicines for sale. He made herbal pills according to the texts. This was the first time that medicine in pill form had ever been sold in Phum Riang. Father ordered a pill-making press from Bangkok. At that time medicine was quite inexpensive, only three, five, or ten *satang*. Bottled medicine was rare. There was one famous compound that made children feel much better. Around here it was called *taan khamoi*. It was for skinny, spindly, malnourished kids. It had to be dissolved in a little alcohol. After a child drank it, he would feel dizzy and his ears would turn red. This medicine spread widely. It was well known in this area. I used to take it. I was forced to take it, but I didn't like its smell."

As Buddhadasa explained, "The formula was complicated, with over ten medicinal ingredients. The special ingredient was *paad chanai*. It was combined with other medicines and then made into pills to be dissolved in alcohol. The paad chanai root contains poison. It's really powerful. It must be pounded and then soaked in water. If this water is sprayed into the canal, all the fish will die. Paad chanai is a vine with tiny leaves. A thick skin covers the root, which has a narrow pith. This medicine was called 'fire-power medicine.' I can remember people buying this medicine more than any other. It could cure all kinds of things, but most of all malnourishment."

The local monasteries were repositories of medicinal knowledge. There were books containing recipes for medicines the secrets of which had been passed from teacher to pupil in a chain spanning many generations. Nguam's Uncle Siang, who lived in Phum Riang before he moved to Chumphon, "also had some knowledge of these matters because he once lived at the same wat as my great-uncle who made traditional medicines."

Besides the medicine monks, there were other healers, Buddhadasa tells us, "wandering healers such as Chinese, Vietnamese, and Indian doctors. Most of these treated chronic diseases, helping the local doctors. With the old ways, some people got better, some died."

By the late 1920s a hospital had been established by an American missionary in the provincial town of Nakhon Si Thammarat, south of Buddhadasa's province. Local people, however, continued to seek help from Chinese or Indian doctors, who charged a small fee. Those who had no money would seek help from Buddhist monks.

During this time in the Tung Song district of Nakhon an Englishman by the name of Frank Exell was working for the Siam Bank. Shortly after his return from a business trip to Phatthalung he wrote, "I started to have the most fearful earache. I tried the usual remedies but they made no difference. There were no doctors in Tung Song. The nearest was the mission in Nakhon but I could not get down there until the week-end." At this time Exell was the only European in town, and the only doctor he knew was an American missionary who lived further south.

Soon the pain became so unbearable that Exell thought of closing the bank early in order to get himself to the American mission hospital. He went home for lunch "feeling worse than ever." He thoroughly upset his cook, a local man, by taking nothing to eat. The cook was certain that Exell must have got an insect in his ear. After the bank manager returned to work, the cook and his servant, a Chinese boy, turned up at the bank. "They had a lengthy discussion with a clerk," Exell wrote. "They had been to see a Chinese doctor in the market [who] they were sure could put me right. And they wanted [the clerk] to talk me into it. Rather to my surprise, the clerk took their side and I decided to have a go. Anything seemed better than a train journey to Ronphibun [district] and then a drive to Nakhon."

When he returned to his house, Exell found that the men had already fetched the Chinese doctor. "A most courtly old Chinaman was waiting for me at the bungalow and was almost apologetic when he asked me to do anything. First of all I lay down on the settee and he had a good look at things but used no instruments of any sort. He then said something to the boy who fetched an egg cup, a bottle of white vinegar and a bowl of hot water. The doctor put beside them a small bundle of very thin wire rods about six inches long. They were the only instruments he appeared to have brought. When I insisted that the rods be put in a solution of potassium permanganate he looked at me a bit askance but gave in with good grace."

Describing the folk remedy which his pain drove him to try, Exell noted, "The egg cup was first of all warmed up in the hot water and a small quantity of vinegar poured into it. A few drops of this in my ear and then he proceeded to select a rod or two. I got a bit worried when he started to insert these into the ear with a twirling motion but his touch was so delicate that I really felt nothing at all. Presently there was a tug and then I felt as if half my head had been pulled away. He produced a waxy lump in the centre of which was the offending insect.

A few more drops of vinegar in the ear and the operation was complete. The charge? About one and sixpence. And that was probably four times as much as he would have charged in the market."

The first modern medical center in Bangkok, Sirirat Hospital, was built in 1888 during King Chulalongkorn's reign. At first, most of the drugs used in the hospital were derived from medicinal plants. As the city became more modern and the number of Western-educated physicians increased, so did the use of Western medicines. This trend continued until local herbal remedies were ultimately replaced by Western drugs in hospitals and health centers all across the country.

But the modern medicine practiced in Bangkok did not penetrate into the outlying provinces for many, many years. For example, out of the five children that were born to them, Nguam's parents lost two. As the Ajahn recalled, "My older brother died; Mother said he died as an infant. The last one died too. I never saw it. Probably born before its time, but there was enough to be a person. It died within a few hours despite the best medical care local custom could arrange. There was probably insufficient sanitation and other mistakes that caused infants to die. Consequently, there weren't so many people, and there was no need for birth control."

In his youth, Buddhadasa's medical school was the great outdoors. Referring to urban Thai people's ignorance of simple domestic remedies, the Ajahn remarks, "If we thought like *farangs* [Westerners], we'd be afraid and rush to the hospital. The old hermits and sages knew a lot about herbal medicine. They passed their knowledge along from generation to generation. In the forest, one had to know how to help oneself. These days people have given up interest in such things. They can't do things right because they don't understand nature." By the time of Buddhadasa's death in May 1993, at the age of eighty-seven, two-thirds of the dense forests in Thailand had been destroyed and many primary sources for herbal medicines had disappeared.

Nevertheless, herbal remedies are still preferred by some Buddhist monks and laypeople, especially those from rural areas. In 1992, just a year before Buddhadasa's death, the National Identity Board, a government agency, finally admitted that the establishment of the first modern hospital marked the beginning of the decline in the use of herbal medicines in Thailand. With the economic crisis of 1997 providing the impetus, herbal medicine began to make a comeback among middle-class Thai.

9

MODERN EDUCATION

N GUAM was eight when he left home to become a temple boy at Wat Phum Riang. By the time he returned home he had acquired so many social as well as practical skills that he thought of himself as a man of the world. By the time he enrolled in the local primary school Nguam already knew how to read and write. The government school was located within the monastic grounds of Wat Neua, known today as Wat Photharam. The school was nearby, so Nguam could walk home for lunch if he wanted. His mother gave him one satang to buy plain noodles for lunch. The natural environment supplied other food. Nguam picked vegetables from a nearby ditch to eat with his noodles.

After the modern system of education was introduced in the provincial town of Chaiya, the governor turned some of the monastery buildings into school buildings. Since there was no janitor, children came to school early in the morning to sweep the grounds and clean the rooms before classes began. "That was fun," Ajahn Buddhadasa recalled. The school at Wat Neua "was the new kind of school that had been improved during the reign of Chulalongkorn."[6]

In Buddhadasa's youth, monks continued to teach school-age children. All schools were to adhere to standards set by the Ministry of Public Education for syllabi, textbooks, examinations, and student uniforms. Ajahn Buddhadasa remembered some of the monks who had taught in the elementary school. "In Phum Riang there was one monk who went to be trained in Bangkok—I don't know for how many days or months—and then came back as a teacher. His name was Khru Wan, and he has since died. His successor was Ajahn Tab Suwan. Each grade had twenty or thirty students. This teacher in particular was talented and skilled in many arts. He could sing. He could draw and paint in the Thai style and render the pictures of the Ramakian. He was able to teach his students to draw, even those hard-to-draw characters such as Tosakan or Palee."[7] Ajahn Tab's drawings, Buddhadasa recalled, "had beautiful lines, which he would fill in with colored chalk. I can still remember his drawings to this day. Later, when I got to see the work of those who were trained to draw classically, I didn't find that any of them were all that much better than Ajahn Tab Suwan. I still feel that he was the best, the most correct, the most beautiful painter, and he didn't pale in comparison to anyone. Other students who could draw well later became artists themselves: painters, carvers, sculptors, and temple decorators."

When Nguam was in his early teens, his father opened another store close to the Chaiya market. His mother stayed with the younger children at the old shop in Phum Riang. While attending the district school in Chaiya, Nguam lived with his father. During this period, when there were "just the two of us," Nguam was close to his father.

"Sarapi Utit, the district school, was more advanced than my old school in Phum Riang," the Ajahn continued. Except for one monk, all the teachers were laypeople. Buddhadasa remembered the novelty of wearing Western-style clothing. "The uniform at that time was a white shirt with black pants, called scout pants; they had to have pockets and belt loops. The shirt was just an ordinary white shirt with a collar."

In an effort to transform Siam into a modern nation, King Vajiravudh promoted a new national identity that owed much to Western ideas of nationalism. The king coined the motto "Nation, Religion, and King" in order to inculcate devotion to the Thai nation, to state Buddhism, and to the absolute monarchy. In 1917, when Nguam was in primary school, the king created a new national flag of red, white, and blue to serve this trinity: red for the nation, white for Buddhism, and blue for the monarch. At the time nobody understood the political concept of nation (Thai: *chat*, from the Pali *jati*) as a territorial entity. People identified themselves by the town or village where they lived. Ethnicity was not that important. Thus, state schools were used to spread the meaning of "nation" to the country's youth and to mold the children into good citizens.

For local boys who were used to living in close contact with their natural surroundings, it was boring to sit in a classroom all day reading books that had nothing to do with their immediate environment. In one of his school reports a teacher wrote that Nguam was restless and often talked to his friends in class. But unlike some children, he did not have to be prodded to come to school, nor did he bully others. He had good manners, and his work was neat and clean. Nguam was an average student but a responsible one. The teacher praised his diligence and good memory.

Ajahn Buddhadasa admits, "Regarding book learning, at that time I never considered myself to be all that good, but I could pass the tests and don't remember failing. But it wasn't much fun to study. At first I was homesick; even before the lunch break I was thinking of home. I was as filled with homesickness as if I were far away from my parents. Studying wasn't fun, but I studied enough to pass the tests fairly well."

Once Nguam began studying at the district school he no longer went back to his father's shop for lunch. For most children, this school was too far away to permit them to run home for lunch, and in those days the school fees did not include meals. "I would find something to eat at school," Buddhadasa recalled, "but at that time kids didn't usually eat lunch very often. Most of the time nobody paid any attention to it. We pretty much forgot about it and so didn't eat anything, because there wasn't much food for sale in the vicinity of the school."

When Nguam was not in school he helped his father at the store in Chaiya, where they sold rice. "Sometimes we had to buy things and send them to the store in Phum Riang. Having two stores required that we have an oxcart, which I sometimes had to drive. Sometimes I also had to look after the cattle. My parents had a hired man who took care of the oxen and drove the cart, but sometimes I took over because it was fun. Taking the oxen out to feed along the railroad tracks was very pleasant. I liked to look for crickets under the rocks along the tracks. While the oxen were eating grass, I would play on the slopes of the railroad track embankments. Actually, this was forbidden. Though it was against the rules, I acted as if I didn't know, because there was plenty of grass there that the oxen liked to eat. Sometimes they would climb up and eat alongside the tracks, and then I would have to chase them down. The railroad officials could be nasty about this, but they left us alone if we let the oxen graze down below. If the man who took care of the oxen wasn't able to take them out early in the day, then I would watch over them until evening, when he would come to fetch them home."

Bullocks were the main ground transportation. The Ajahn described the kinds of carts that local people used. "In our area back then, the carts used two oxen. We chose two beasts that got along with each other and were of equal size. Some people only used one ox, but if two were used the cart would go faster and more smoothly. Each ox complements the other's strength. They were slender, quick oxen, not heavy or ponderous with sagging bellies, so they pulled well. I used a small piece of bamboo to crack at them. Actually, driving the oxcart wasn't my duty, but I liked doing it because it was different and fun."

A young disciple of Ajahn Buddhadasa's, curious about how he spent his time when he was in his teens, asked him if he had ever misbehaved before he became a monk. This was in the early 1980s, a time when many teenagers and young adults in Thailand were getting into all kinds of trouble by stealing cars or motorcycles, driving when drunk, or taking drugs. "What do you mean by misbehave?" the Ajahn asked in a critical tone. "What level of misbehaving are you talking about? When I was a teenager there was no such thing as stealing or thieving or getting into fights and beating people up; there was none of that. I didn't even know how to do such things." The worst thing Nguam ever did was to take what was not given, thus breaking the second precept. "Maybe before it got light I would go and sneak a couple of those beautiful roses on the other side of our fence," the Ajahn recalled with a chuckle, "but that was before it got light. Our neighbors planted them along the fence between our houses. Even if they saw me take a few, they wouldn't say anything, although they weren't exactly happy that I took them. We would have to consider that stealing, so that kind of misbehavior happened."

In 1922, not long after Nguam completed his third year of secondary school, his father died. "I guessed that he must have had a stroke," Ajahn Buddhadasa said later, "because he said he had an intense headache, the kind that people speak of as causing them to pass out. I went to get a massage doctor, but I wasn't fast enough, and he died within just a few minutes. Death was probably the result of the bursting of a major artery in his brain." Recalling his father's easygoing manner and the joy he found in his work and hobbies, the Ajahn said, "My father wasn't a particularly tense person; he took things pretty easy. He was always thinking of ways to improve and advance his work, which was the family business, but he didn't do anything in an intense or tight way."

Nguam was sixteen when he left school and became the manager of the store in Phum Riang. "After Father died we gave up the store in Chaiya, and I went back to stay with Mother in Phum Riang." As the Ajahn recalled, he did not have time to feel sad. "I was just too busy making the funeral arrangements and seeing to all the rest." Nguam had learned the vocation of his family by working alongside his father. As the eldest son, Nguam was expected to take charge of his father's business so that his younger brother, Yikoei, could go to school. "I had to help with the family's burdens. If we all studied, then nobody would be at home to help Mother. I was given the responsibility of overseeing everything, because Mother was already old and was sick for much of that year. She had aching knees. This trouble later went away. She was cured after she took a traditional medicine."

10

FINDING FOOD

S THE ELDEST CHILD, Nguam spent most of his youth working at his parents' store. "I wasn't just a merchant," Ajahn Buddhadasa recalled. "I was also a laborer. I had to carry things to the homes of important people, such as the government officials who bought twenty-liter cans of kerosene. I had to carry them home for them. We didn't have any hired hands then, didn't have a truck," the Ajahn said with a laugh (there were no trucks of any kind back then). "I was always busy, and the work was heavy. I even had to split all the firewood that we used at home. Mother would buy warped and twisted driftwood that was brought in by boat. I had to cut these half trees into suitable pieces and then split them before storing them beneath the house. It was a lot of fun splitting the driftwood. It was totally dried out, and the axe might bounce off when you hit it. Or I would put the axe down, blade up, on the ground and then smash a piece of wood down on it. Then the wood would split. That was fun."

Occasionally Nguam got a break from work when his parents took him to visit his mother's relatives in Tha Chang, a district south of Chaiya. "Every once in a while I would go to visit them, and sometimes our relatives there would come to visit us. Each year we might go back and forth two or three times. On rare occasions all the aunts and uncles, even the grandparents and great-grandparents, would get together, which made everybody very happy. They were delighted to see and enjoy all the children. This was one of the ways that we got to go out onto the sea."

When Nguam was in school, the teachers would sometimes take the students on field trips to the seashore. At other times Nguam and his friends would go on their own. As the Ajahn recalled, "Occasionally I would go out to catch crabs or fish. It was like an adventure, because my family did not allow me to do such things. So when I escaped, it was like escaping to another world and studying all kinds of things I had never seen before."

"We got plenty of crabs and fish. We got the horseshoe and king crabs that climbed up to eat *pak bia* grass [an edible medicinal plant] when the water level rose a bit. There were shellfish as well. Children could catch a fair amount and take some home with them. But I never went out there intentionally because my mother absolutely forbade it. If she knew I was fooling around like that, I would be severely scolded.

"When I was a little older, I would sometimes pretend to be going to visit somebody in Takrob township on the banks of Phum Riang Canal, and along the way I would catch *samae* crabs." These are small crabs that live in mud flats. "That was a lot of fun. When the water level rose a little bit, the sand crabs had to leave their holes because the water flooded them out. They would sit at the mouths of their holes and wait for the water to recede. My friends, who were more experienced, could catch them easily, but I had never tried catching them before. My friends would act nonchalant, as if they weren't doing anything in particular, then quickly grab the crabs and put them into the earthenware jar we carried. We would carry the jar in one hand and grab the crabs with the other. If we did this slowly and awkwardly, the crabs would pinch us. If we were quick, they didn't have time to get us. I had so much fun. Before long the jar was full. If we were pinched once in a while, well, that was no big deal. That's how things went. For me it was a kind of education."

Nguam had a curious mind and liked trying new things. "I loved to learn about things I had never seen. How do you clean crabs? How do you make fermented crab paste? I had never seen that done. This was like going to a vocational school. People used big baskets that could hold many crabs. The crabs were dumped out of the jars into the basket, which was then set in the river to keep the crabs alive."

Many fishermen lived in the area where the Phum Riang Canal emptied into the sea. Nguam and his friends enjoyed going to the nearby *poh* factory. A poh is a method of trapping fish in which wooden stakes are driven into the sea floor, not far from shore but often in water over ten meters deep. The stakes are right next to one another. On one occasion Nguam stayed overnight at the poh factory. The Ajahn recalled, "The person who took us to watch was a friend of the poh plant owner. Lots of people went to watch them pickle the crabs. The crabs were dumped into this huge basket until it was half full. And then, by agitating the basket, the crabs were rinsed in water while still alive and then put into jars. Brine was then added to the jars, which were sealed with a wooden plug, and the crabs stayed sealed in the jars and fermented. I didn't claim my portion but gave it instead to the distant relative who had brought me to watch. He was the one who arranged for the boat, and I just went along for fun."

The Phum Riang Canal, full of water all year round, is about ten kilometers long and ten meters wide. In the 1920s birds and fish were still very abundant. For Nguam it was a magical time. The Ajahn recalled that he "loved to visit the little canal that went from Phum Riang to the villages of Takrob and Giew. The stream was just wide enough for a boat to pass through. What I liked most were the Java doves. Around there, if you got off on a sandbar to heed nature's call, you would find Java doves calling raucously everywhere." By the 1980s, however, the Java doves had disappeared. "Recently, I asked around and learned that not one was left."

There were plenty of small freshwater fish, such as *kradee*, which the Ajahn described as like "an army in the river. When the water level went down with the tide, one could take a fine sieve basket and scoop up the kradee. In one catch there would be far more fish than one could eat. Once we cut off their heads, we would put them on wood skewers, and after drying them in the sun for awhile we fried them in oil until they were crispy. We ate them with tamarind shrimp paste and neem shoots. That was enough to make our bellies bulge. We were so hungry and tired after catching them. It was cool, because it was fun." But because of his duties at his father's shop, the Ajahn said, "I could only go there once in a while."

On subsequent trips Nguam borrowed a casting net from the poh factory and was able to catch fish right in front of the plant. "I would pull them up onto the beach," the Ajahn recalled, "and in just one cast have more than I could eat." In this region where he used to live, fresh food was always available. "There were all kinds of crabs, fish, and squid—many different varieties, including the hard-shell squid that they dried and pulverized to make toothpaste. These squid are boiled alive and come out unbelievably crispy—almost as crispy as a crisped Chinese pear. They are delicious, even without any sauce to dip them in. One can even eat the squid with coffee, using the same water for brewing the coffee as for boiling the squid."

When the Ajahn described eating squid to people who had never eaten them, they were skeptical. "Some people don't believe us and assume the squid will taste terrible, wondering how anybody could eat them, but they're unbelievably crunchy and really sweet as well. If you have never eaten them, you won't believe me. But if the squids die before they're cooked, the flavor is just the opposite, because then they become sticky and stinky. Everyone is surprised and impressed by crunchy squid. Nowadays there just aren't the same opportunities as in the old days to boil them alive with coffee. Before I was ordained I really liked to eat them."

Another food found in nature that Nguam loved was "honeycomb with larvae still in the cells." This craving followed him into the monastic life. "I always wanted to eat those larvae even after I was ordained. But I never had the chance. I couldn't ask anybody to bring me raw bee larvae to eat, because that would have been a violation of the Vinaya [the monastic code of discipline] in so many ways. But people understood this, so they would bring me the kind that had already been roasted with a little salt." Ajahn Sophon, a monk who lived at Wat Boromthat in Chaiya, was an old friend of Buddhadasa who shared his taste for honeycomb, a taste that Ajahn Sophon too had acquired in childhood. Ajahn Buddhadasa empathized with his friend's craving for honeycomb with larvae in the cells. "He liked it just as much as I did, but like me, he didn't have much chance to eat any. But Ajahn Sophon had a lay disciple who knew his tastes and would prepare some for us whenever there was an opportunity. They would take the bees' nest and wrap it in banana leaf, then put it in a wok to sort of bake it. The larvae weren't completely cooked—kind of half cooked, half raw—but it was enough to kill them. I really liked such food. Even as a monk, I had the habit of eating raw foods. The smaller the bees were, the better."

People who grew up during the Jungle-Village era, like Nguam and his friends, found a great deal of their food in the natural environment. The insects and other animals the boys captured were not considered peculiar foods. People knew perfectly well what they were eating. Decades later, whenever Ajahn Buddhadasa told stories about the foods he had eaten to a younger generation used to packaged food, the youngsters certainly thought the food weird.

11

LOCAL ENTERTAINMENT

Y OUNG MEN in their teens spent their leisure time with male friends more often than with girls. Ajahn Buddhadasa recalled that "young people, for the most part, lived their lives according to the circumstances of their families. Those of us from merchant families—and there weren't that many shops in town—tended to play together. When we got bicycles, then others of the same age tried to get bicycles of their own. And we enjoyed ourselves in the ways of rural people of that time. Nobody studied very much."

Nguam had to earn cash for his bicycle, which he used for work as well as for fun. "Mother trained me to be self-reliant. She said that it was not her duty to give me a bicycle. If I wanted one, I had to get it on my own. I learned to use a sewing machine, and Mother gave me money for sewing cloth. It took several months of savings before I could buy a bicycle." Around 1920 a good bicycle cost 90 baht, but "the best brand of bicycle cost 150 baht. I could not afford that."

Nguam never drank, never smoked, and never chased girls. Comparing the courtship rituals between the southern and northern provinces, the Ajahn tells us that "customs like serenading young women, as they did in the North, were impossible in our area; it went against people's sensibilities. And I think that was true throughout the South. For the most part, back when I was a young man, the parents would find and choose your marriage partner. And everyone went along with their choices. Of course, the adults would ask their children if they were willing. My older relatives were on the lookout for somebody for me. They found me a partner, and although things never got to the point where we became engaged, there was an agreement. At the time I had never laid eyes on her. For a while I didn't even know her name. She lived in the same province but wasn't from Phum Riang."

Although Nguam spent much of his free time working at his father's store, occasionally he would attend the temple festivals. In Phum Riang, when Nguam was a youth, there were no movie theaters. "There was a movie from Japan shown once, a long time ago, and that was it," Ajahn Buddhadasa recalled. "Of course there was the shadow theater—that was more traditional. And once in a while *manora*, a southern dance form, and *likay* were performed at the wat. That was a local form of likay, not the classical likay from Bangkok."[8] Local people called this dance-drama *nora*, and it was performed during temple festivals, at ritual ceremonies or other religious celebrations.

Nora dance performances and shadow theater were the main sources of entertainment for Nguam and his childhood friends. Both shadow theater and nora performances were based on Buddhist, Hindu, and animistic beliefs. Most nora and shadow-theater masters had been trained or educated in a wat and were expected to possess spiritual knowledge for self-protection, so that when they were performing, people who might wish them ill could not use black magic against them—magic that might cause the masters to blank out, forget their lines, and thus ruin their performances. Local people respected nora masters and shadow-theater masters, not only for their skills as storytellers and their knowledge of art and ritual, but for their spiritual powers as well.

Shadow theater shows began at night and lasted until dawn. The shadow master, with the help of his assistants behind the screen, manipulated an array of two-dimensional puppet figures cut in intricate, lacy patterns from buffalo hide. The audience viewed the puppets through a screen illuminated from behind. Only the shadows of the puppets were visible. The performer achieved dramatic effects by moving the puppets and varying their distance from the screen. The master spoke all the parts and created all the sound effects. Besides learning to manipulate the puppets, an aspiring master also had to memorize hundreds of pages of traditional prose and verse from the Ramakian or the Jataka stories. Shadow theater served both as a source of entertainment and as a way to communicate social criticism. Not only did a master use a different voice for each character; he also added improvisations that gave his performances local and topical meaning. Today such shadow performances are rare; the art of shadow puppetry in the South is dying out. Television, movies, and video games have become the main sources of entertainment for youngsters.

"Shadow theater started in Phattalung," Ajahn Buddhadasa explained. "From there it went south to Java and moved north into this area [Chaiya]. It was called *nang talung*; that is, 'Phattalung theater.' In India it's called *chayanatika*; that is, 'shadow theater.' Shadow theater originated in India, where it was very popular and common. In India, in this kind of theater, no matter what the subject matter, the educated male characters always spoke Sanskrit. Ordinary villagers, servants, and women spoke Prakrit, the vernacular. This style carried over into our shadow theater."

During Buddhadasa's youth, people still spoke their local dialects. Chaiya children learned Bangkok Thai in the government schools. Shadow theater served as a vehicle by which to transmit the "national" language to local adults whose only schooling would have taken place at the wat and in the vernacular. In the Ajahn's words, "the shadow theater taught the villagers how to speak the Bangkok language. Rural people never had a chance to go to Bangkok and seldom heard Bangkok people speak."

"In shadow theater," Ajahn Buddhadasa continued, "the main characters, usually monks and hermits and members of the aristocracy, spoke the higher language, namely Bangkok Thai. If one looks at the old shadow theater of India, even the lead female character spoke Prakrit, which shows that the caste system was still very strong. In our shadow theater there were two languages: Bangkok Thai and the local language, which changed from area to area. The villagers learned to speak Bangkok Thai from these shadow theaters. They spoke with an accent, naturally, and called it 'speaking official.' If they didn't speak it clearly, it was called 'tainted official.'"

Nguam and his younger brother, Yikoei (Dhammadasa), enjoyed different kinds of entertainment. When he was in his teens, Nguam's secret passion was to be a musician. "Music occupied a big part of my inner life, but I had no chance to practice. I just liked it somehow. Dhammadasa didn't like it at all; he probably hated it. But I loved music, loved songs utterly, completely, you could say. But Mother forbade us to have any musical instruments in the house, so I never had a chance to learn how to play or practice. I would go to other houses where people practiced instruments to watch and to practice. I liked the easy instruments like flutes and accordions, the ones for which you used the fingers to make the notes. With my voice I could imitate the sounds of the instruments that accompanied all the songs I knew, but I couldn't practice because of Mother. I always had to give the instruments that I borrowed back to their owners. Mother thought music bad; for her it led to decay and deterioration, just like fish fights or cockfights. Music was the same kind of thing in her mind."

In secret, Ajahn Buddhadasa practiced singing. "I had to escape to practice at a house where they were serious about singing. Back then there was a man named Pho who was crazy about songs; he would practice every song until he mastered it, and he was the lead singer in all the bands in our area. They all wanted Pho as their singer. All the different musicians insisted on having him, but in the end he came down with venereal disease and died. Phum Riang had many people who were good at singing and making music. Another fellow, named Nut, could do response calls and sing the harmony, the second part of a song, better than anyone. I think he came from Bangkok; he was also quite a talented flute player."

Nguam's interest in music remained with him long after he became a monk. In the mid-1950s when tape recorders became available in Thailand, Ajahn Buddhadasa turned to the new technology to pursue his keen interest in traditional Thai music. "After I got a tape recorder I used it to study the various levels, or voices: the first, second, and third." Thai classical music, which involves the singing of poetic verses, is very intricate. Buddhadasa was curious about the structure and form of the music. He listened to the songs on tape to study lyric poetry, lyric composition, and the succession and arrangements of sounds. Studying music sharpened his ear and helped to shape his rhythmical inventiveness in writing poetry.

While other boys were engaged in boxing competitions, Nguam learned to play Thai chess. Whenever he had leisure time at their store in Chaiya, Nguam's father enjoyed playing chess, and Nguam became fond of the game. But in their house in Phum Riang, Ajahn Buddhadasa says, "Mother didn't even allow Thai chess; we couldn't bring a board into the house." As with the music, Nguam had to sneak out to play chess with his friends. After he became a monk, he went to Bangkok to study Pali at Wat Pathum Kongkha. To his surprise Phra Nguam found that he could play chess with his fellow monks. "Back then chess was being played in almost every monk's kuti," Ajahn Buddhadasa recalled with a laugh.

In his old age Ajahn Buddhadasa extolled the benefits of Thai chess. "I myself think that chess ought to be in the curriculum for all children, that they should learn how to play as part of their studies, because it will make them think; it will help them to be intelligent, clever, and agile of mind. I'm talking about Thai chess—I don't know if that happens in European chess. It makes one well rounded and develops mindfulness and clear awareness. It gives you a head like that of a general. The principle is to chase the opponent's pieces until they are cornered. One has to keep trapping the opponent until his situation becomes hopeless and he gives up."

12

DHAMMA DEBATES

WHEN ASKED if, as a young man, he had ever flirted, Ajahn Buddhadasa replied, "As far as being a lady's man, I knew nothing about that. I didn't have time to go flirting and chasing after women; there was always work to be done. I didn't court any girls. At night I never went anywhere and didn't have relationships with women. Of course, I was attracted to and liked some of them. But there was never a chance; I only thought of them in my heart. Besides, I enjoyed other things. Before I was ordained, I enjoyed the work of helping Mother sell things at the store, and there were always things to discuss. I was a kind of Dhamma discussion enthusiast."

In the early decades of the twentieth century there was no such thing as a bookstore of the kind we see today. But Buddhadasa's parents sold books along with rice and kerosene in their general store in Phum Riang. Nguam thus had access to a steady stream of new books that his parents ordered from Bangkok.

"I read various things," Ajahn Buddhadasa recalled, "because our home was a store that sold books, among other things. The best-selling ones were about royal lineages and histories. And then there were books on numerous matters that readers ought to know about. They were called 'quarter books' because they cost twenty-five satang each." At a time when a horseshoe crab cost one satang, these books were not cheap. "Modern books from Europe that had been translated also began to come our way. These were published by Thai Printing in

Bangkok. These modern books were probably difficult to sell, so they had salesmen work the markets in the provinces and even smaller towns. Our shop was pressured into taking some of them to sell cheaply, some for only one satang apiece, which was about the cost of the paper they were printed on. Hardly anybody bought these books. Some people ordered books from Bangkok. Among the translations that reached us were *Soraida* and *The Thousand and One Days*.[9] I'm pretty sure these were the kind of books that didn't sell. I read them, but they didn't stick in my mind. They were just something new and strange."

Buddhadasa's father's connection in Bangkok was Siang, his younger brother. At the turn of the twentieth century Siang became a monk at Wat Phum Riang. When Nguam was born his uncle Siang was still in the robes. He knew Sanskrit and could read Pali texts written in the sacred Khmer alphabet. When the old abbot of Wat Phum Riang died, local people appointed Siang abbot of the wat. After serving as abbot for two years, Siang realized that he did not like being an abbot. He then went to Bangkok to further his studies and was appointed secretary to the abbot of Wat Pathum Kongkha.

Living in the capital city gave Siang access to the writings of the best-known journalists and essayists, especially Thianwan and K.S.R. Kulap.[10] Both writers were commoners who had spent time in jail because they were critical of the social, economic, and political conditions under the absolute monarchy. Their books were available at Chaiya Panich, Nguam's father's store in Phum Riang. "Mother received these regularly for one baht a year," Ajahn Buddhadasa recalled. "Uncle Siang would order any books that seemed strange or interesting and send them to us. Uncle was interested in lots of things and was a regular reader. He wanted to know this and that, and then would inform his kinfolk in the backcountry—or as much as he thought would be to their benefit."

Before he was ordained as a monk, Nguam read the new academic texts called Nak-dham.[11] The Chaiya Panich store became a place where people gathered to discuss new books, and Nguam was eager to share his knowledge of Dhamma with anyone who showed an interest. Recalling his precocious youth, the Ajahn said, "Various adults would come by in the morning to discuss Dhamma. I acted as if I were a real Dhamma teacher. I had to be able to answer their questions and debate with them. There was one government official, whose home was near ours, who had to pass our store on his way to work every day. And then there were other people living near us who were relatives. If I saw a certain old man come in, I knew he would tease me and banter about Dhamma. And by the time he made a move to go on his way to work, an hour would have passed. Some men even came to our home. I had to buy and read the Dhamma studies books of the first, second, and third levels and even read some of the Abhidhamma." Many monks as well as laypeople considered the Abhidhamma to be the hardest text of all to understand. "At that time," the Ajahn recalled, "I was a lot younger than any of them, most of whom were rather old. But I usually spoke more correctly because I had books to read. They spoke more along the lines of guesses and hypotheses. I always enjoyed speaking when others were listening."

By this time, in obedience to the Prince Patriarch's rules, all monasteries in Bangkok were using the new Dhamma texts for the instruction of novice monks. Buddhadasa recalled the excitement of new ideas drawn from his reading: "That was a wake-up time with regard to understanding Dhamma. They had started a new system of Dhamma studies that was spreading throughout the country and was just reaching our area. Everybody was fond of discussing it. The government official who lived near us liked to associate with the teachers of Nak-dham at the wat and then would take advantage of others. It wasn't really a big deal; I simply enjoyed objecting and arguing with him. I pretended to dispute and disguised my teasing. There were some intelligent, educated people who didn't know much about these Dhamma studies who were willing to support him. Others got angry. Some older people took my side. Back then, this is how we enjoyed ourselves in Phum Riang."

While teenagers today may think that it is boring to debate the teachings in the Dhamma textbooks, for the Ajahn "the fun part was to explain it to others." That seems much like young people today patiently explaining computers and DVDs to their seniors.

Among the books that young monks and novices studied in Nguam's day and continue to study today is the *Navakovada* (Instructions for Newly Ordained Monks and Novices). Another text is the *Buddhapavatti* (The Life of the Buddha). In the new version of the *Buddhapavatti*, written by Sangharaja Wachirayan, Lord Buddha is portrayed as a wise earthly teacher rather than as a divine being endowed with supernatural powers. The life of the Buddha is also anchored in the historical, sociological, and geographical context of his time. Young monastics also studied the *Buddhasasana-subhasita*, a book of five hundred Buddhist proverbs printed in Pali with Thai translations.

The Nak-dham texts were considered an important innovation both because they were written in Thai and thus accessible to lay readers and because they left out that which goes beyond ordinary human knowledge. The Sangharaja's rationalistic approach to the Dhamma generated much debate between the younger and older generations, a debate that continued long after Prince Wachirayan had passed away.

In his article "Buddhism for the Next Century," adapted from his book about the future of Thai Buddhism, published in 2003 and dedicated to his teacher Buddhadasa, Phra Paisal writes, "In the past hundred years Buddhism has been transformed to fit with modernity. Ironically, while superstition was supposedly removed from Buddhism in the process of purification, western rationality, scientism, and nationalism replaced it, resulting in the removal of transcendental and ultimate aspects. In other words, traditional superstition was replaced by modern, foreign superstition. Despite its emphasis on morality, official Buddhism has failed to strengthen the actual morality of Thai society."[12]

In Nguam's day, one of the most important Buddhist traditions in Siam was the temporary bhikkhu ordination, when young men became monks before getting married and becoming householders. Having young men live as monks for a year or so was a way of preparing them to be mentally and morally fit to take on the responsibilities of adult life. Ordination was also a way to bestow merit upon the monk's parents. On July 29, 1926, when Nguam turned twenty, he was ordained as a monk in keeping with the custom of expressing gratitude to his parents. His preceptor gave him the Pali name Indapanno.

FIG. 13. BUDDHADASA NEWLY ORDAINED, 1926.

After the ordination ceremony at Wat Nok (also called Wat Ubon), Phra Nguam went to live at Wat Phum Riang. "Because of all my talking and reading about Dhamma, I had learned a fair amount even before being ordained, and after that I hardly had to study. When I was set to work on the first level of the Nak-dham course, I hardly had to do anything, because I had already read it all for the discussions and debates in our shop."

Several white-robed female renouncers (Thai: *mae chi*, often "nuns" in English) resided at Wat Phum Riang. The nuns were well supported by the local community. As Ajahn Buddhadasa recalled, "When the locals came to the wat to offer food, they usually went to the kuti where the nuns lived. It was convenient that way. Their kuti was large. Then the nuns would put the food in containers and bring them to the dining hall. The best-known nun was Mother Phak. She was about the same age as my mother. She used to be a wandering ascetic, following her teacher on thudong along with a male white-robed renouncer. In Phum Riang she was the only nun who went on alms round. She was much revered by the locals. During her alms round she got more food than the monks. When I was ordained she was quite old and no longer went on pilgrimages. She stayed put and took care of the wat, beloved by the locals. Her lay supporters provided her with whatever she needed."

During his first rains retreat at Wat Phum Riang, Phra Nguam gave nightly sermons in which he explained the Buddha's teachings in simple language. The young monk also trained himself to preach the Milindapanha.[13] Mother Phak and the other nuns, who often came to hear Phra Nguam preach, cheered the young monk on in his effort to put new life into the old sermons.

Phra Nguam's original intention was to ordain for three months during the rains retreat. But at the end of the retreat he found that the monastic life suited him so well that he decided to remain in the robes. By this time Uncle Siang had long since disrobed and left Wat Pathum Kongkha, but he still maintained his connection with the monks at the monastery in Bangkok. "It was this connection," Ajahn Buddhadasa says, "that enabled monks from Phum Riang and Chaiya to study at that wat." A few years later Uncle Siang arranged for Phra Nguam to further his education in Dhamma at Wat Pathum in Bangkok. "My uncle," the Ajahn recalled, "was an adroit, active person who took the time to help others. He had more opportunities than Father, who never had a chance to go to Bangkok. Uncle was at ease both reading palm-leaf texts and writing in the Khmer alphabet." Before state Buddhism superseded all local variants of the religion, the Khmer script had been regarded as sacred. Today only a very small number of monks, mostly the very old, are able to read Pali palm-leaf texts or write the Khmer alphabet.

In spite of his early enthusiasm, Phra Nguam soon became disillusioned with the academic Dhamma studies program and monastic life in Bangkok. In May 1932 he left Bangkok and moved to an abandoned temple about one kilometer from the Phum Riang market. Here, in a natural setting, Phra Nguam established Suan Mokkh, "The Garden of Liberation," and took up the name Buddhadasa. The young monk began to read the Tipitaka on his own and explored the connection between the study of the Buddhist canon and the practices of the forest tradition.

13

THE CULTURE OF SILA-DHAMMA

THE PROVINCIAL administrative system for the southern region was centered on the larger towns and the outlying areas that surrounded them. When Phum Riang was the major town of Chaiya, Ajahn Buddhadasa recalled, "many government officials built homes and brought Bangkok tastes and culture with them. We became acquainted with this culture more quickly than those who lived in outlying districts. For example, it was due to the Bangkok influence that the chili sauce made in Phum Riang was different from the chili sauce made elsewhere in the area. If one ate chili sauce in another village and it tasted the same as ours, this showed that the person who made it came from Phum Riang. When I asked where the cook came from, my guess was seldom wrong."

Another innovation that government officials brought to Phum Riang was the Bangkok style of dress. Europeans in Siam tended to consider uncivilized someone who wore only a wraparound lower cloth. The Siamese court responded by adopting European fashion. Before King Chulalongkorn and members of the nobility adopted various items of Western apparel, men and women in Siam dressed more or less alike. Both wore a *jong kraben*, a long piece of cloth that was put around the waist, gathered up in front, and twisted into a long "tail" that was then passed between the legs and tucked into the fabric at the small of the back. Another lower garment worn by both men and women was a *panung*, an unsewn strip of cloth that was wrapped around the body and tied in a knot at the navel. The women in King

Chulalongkorn's court, who cut their hair short, wore the trouserlike jong kraben with blouses or short jackets derived from Western models.

Some Europeans who lived in Siam found the very short hair worn by Siamese women unattractive. In 1920 King Vajiravudh, who was educated in England, encouraged the women in his court to let their hair grow long and wear a skirtlike *pasin*. A pasin—often called a *pathung*, meaning tube cloth—is a Bangkok variant of a lower garment in which the cloth is sewn together like a skirt. From then on the pasin became the national dress for women, replacing the jong kraben. Government officials wore European style cotton shirts and trousers, and their wives wore blouses with a pasin or pathung.

The people of Phum Riang dressed simply, according to their various customs. Ajahn Buddhadasa recalled that during his youth most men wore loose-fitting Chinese trousers. This pajama-like garment was comfortable to wear at work as well as at home. "A few men wore the jong kraben, as women still did. Women who wore the pathung were seen as different. At home, women wore blouses that were open at the neck. Outside the home, or if dressing up, they wore long-sleeved shirt-jackets in the style adopted by the government officials who came from Bangkok. But ordinary people didn't wear tailored shirts—they were too expensive." Male villagers continued to go about barefooted and bare-chested according to their own custom. "Even when they went to see an official at the government office, they didn't have to wear shirts. They might wear a *pakhama* [a simple piece of cotton cloth] over the shoulder and across the chest. Shirts weren't necessary at the wat either; one wore a pakhama over the shoulder." Buddhadasa's mother, Khleuan, wore an open-necked blouse and a jong kraben. Her hair was short, like that of most Siamese women. Xiang wore Chinese pants and had long hair, both of which were the Chinese custom.

Speaking of Phum Riang's compassionate culture, Buddhadasa singled out the sense of responsibility people felt toward their community and those who lived in it. "When someone had an accident or faced serious danger, everyone would help until the crisis was over. The whole village would be concerned, unlike today."

State education gradually turned the younger generation away from the good things in local culture. As they established themselves in cities they began to lose their ties with their villages and felt less obligation to their community. Young men of Buddhadasa's generation found Western culture, with its scientific discoveries and rational thinking, intriguing and stimulating. Since Siam had never been colonized, the full impact of Westernization had yet to be experienced.

From the late 1950s until the late 1990s the growth rate of the Thai economy was one of the fastest in the developing world. This growth came from intensive exploitation of natural resources and the people. Ajahn Buddhadasa saw how the Western economic values that had shaped the National Development Programs and brought the consumer mentality to Thailand had overturned the old values, putting rampant materialism in their place and creating a situation in which people were estranged from their own cultural roots. The Ajahn was concerned that rapid commercialization had ruined the local culture of Chaiya. He illustrated the profoundness of the transformation by referring to an accident that occurred in the early 1980s. "A truck overturned in a ditch near here, and people pilfered the shirts, the pants; they took everything, even as the driver was dying. There was no way this could have happened back then."

Village culture was still strong when he was a youth, the Ajahn said. "People would gather around to help, nurse, and care for others, to feed them and share what they had. Even a stranger who wasn't a relative did not need to be afraid if some accident occurred. Sure, maybe we didn't have cars and trucks, but if that kind of vehicular accident had occurred then, you could be confident that friends would be there to help you survive and be safe. A traveler who fell sick and finally died in a shelter at the wharf had all kinds of help because of the belief that one would earn a lot of merit (*puñña*). Now nobody's interested in helping or making merit. They'll just have someone from Po Tek Tung collect the body."[14]

In Buddhadasa's youth the Sangha was a moral force in the local community. "The influence of Dhamma and religion were profound when I was a child. There were many wats and monks. Phum Riang had four or five wats not far from one another, and each wat housed on the order of twenty or thirty monks who had been ordained for three or four years before disrobing." Ajahn Buddhadasa's remarks reflect a time when the wat still maintained a close relationship with the local community. Today only a very small number of men are ordained as monks, and when they become monks temporarily, as was long the custom, it is usually for only one three-month rains retreat or even less.

FIG. 14. REVERED MASTERS IN PHUM RIANG: AJAHN SAK, ABBOT OF WAT HUA KHU, AND AJAHN THUM, ABBOT OF WAT NOK, 1926.

Two of the most revered abbots in Phum Riang who were active during Buddhadasa's youth were Ajahn Thum of Wat Nok and Ajahn Sak of Wat Hua Khu. Both Buddhist masters were steeped in local tradition. They taught by example, emphasizing the practice of moral discipline (*sila*), generosity (*dana*), and mental development (*bhavana*). As Ajahn Buddhadasa later recalled, "Venerable Teacher Thum was an astrologer and accomplished meditator. Before he became abbot he was a wandering ascetic. The abbot allowed a son of one of his relatives to live with him. This unfortunate boy had leprosy. His duty was to boil the abbot's drinking water. Although others feared to be in such close contact with lepers, the Ajahn's attitude was that if there were any germs, they were probably killed by the boiling water. Ajahn Thum had real compassion for the unfortunate."

Ajahn Sak was also a meditation monk known for his compassion. As Ajahn Buddhadasa described him, "Venerable Teacher Sak was unselfish. Local people, Muslims as well as Buddhists, always turned to him in time of illness. For critical cases they woke him up in the middle of the night," because the wat was open to laypeople at all times. "The abbot got up immediately and went to their houses to attend to the sick." Ajahn Sak died in 1930 when Buddhadasa was twenty-four years old. Ajahn Thum died shortly after Buddhadasa established Suan Mokkh in 1932. State Buddhism proved ineffectual in influencing old masters such as Ajahn Thum and Ajahn Sak, monks whose virtuous presence had strengthened the moral conduct of members of the community. Among the locals both elders were considered holy (saksit).

Recalling the local economy of his youth, Ajahn Buddhadasa observed that "many villagers have been fishermen since ancient times, but they didn't fish like people do today. They fished to get just enough to sell within the village and perhaps in a few nearby villages. The fishermen had enough to eat and live on. There were plenty of shrimp, clams, crabs, and fish." But commercial fishing and industrial fish processing or freezing have led to overfishing and a catastrophic loss of fish species in the Gulf of Thailand. "Now they fish to send their catch far away, and so there is never enough. The fish are increasingly difficult to find, and the price is two or three hundred times what it used to be. Back then two horseshoe crabs cost two satang. Now just one costs a whole baht." (There are one hundred satang in a baht. In the early 1980s twenty baht were equivalent to one U.S. dollar.)

When Buddhadasa was young most people lived simply. They took only what they needed from the natural environment. Wooden carts and metal tools were made in the village. Women continued to weave silk and cotton into designs that Phum Riang was famous for. As the Ajahn pointed out, "Ordinary villagers weren't wealthy, but there was enough work for them to make a living, to have enough to eat from day to day and month to month. There wasn't anything to make one rich, and the wealthier ones didn't really have all that much anyway.

Having one thousand baht back then was enough for one to be considered wealthy. Those with a monthly income of four or five hundred were considered well off."

In the early twentieth century, rice had become the major export crop and the greatest source of tax revenue for the government. "The wealthy folks usually had rice fields to rent out, and at the end of the year the renters would pay up. Those who received more rice-field rent than others were the wealthy ones. Back then people staked out rice fields. They hired others to erect the dikes. Those who had money bought up rice fields at cheap prices. If people needed to sell, they did so at a low price, and somebody with extra money would buy. So those with extra fields rented out their excess, dividing the harvest fifty-fifty with the renter, which is a huge advantage for the owner of the land, who got half of the harvest—just as much as the actual farmer who did all the work. Some people made other arrangements. For example, for a certain rented field an owner might want to receive thirty bushels of rice. In years when the harvest was poor, there were some landowners who were considerate and didn't make the tenant farmers pay the rent they owed. The governor and his family had lots of rice fields. There were times when they used their advantage and oppressed others."

Under the absolute monarchy, the driving forces of society were civilian officials. "People lived in fear of provincial government officials," Ajahn Buddhadasa tells us. "Ordinary people were shy and afraid. Those local bureaucrats wielded a lot of power on behalf of the government, so those who were government officials constituted a separate class. Still, we all had to rely on one another. The officials didn't go so far as to be enemies of the common people. Of course, there were some cases of injustice that, once they became onerous enough, would finally impel the central government administrators to send a senior official to investigate and then punish the offending provincial official. This did happen but only occasionally.

"I never heard of villagers objecting on their own behalf, mainly because they were afraid. They didn't object or complain. This situation was good in a way. That is, people didn't want to do anything wrong. They were careful not to stir up trouble. Those who liked to get into scrapes or create legal problems were few and far between, because it wasn't worth it to make trouble. There were hardly any criminals. I suppose the would-be criminals were afraid—afraid of the governor. Criminals and tough guys didn't have friends. They couldn't have any in the rural towns beyond Bangkok. If there were any of these lowlifes in our area, they had to live in the woods or some isolated place. They couldn't exist in a market town like Phum Riang."

Among civilian officials, the rank of *chao khun* was much higher than the rank of someone bearing the title *khun phra*. The system of government-granted honorific titles was abolished in 1932 when Siam became a constitutional monarchy. However, the practice of granting honorific titles within the monastic community has remained intact to this very day, and no prime minister yet has dared to challenge the custom. Ajahn Buddhadasa pointed out that "villagers called the government officials 'chao khun' and 'khun phra' according to their rank. The governor of Chaiya was called 'Chao Khun Chaiya.' Commoners addressed them as 'master' (*nai*). If you came from a family of no particular consequence and spoke to a member of a powerful family, you would have to address him or her as *pho nai*, literally 'father master,' or *mae nai*, 'mother master.' Even the little children of the powerful had to be addressed as masters—as 'pho nai' if the child was male, and 'mae nai' if female. Still, people of both high and low status lived together amicably. These forms of hierarchy didn't provide cause for people to revolt. All people helped each other according to the circumstances."

The wat was then the social center of the community. The people of Phum Riang faithfully followed the Buddhist custom, each according to the family's means, of giving alms food to monks in the morning. The rich offered food every morning, the poor occasionally. Most householders gave whenever they could. "Making merit and giving alms were strong traditions. If one had plenty to eat, then one would give alms-rice every day. If the householders were known as 'Father This' and 'Mother That,' then they had to give alms. They would be mortally ashamed if they didn't." The Ajahn recalled the practice of placing rice-giving benches in front of houses, a custom that has vanished. "In front of each house was a small bench that held the rice bowl. The bench was made of a couple of uprights with a board nailed on top. At first these benches were movable, and people would bring them out each time they gave alms. Later, the rice bench was made of posts driven into the ground. It was strong enough for someone to sit on. Every household that had enough food had to have one of these benches."

In 1926, when Buddhadasa was ordained as a monk, the practice of putting up rice-giving benches in front of the houses still existed, and he received alms there regularly. Fifty years later, however, the practice of giving alms, a tradition that had existed for generations, was completely neglected. "There is no almsgiving because people just didn't carry on the tradition." All across the district people got too busy to bother giving alms to the monks. By the 1980s the almsgivers had almost disappeared. "You can hardly find a single one now in Phum Riang."

Another practice of generosity was the building of shelters (*sala*) for wayfarers: by the roadside, out in the forest, or at the foot of a mountain. Ajahn Buddhadasa referred to this practice as due to a "culture of morality," which was based in and permeated by sila-dhamma. "A traveler could always find a sala in which to spend the night. In these shelters the traveler would find uncooked rice and other food staples, clay pots for cooking, braziers, mats, and pillows. These things were left there for any traveler to use. Nobody would ever steal from a shelter. This custom of local hospitality disappeared with the arrival of the new culture of materialism."

An important coming-of-age custom in Siam that has now disappeared completely was the wearing of topknots. Traditionally, not long after the removal of the topknots at the age of twelve, boys were ordained as novices, and monks took charge of their education. For the female child this was an equally important ceremony that marked the end of her girlhood and her entrance into the condition of womanhood. The last time Buddhadasa saw all schoolchildren in Chaiya wearing topknots was in the 1930s. Barely two decades later, in 1950, Ajahn Buddhadasa mourned the loss of this honorable custom. "I feel that the custom of wearing topknots and cutting them off at a certain age is a good cultural trait that should have been retained. Wearing the topknot served as a reminder to the child that he or she is too young to be interested in the opposite sex. These days, without the topknot as a reminder, boys and girls act like young men and young women from the time they are babies! The consequence is what we see today. We need to come up with a custom to replace topknots."

Buddhadasa considered the local culture of Chaiya to be healthy, balanced, and wise. "In summary," the Ajahn tells us, "people at that time coexisted peacefully." Houses were generally very simple and easy to construct out of materials found locally. "Natural resources were abundant. There was plenty of fish and other food to eat without worry. There were wats and religion to support hearts and minds."

FIG. 15. AJAHN BUDDHADASA AND FRIEND AT SUAN MOKKH.

PART II

AJAHN PANYA
(BOYHOOD NAME: PAN)

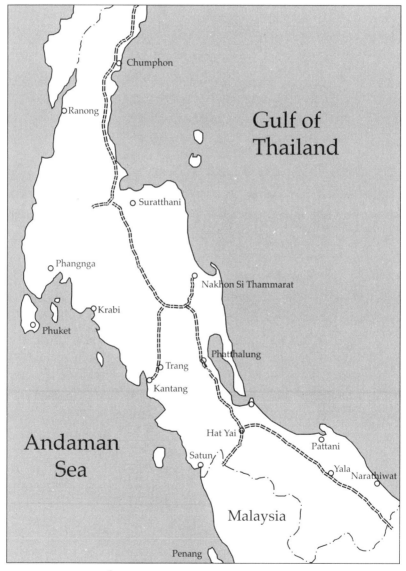

Gulf of Thailand

Andaman Sea

Malaysia

Chumphon

Ranong

Suratthani

Phangnga

Krabi

Phuket

Nakhon Si Thammarat

Phatthalung

Trang

Kantang

Hat Yai

Satun

Pattani

Yala

Narathiwat

Penang

FIG. 16. PENINSULAR THAILAND SHOWING RAIL LINES.

14

VILLAGE LIFE IN MUANG LUNG

I N 1936, four years after Buddhadasa established his forest
monastery in Chaiya, a young monk named Phra Pan came
to spend the rains retreat with him. From then on the two
southern monks became Dhamma brothers and vowed to
work together for the Buddha. Buddhadasa was then thirty years old;
Phra Pan was twenty-five. It was the beginning of a spiritual friendship that lasted until Ajahn Buddhadasa's death in 1993. In 1960, more
than two decades after his first visit to Suan Mokkh, Ajahn Panya
became the first abbot of Wat Chonprathan, a new monastery in Nonthaburi province, north of Bangkok.

Phra Pan's monastic name is Paññananda (in Pali, "One Who
Delights in Wisdom"). After he became a preacher, people generally
called him Ajahn Panya, a shortened form of the Thai pronunciation
"Panyanantha."

Ajahn Panya was born in 1911 in Phatthalung. He was the fourth
of five children. His parents, Wan and Khlai, named him Pan. The village in which Pan grew up was surrounded by high hills, wide pastures, and dense forests. It consisted of only ten households, which were
like one extended family. "The air was clean," Ajahn Panya tells us.
"Villagers worked on farms. The soil was fertile; no need for fertil-
izers. It rained according to the season. Rainwater was used for drinking and irrigation. Once we finished planting rice, we grew vegetables
and fruit trees. Then it was time to harvest the rice. Once the harvesting season was over, we gathered vegetables and fruits to eat and

distribute to neighbors. Surplus produce was used in exchange for necessary goods. The way of life in these agricultural societies was free of competition, and all produce was shared. People lived off their farms, and life was simple and straightforward."

Wan and Khlai considered themselves well off, since they had more than enough to eat. Their son, Pan, grew up in a harmonious environment. "My parents spoke little," Ajahn Panya recalled. "They never fought or argued, never used bad words. I never heard them quarrel with neighbors. They were friendly and helpful to anybody who had problems. They helped others as much as they could."

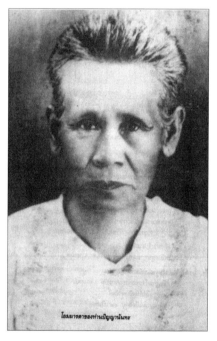

FIG. 17. KHLAI, AJAHN PANYA'S MOTHER.

Pan's parents were known for their generosity. They owned more than one hundred head of cattle and twenty water buffaloes. They were willing to lend eighteen of their buffaloes to neighbors who needed to plow their fields. They used only two buffaloes to work their own fields. Nevertheless, if anybody was in need of buffaloes, they would lend out their last one. Pan learned from his parents that other people's needs came first. "Those who turn to us," his parents said, "must really be in need. For our needs we can always look to some other source." At the end of the plowing season neighbors usually returned the buffaloes without offering any payment. Pan never heard his parents complain.

Wan and Khlai extended their hospitality even to strangers. Sometimes as many as fifteen people from far away might show up unexpectedly in their village. The couple willingly offered these strangers food and shelter. Ajahn Panya recalled, "On such a day my mother would get up earlier than usual to prepare breakfast for these travelers and also give them lunch to eat on the way. Mother was a good and resourceful hostess. Offering food and shelter to strangers made Mother happy; she gained friendship. These travelers often gave her unusual foods or gifts from other places. These were not given as payment but out of affection."

There were two monasteries near the village, Wat Nanglat and Wat Khoknian. Pan's house was located between them. Wat Nanglat was the monastery of his ancestors. When Pan's relatives wanted to be ordained or make merit, they would go to this wat.

Pan grew up in an agrarian society in which families, friends, and neighbors truly depended upon one another. Money played only a minor role and was used primarily to pay taxes and buy cattle or metal tools. Ajahn Panya recalled the tradition of exchanging labor in his village, "During the plowing and harvesting seasons, farmers took turns helping one another in their fields by offering to perform the labor required. The work needed was given free of charge. It was considered rude to pay for such help." These communal projects also provided occasions for young men and women to work side by side.

Villagers of all generations worked and played together. During festivals they would cook special savory dishes or sweets and distribute them at the monastery. Even when there was no special occasion, if a man killed a deer or caught a very large fish he or his wife would cook a big pot of curry and then send his children to distribute a bowl of it to every household. Such acts of sharing and generosity influenced Pan's character, even though the young boy had not yet learned to appreciate his village's customs. "As a child I got tired of walking to every house to distribute curry or sweets," Ajahn Panya recalled. "Whenever my parents got some special food, such as a piece of meat, they would cook a big pot of curry. If they got a few durians, they would make a big bowl of durian with sweetened coconut milk. If they caught a lot of fish, they would divide the fish into portions. Then we children would have to walk from one end of the village to the other to distribute meat curry, durian sweets, or raw fish to every house. This happened often." Pan could not really avoid this duty. Whenever he saw his parents putting fish in piles, the boy thought, "More work for me today. I'll have to run around again."

Following the Dhamma practice of the four "conditions for social welfare" (sanghahavatthu), Pan's parents taught him to practice generosity, to speak kindly, to render service to others, and to treat everyone equally.[15]

LIFE WITH GRANDMOTHERS

RANK K. EXELL, the British schoolmaster who took a job as a bank manager in Nakhon Si Thammarat in the late 1920s, often went to visit Phatthalung. He noted that "the Siamese had two qualities of which any people can be proud. These were their respect for age and their fondness for their children. Aged parents were an accepted responsibility and there was no pleasanter sight than the smile on the wrinkled face of a grandmother as she watched her grandchildren at play."

In his formative years Pan was very close to two grandmothers, both of whom had grown up in a culture in which stories about ancestors and local Buddhist masters were kept alive through constant retelling. Ajahn Panya credited these two with planting the seeds of his vocation. "The impetus that turned me to the monastic life came from my family, who raised me according to their custom." Although neither of his grandmothers could read, "they knew so many stories from the past that they never ran out of Dhamma lessons to teach us. They grew up in a society that was steeped in oral tradition. Women of their generation acquired knowledge not from reading books but from hearing stories told by village monks and elders. They were content with their lives and were able to pass on their wisdom to the grandchildren they helped raise. These two grandmothers instilled a love of Dhamma in me."

Ajahn Panya's eyes lit up at the memory of his grandmothers, who called him Doggie. "When I was a child two old women had the most

influence on my heart and mind. I called them Big Grandma and Little Grandma. Little Grandma, Yai Num, was my real grandmother; I
was her only grandson. Big Grandma, Yai Nu, was Yai Num's older
sister; she had no grandson of her own. These two grandmothers lived
in the same house. When they slept they put me in the middle."

Every night one of the grandmothers would remind her grandson
to put his palms together and bow to his pillow. When he heard one
of the grandmothers ask, "Doggie, did you bow to the pillow yet?"
Pan had to get up and bow before he was allowed to put his head on
the pillow. No one ever explained to Pan the meaning of the gesture.
The Buddhist ritual of focusing one's mind before going to sleep only
became clear to Ajahn Panya with hindsight. "I did not understand it
then," he tells us. "After I was ordained I realized that to bow to the
pillow is to pay respect to the Buddha. The ritual helped focus my mind
on the Buddha-dhamma."

Ajahn Panya's skill as a preacher may have been fostered in his
youth by the stories his grandmothers told him. The stories filled the
boy's world with ancient landscapes and people coping with adversi-
ties. If Pan could not fall asleep after bowing to the pillow, his grandmothers would tell him tales such as "The Golden Swan" and "The
Four Jampa Trees." These two stories were well known in villages
throughout the Central Plains and the Northeast. "The Four Jampa
Trees" was especially well known in Lao villages. "The Golden Swan"
is a long tale, and it probably took several nights for one of Pan's
grandmothers to tell it. Besides telling him folktales, Pan's grandmothers sometimes sang old lullabies that had been passed down for generations. Both tales and songs were laced with Dhamma teachings.

In Pan's village both the young and old were awake before sunrise
to do their chores. At the crack of dawn the monks would walk in single file into the village to receive almsfood. All children got up along
with the old folks. Every morning his grandmothers rose early to prepare food for the monks. Pan, too, got up early to wait for the monks
to come by for alms.

Boys as well as girls were expected to help around the house. Pan
did such chores as cooking rice, planting vegetables, watering plants,

and pounding rice. Every house kept a big mortar that was made from a section of a tree trunk. The pestle was a long length of wood attached to a shorter, heavy crosspiece. Pan raised the pestle by stepping on one end and then stepping off, letting the other end drop into the mortar to crack the husks. It was hard, time-consuming work. Yet it was fun for Pan to help his mother by stepping on and off the heavy pestle. "It was good exercise," Ajahn Panya said.

Villagers normally worked seven days a week except when there was a festival at the wat. Farmers and buffaloes got a break from their work on holy days (*wan phra*), which occurred four times a month in keeping with the phases of the moon. On holy days no fishing or hunting was permitted. There were no classes for temple boys because the monks were busy giving sermons. The young as well as the old went to listen to the sermons at the wat. Old people who normally followed the five basic precepts stayed overnight at the wat to practice meditation and observe the eight precepts, namely, not to kill animals, even the tiniest insects; not to take what is not given; not to engage in sexual activity; not to engage in idle talk; not to use intoxicants; not to eat after midday; not to dance, sing, play musical instruments, watch shows, or adorn the body with jewelry; and not to use high or luxurious beds or seats. Spending the whole day in the wat gave people a genuine break from their ordinary routines.

On these holy days the two grandmothers always took Pan to the wat to participate in religious activities. "I went to the wat so often," Ajahn Panya said, recalling his boyhood. "The wat was a site for festivals and my playground. Even though children spent a lot of time just running around in the wat compound, it was a good environment for them. Hearing the sermons and the sound of monks' daily chants had a good effect on their minds."

16

BUFFALO BOYS

ILLAGE CHILDREN began tending water buffaloes at the age of five or six. Water buffaloes were the most important domestic animals for local farmers, who used them to plow paddy fields. In the morning the children took the water buffaloes out to graze. At night the buffaloes were brought back to the village and shut in their pens.

While traveling in the area known today as Southeast Asia, Westerners got to see water buffaloes up close. Peter Thompson, who worked for Siam's Survey Department, wrote in 1905, "They are formidable-looking beasts, with their immense spreading horns, which get very much in the way when they are yoked together. A pair of horns has been known to measure as much as eight feet six inches from tip to tip, measured round the curve."

Out walking one evening, the Englishman Harold Hall encountered a herd of buffaloes heading home. Finding himself surrounded, Hall discovered that in spite of their appearance "water buffaloes are absolutely tame." Hall, who lived in Burma in the 1890s, noted with amazement, "You can see a herd of these great beasts, with horns six feet across, come along under the command of a very small boy or girl perched on one of their broad backs. He flourishes a little stick, and issues his commands like a general. It is one of the quaintest imaginable sights to see this little fellow get off his steed, run after a straggler, and beat him with his stick. The buffalo eyes his master, whom he could abolish with one shake of his head, submissively, and takes the beating, which he probably feels about as much as if a straw fell on him, good-humouredly. The children never seem to come to grief."

FIG. 18. WATER BUFFALO.

In Siam many abbots of town and village monasteries spent their boyhood tending water buffaloes. Pan began taking care of buffaloes when he was about six years old. Each day before the sun came up he took two water buffaloes out to graze. Such a chore could be daunting for children who believed in ghosts, but they could not say no. Ajahn Panya recalled how he faced his fear. "The most unsettling thing was to have to get up very early during the plowing season. The buffaloes had to be in the paddy field before sunrise. I had to take them out to eat. I was afraid of ghosts but dared not tell my father for fear of being scolded. I didn't like it when my parents told me to do a task at night when it was pitch black outside. I was afraid of walking in the dark, so I hung on to one of the buffaloes. Wherever he went to graze, I went with him and watched. I talked to him as I would to a human companion. I thought if anything happened I could always climb on his back and make him run. But nothing ever happened. Sometimes I saw something in the darkness that looked like somebody standing there. I hung on tightly to my buffalo while eyeing the thing carefully. The mystery finally unfolded when the sun came up. It was just a stump, not a ghost as I had feared."

Children given the responsibility of caring for buffaloes became sensitive to the animals' well-being. These great animals were Pan's friends. "The buffaloes' happiness was my happiness," the Ajahn recalled. "I could tell at a glance if they had had enough to eat. Watching the buffaloes submerge in a waterhole gave me joy. On days when the buffaloes did not get enough to eat I felt terrible. My heart sank."

FIG. 19. TENDING THE WATER BUFFALO.

Taking care of buffaloes could be pleasant, especially if the boys caring for them were working together in a group. The task gave the youngsters the opportunity both to be away from the watchful eyes of adults and to expend their youthful energy outdoors in the fields and forests. Luang Ta Chi, now abbot of Wat Thai in Washington, D.C., spent his youth tending water buffaloes in northeastern Siam. Born in 1925, the abbot remembers the performance of this task as among his happiest childhood experiences. He recalled how the village boys of Ban Phon Ngam learned about their immediate environment. "We usually got up early in the morning and rode the water buffaloes up Sweet Vegetable Hill. There were zigzag trails going uphill along which we guided the buffaloes. The slopes were covered with big trees, but the hilltop itself was a flat meadow. Once we got the buffaloes to the top we were free to do whatever we liked. We hung out all day playing, running around, climbing trees, picking mushrooms, looking at birds and animals, and so on. In the late afternoon we rounded up the buffaloes and rode them back to our village."

When traveling by road from Bangkok to other provinces today, one rarely sees water buffaloes in the rice fields. Nowadays most farmers plow their fields with a machine they call an "iron buffalo."

17

LEARNING THE FIRST LETTER

PAN STARTED learning the Thai alphabet at the age of seven in his village in Phatthalung. Pan's first teacher was his father, Wan. In local traditions, learning to read and write was not separate from learning Dhamma. Both the teacher and the book were treated with the kind of respect that was usually reserved for objects of religious veneration. Before Pan took part in the sacred ritual of learning his first letter, Khlai gave her son a bath and dressed him in a white robe. The lesson began with religious ceremonies on a Thursday, an auspicious day for learning. Children recited Pali invocations calling upon the name of the Buddha. The traditional offerings, Ajahn Panya recalled, "consisted of nine portions of areca nuts and nine candles (which my mother made) placed on a white cloth over a small, low bench. I sat on the floor and prostrated myself three times. Once the candles were lighted, I prostrated myself three more times. Then I sat on the floor with my palms together. An old uncle, Duang, recited the verse paying respect to the teacher and asking for permission to study. I repeated after him. The whole recitation took about fifteen minutes. Then my father covered my right hand with his to help me hold a pencil. The pencil was homemade. I drew my first letter on a slate. This was the same slate my father had used when he studied at the monastery." Not only did Pan learn the first letter that day, he also learned the Dhamma principle of showing respect to one's teacher and expressing gratitude for the teaching (in Pali, *katannu katavedita*).

Sitting in his house, built on stilts, Pan spent the whole day writing the first letter. He practiced writing just the one letter all day, taking an occasional break to play outside. As Ajahn Panya recalled, "Sometimes my father got mad at me because I did not do it right. He grabbed my hand and rapped it against the slate. But it was not a serious punishment. This was how I learned every day." Each day Pan learned to write a new letter, proceeding one by one. In a short time he was able to write the entire alphabet of forty-four consonants and thirty-two vowels. Pan learned to write words before he became a temple boy at the village wat.

During this same year, in 1918, Khlai's younger brother, who had just graduated from the state school in Lam Pam district, returned to his natal village and was ordained as a monk at Wat Nanglat. Pan called him Luang Na (Venerable Younger Uncle). Abbots of Wat Nanglat had always been known for their knowledge of herbal medicines. According to a local saying, "If you wish to study medicine, go to Wat Nanglat; if you want to hear the Mahachat (the Great Birth story), go to Wat Tamira." Pan's parents sent him to Wat Nanglat to serve as a temple boy, and Pan lived with Luang Na. The monk taught Pan to read the standard textbook published by the Ministry of Education in Bangkok. By the time Pan enrolled in the state primary school, he had already learned to read and write from his father and his uncle.

18

PASSION AND COMPASSION

VILLAGE BOYS who lived at some distance from the train station in Phatthalung used to be eager to look at the steam locomotives, the railway cars, the warehouses that had popped up around the station, and the colorful people who came and went. One such boy was Pan, and his desire to hang out at the train station soon got him in trouble.

When Pan was a temple boy at the wat in his village, he suffered epileptic seizures several times a month. His mother went to consult her cousin, Ajahn Phum, a physician-monk at Wat Khuha-sawan. Inasmuch as Ajahn Phum was willing to try to heal the boy, Pan's parents moved him to that wat. "Luang Lung" (Venerable Elder Uncle), as Pan called Ajahn Phum, was especially noted for his compassion. He had saved many lives with his medicinal knowledge, and local people were impressed with his skill and the gentle way he treated them. The local wat was like a health clinic. When children got sick their parents brought them to physician-monks to be healed.

After Pan had settled in at Wat Khuha, Luang Lung brewed a pot of herbal medicine that the boy was to drink every day. As soon as Pan swallowed the bitter liquid he reached immediately for some honey or sugar to get rid of the bad taste. After three months of drinking pots of this dark herbal liquid, his epilepsy gradually disappeared.

Normally Luang Lung spoke little. Though compassionate, he was a strict disciplinarian. Breaking the rules demanded swift punishment. Temple boys could be troublemakers, and whenever they got too loud or rowdy Luang Lung would hit them with the closest thing he could lay his hands on. If the boys were not mindful when attending the teacher they got slapped. As a child Pan had always been outgoing and fun loving, but after having lived with this strict uncle for many months, Pan got bored and thought of running away and going back home. Fear of parental punishment was what stopped him.

During Pan's boyhood, parents, schoolteachers, and monks still shared similar values concerning child rearing. "Spare the rod and spoil the child" was as much a guiding principle in Siam as it was for a while in Europe and North America. S.G. McFarland, an American missionary who lived in Siam during Chulalongkorn's reign, referred to the Siamese method of "teaching to remember" as "rattan discipline." As an example, McFarland pointed to an incident that took place in Bangkok in the 1880s. "One day a man brought his boy to put him into the 'King's School.' After the arrangements were all made and he was about to say 'Good-bye' to his boy, he turned to the principal of the school and said, 'Please whip him a great deal; I want him to learn fast. If at any time you think he deserves one dozen, please give him two dozen, and if you think he deserves two dozen, please give him four dozen. Don't let him be a dunce.' And with this loving injunction he took his leave."

Although Pan's parents never actually thrashed him, they fully expected the monk to discipline their son. When Pan's father took him to serve as a temple boy, he said to Luang Lung, "If my son is naughty, give it to him. Don't let him get away with anything."

At Wat Khuha every act of disobedience, no matter how minor, was punished. One day Pan skipped his daily chores and ran away to the train station just for fun. Having lived until then only in his natal village, Pan had never seen a steam engine before, and he was curious. Luang Lung sent some of his lay disciples to look for the boy. They found him and brought him back to the wat. Luang Lung then gave Pan a sound thrashing. The punishment did not stop the boy, however. He soon tired of the solemn atmosphere in the wat and ran away again. This time the Ajahn's men knew where to find him, and Pan got the same punishment.

The third time, Pan ran away during the day and stayed overnight in a warehouse near the train station. It took the men a while to find him. Afraid that Pan would become associated with bad boys and grow up to be a bandit, Luang Lung punished him severely. Many bandits in the South had been temple boys in their youth. Local monks had seen that a boy endowed with intelligence and willfulness could turn out to be either a fearless abbot and a strong leader of the community or a notorious bandit leader who hid out in the jungle.

Pan's punishment was administered in a room in Luang Lung's kuti. When Luang Lung was finished, he confined the boy to the kuti, keeping a sharp eye on him all the time, making it impossible for Pan to attempt escape. Some days later, however, when Luang Lung left to have a meal at a sala some distance from his kuti, Pan squeezed his body through a small hole in the wall, then walked across the hills toward the north and west. To make sure that nobody spotted him, Pan took the least used paths and walked all the way home.

By the time Pan got home a deep cut on his bottom had become infected. There were no ready-made medicines to treat such wounds. Pan's mother used holy water to clean the cut and eventually got rid of the infection. Believing that a strict diet would help the skin regenerate, she put Pan on a diet of rice and *kruat* fish for a few months until his wound had healed. Once Pan had recovered, his father asked him if he wanted to go back to Wat Khuha. Pan refused. This time Pan's parents did not intervene; nor did they get angry with the monk for beating their son so hard that the boy ran away from the wat.

Pan's father enrolled him in a government school about two kilometers away. Wan himself had had no formal education; he had learned to read and write from monks at the monastery near his village. Education at the wat was open and loosely structured. At the onset of the rainy season a boy might leave the wat to help his family in the fields and later return to school to continue his studies. Working in the fields was as important as learning from texts.

Adhering to a fixed schedule, the state-run school system did not allow students to help parents in the fields. Furthermore, by following the Western calendar, state schools held classes every weekday. This took children away from the wat on holy days, which more often than not fall on weekdays. Primary school textbooks made no reference to local crops or agricultural seasons. The state school curriculum emphasized the modern and scientific. In addition to math and science, textbooks described typical European environments, illustrating household niceties such as bathtubs, fireplaces, and furniture.

Going to a state school was a new experience for the children of Pan's generation in Phatthalung. All teachers there were civil servants. The children who attended the school walked back and forth from their villages. Pan was eight years old when he started the first grade. There were fifty students in the elementary school. Since Pan had already learned to read and write from his father and his uncle, he was well ahead of his classmates.

Pan proceeded to the third grade at the age of eleven. His third grade teacher, Leng, was very strict. In the hour devoted to arithmetic, every time Pan failed to add the assigned numbers correctly he was struck with a switch, twice, on his hand. Pan hated the punishment. One day he decided not to go to school. He left home as he did every morning, dressed as usual in his uniform. Instead of walking to school, however, Pan spent the whole day in a meadowy area with patches of tall grass and dense brush. There he could roam around without passersby seeing him. Before being sent to the government school Pan had spent his days outdoors tending water buffaloes, free from adult supervision. So it was very difficult for him to be cooped up all day in a schoolroom. Out in the woods and fields in the company of wild animals he never felt bored.

Pan skipped school for seven days. Late each afternoon, when the other children from his village passed through the forest on their way from school, Pan joined up with them and went home.

Wondering what had happened to Pan, his teacher decided to write a letter to Pan's father and asked a student named Paen to deliver it. When Paen arrived at Pan's house, he saw Pan in the kitchen cooking rice on a charcoal stove. Since Pan's parents were out, Paen simply left the teacher's letter with Pan. As soon as Paen left, Pan opened the letter and read that Teacher Leng was asking the boy's parents to send

Pan back to school. Pan threw the letter into the fire, thinking no one would find out.

But an uncle of Pan's named Muang happened to see Paen carrying the letter to Pan's house. At dusk Uncle Muang stopped by for a visit and asked Pan what was in the letter. Pan's father, Wan, had just got home, and thus found out that his son had been skipping school. Normally a man of few words, Wan complained to Uncle Muang, "The boy is no good. The government put him in school, but he dislikes it. What will he do with his life? Is he going to be like a water buffalo?" Pan sat silently listening to his father's lament.

The next day Pan got up, put on his school uniform—a white shirt and short pants—and walked to school. As soon as Teacher Leng saw the boy, he asked, "Why did you cut classes?"

Pan replied, "I am afraid of your switch."

His teacher reassured him, "I will not hit you from now on. Be attentive to your studies."

From then on until the day he graduated from the primary school Pan never skipped classes.

Back then, the primary school consisted of three grades. After completing these, Pan enrolled in the secondary school in Lampam, a subdistrict about ten kilometers from his village. While attending the Lampam school, Pan, along with other boys whose homes were too far away from the school for them to walk back and forth each day, lived at a monastery a short distance from the school. The boys paid nothing for room and board at the monastery, but they had to buy notebooks, pens, and black and red inks for the calligraphy exercises they were called upon to do at school.

On one occasion, when he was a seventh grader, Pan had to travel home to get some money. As he was walking past Wat Khuha, it began to rain hard. Pan had no choice but to go into the monastery for shelter. Ever since his severe punishment several years before, Pan had not seen Luang Lung. Reminded now of the punishment inflicted upon him, the boy was scared to death. As soon as he caught sight of Luang Lung, Pan began to shake as if possessed by a spirit. He was so frightened that his hands shook while he bowed down three times before the monk.

"Why are you shaking?" Luang Lung asked the boy.

"I'm afraid you might beat me again," Pan confessed.

"Don't be afraid. I won't beat you ever again."

Luang Lung told Pan to spend the night at the monastery. Since the boy was covered with dirt from walking through mud in the rain, the monk helped him take a bath before bedtime. Pan was surprised by Luang Lung's tenderness. "Gently, Luang Lung dipped water from the earthenware jar outside the kuti," Ajahn Panya recalled, "and poured it over me from head to toe. His manner and his eyes were so tender. What a complete change! Six years ago when I last saw him his anger was so wrathful, like a fire that burns everything to ashes. But underneath his hot temper is compassion, as cool as rainfall. All my apprehension disappeared as the water flowed over my head. His eyes were full of kindness, expressed from the depths of his heart."

At home Pan usually slept between his two grandmothers, who lulled him to sleep with old folktales. At the wat the monks and temple boys slept on simple mats, just as they did at home. Temple boys like Pan who were related to a monk at the wat usually slept in that monk's kuti; the rest bunked with other monks or slept in a hut designed for them. "That night," Ajahn Panya said, musing upon the warm feelings he felt for the monk, "the friendship that had run dry was renewed. Although I did not get to put my head on grandmothers' arms, sleeping right next to Luang Lung I felt just as happy as I was at home."

In the morning Pan told Luang Lung he needed to go home to get money. There was no way for him to get there except on foot, and Pan's home was hours away from Wat Khuha. The monk told Pan, "You don't have to walk all the way home." Luang Lung then took Pan to a wooden box where he kept all his money and told the boy to take as much as he needed. Pan took two baht. Luang Lung laughed, "Is that all?" Pan prostrated himself before Luang Lung and walked back to the school.

19

Food for Body and Mind

ABOUT A HUNDRED students, all boys, attended the secondary school in Lampam. Most girls received some elementary education at the village schools but did not further their studies, as their parents wanted them to help at home. Parents sent their sons to the secondary school so that they would become more literate. They expected the boys to be ordained as monks, at least temporarily, so that there would always be monks at the local monasteries. Monks were looked up to as the most knowledgeable people, and they often served as community leaders and healers. The only libraries to be found in rural Siam were housed in the monasteries.

At the school in Lampam students studied arithmetic, geography, history, ethics, and English. The English class was assigned a book written by B.O. Cartwright. (During King Chulalongkorn's reign Cartwright served as the official English tutor in the School of the Royal Pages in Bangkok.) In the hour devoted to ethics, students learned moral precepts and Dhamma principles. They had to memorize various Dhamma terms in order to pass the exam. There were no multiple-choice tests back then. Students had to explain things in their own words and were taught to write clearly. Through rote learning the students developed serviceable memories. They became skilled in reading comprehension and were encouraged to practice elegant handwriting.

Every school day a student was expected to bring notebooks, textbooks, a bottle of black ink, a bottle of red ink, and two pens—one fine-nibbed and the other broad-nibbed. The fine pen was used for underlining, the broad pen for writing. The pen handle was made of bamboo. Carrying their school supplies back and forth often led to ink-stained clothes. Not all textbooks were available in Phatthalung. If the teacher had the only text, the students had to copy the contents into their notebooks by hand.

In 1920 school started on May 17, but Pan's father did not bring him to school until June 5, with the result that Pan was behind his classmates. The first day Pan came to class the teacher called on him to stand up and read aloud from the English text. But Pan could not read English. The teacher told Pan to come to his house after school. Every day Teacher Kitcha tutored Pan in English until he had caught up with his classmates.

Forty students, including Pan, were from out of town. Since the school was far away from their villages, these boys lodged at Wat Yang as temple boys. The monastery, located within walking distance of the school, thus served as a dormitory for the out-of-town students. The abbot of Wat Yang was Ajahn Suk, and his deputy was Ajahn Phum. Ajahn Suk was skilled in carpentry, woodcarving, and basketry, and he made the furniture, baskets, and other containers that monks and temple boys used every day. Ajahn Phum was more like a guardian for the temple boys. Whenever Ajahn Phum was free from his monastic duties he would supervise the boys while they did their homework. If a boy was weak in any subject, Ajahn Phum would tutor him.

Temple boys received some of the food that monks collected on their daily alms round. At Wat Yang, where the boys outnumbered the monks, there was insufficient food to feed all forty of them. So every morning before they went to school, the temple boys took turns cooking their own breakfast, and every afternoon after returning from school they again took turns cooking. Most boys, including Pan, had already learned how to cook from their mothers or grandmothers. Those who had never cooked at home got their training at the monastery.

The temple boys ate the same food every day: rice and vegetable curry. The rice was given to the monks by laypeople. Vegetables, fruits, and coconuts were given by nature. A vegetable known as *phak bung* grew year-round in a big pond near the wat. The area surrounding the monastery was full of coconut trees. All the temple boys had to do was climb the trees and pick them. Ajahn Panya recalled, "We never ran out of phak bung and coconut milk, even though we cooked the same curry every day all year. We became vegetarians, since fish, pork, and chicken were hard to come by."

Temple boys did not plan ahead. Sometimes they did not realize that they had run out of rice until dinnertime. One evening Ajahn Phum noticed that quite a few of the temple boys were up in the tops of the coconut and guava trees. "Why aren't you in the kitchen cooking?" he asked. The boys replied, "We ran out of rice, sir." After hearing that the boys had nothing to eat, Ajahn Phum immediately went to his kuti, put on his outer robe, grabbed a big umbrella and headed out on foot to one of the boys' villages, ten kilometers away.

The next morning Ajahn Phum returned with four bags of rice. The bags were made of fibers woven from *krachut*, a sedge with round, hollow stems that grows in great abundance in the ponds and marshes of Phatthalung. Sixty years later Ajahn Panya vividly recounted the scene of his teacher returning to the monastery with four bags of rice for the temple boys. "Whenever we ran out of rice, the Ajahn never failed to feed us. The sight of Ajahn Phum carrying rice sacks will remain forever in the memories of us temple boys."

After the boys had their supper Ajahn Phum usually gave them a Dhamma talk. Then, at dusk, the boys formed into groups of three. Ajahn Phum distributed oil lamps. While the boys read their books the monk walked among them to make sure that they were not playing around or falling asleep but remained focused on their studies. Around 9 P.M. all the oil lamps were extinguished, and the temple boys were sent to bed.

One advantage of living at the wat for temple boys was that they got to hear Dhamma talks or stories laced with Dhamma. At the state school the lay teachers taught secular subjects; at the monastery the monks imparted the way of Dhamma and moral discipline. For generations before the Western system of education became compulsory, which occurred during the reign of King Vajiravudh (1910–25), the Dhamma was not taught separately from more mundane topics. The two were interwoven.

20

MOONSHINE

ALTHOUGH the sale of whiskey and other spirits was a state monopoly in Siam, this did not prevent some people from distilling their own and concealing it. One morning, Ajahn Panya relates, a number of temple boys were cooking in the kitchen as they normally did. Klan, the oldest, went into a nearby forest to look for edible plants. He came across a big earthenware jar full of rice whiskey that a villager had made and then hidden. Using the empty tin can that he always carried with him, Klan dipped into the jar and drank the liquid. Struck by its taste that was at once sweet, sour, and bitter, Klan dipped into the jar again and then filled the can and carried it to his friends. At the wat the temple boys who sampled the liquid liked it so much that they gathered their tin cans and went back to the grove for more. In time they had emptied the entire jar.

When the moonshiner discovered that his whiskey was missing, he immediately went to see Ajahn Phum. "Your temple boys are terrible. I hid my whiskey, but they found it and drank it all up."

"Well, the stuff is illegal. No use in hiding it," Ajahn Phum remarked.

Ajahn Phum went to observe the temple boys from a distance, but he did not put in an appearance. Having drunk the whole jar of whiskey, the boys were pretty tipsy. They laughed and talked loudly.

With great self-confidence, Klan advised his friends, "If the Ajahn calls you, you should chew on some raw rice before you go to him. The rice will absorb the smell of the liquor."

Pan was so dead drunk that he threw up all the food he had eaten earlier, as did others. A young monk named Dam, whom the boys called Luang Phi (Venerable Brother), passed by. Luang Phi asked, "What exactly did you eat?" Pan quickly came up with a lie. "I bought two packs of *khao mak* from Uncle Chuen and ate them both." Khao mak is a snack made of fermented rice wrapped in banana leaf, and Uncle Chuen was a vendor who had a food stall just outside the wat. Luang Phi asked no further questions and continued on his way to his kuti.

Pan knew that he had violated two of the five precepts that temple boys must observe; he drank alcohol and he told a lie. These two precepts are related. The alcohol removed his sense of shame.

The next morning the boys again cooked rice in the kitchen and sat down together for breakfast. While they were eating, they overheard Ajahn Phum say to the abbot, Ajahn Suk, "Last night I learned something new."

"What was that?" asked Ajahn Suk.

"Chewing raw rice eliminates the smell of liquor on the breath," replied Ajahn Phum.

The temple boys eyed each other warily. They ate their breakfast quickly, got dressed, and walked to school. All day Klan, Pan, and their friends were tormented with anxiety, not knowing how the monk was going to punish them. They were unable to concentrate on their studies.

As soon as they finished dinner the boys heard the temple bell ring loudly. Klan and his friends knew that it was a call for a meeting. The critical moment had finally arrived. Once all the boys were assembled, Ajahn Phum gave them a long, stern lecture. Then he called out the boys' names one by one and scolded them. To one boy he said, "Your father is an alcoholic. Do you want to be a drunk like your father?" To another: "Your grandfather was addicted to liquor." To yet another: "Your dad is always dead drunk. Do you want to follow in his footsteps?"

After Ajahn Phum singled out each boy for a public scolding, he then rewarded each of them with three stiff whacks with a stick.

"That was the first time in my life that I tasted liquor," Ajahn Panya tells us. "I learned that a drunk was a good-for-nothing. From then on, as temple boys we never touched liquor again."

One advantage of having the boys live at the wat is that their behavior was monitored by the monks. Decades later, the temple boys who had gotten drunk and were whipped by Ajahn Phum turned out to be respectable adults. Pan became Ajahn Panya, abbot of Wat Chonprathan in Nonthaburi, known as one of the most outspoken preachers in mid-twentieth-century Thailand. Klan, who first discovered the whiskey in the woods, grew up to be a schoolteacher, and Klan's son, Sing, was ordained and lived at Wat Chonprathan. Later, in the 1990s, Phra Sing became abbot of Wat Umong in Chiang Mai. Plaek, another temple boy who drank the liquor with Pan, grew up to be a Supreme Court judge.

21

BECOMING A MAN

IN 1926 when his father became gravely ill, Pan, as the eldest child at home, felt obliged to help his mother plow their fields. At the approach of the rainy season Pan left the district school for good and went back to his village to become a farmer. His formal education thus ended at the seventh grade.

The very first day Pan went out into the rice field by himself he learned that plowing was not easy work. The boy had two oxen in harness. As Pan plowed, the plowshare began cutting deeper and deeper until finally it got stuck. Unable to pull the plow any further, the oxen simply stood still. In desperation Pan lashed the oxen, and the pain startled them enough so that they jerked forward. The jerk caused the blade of the plow to break from the handles. Pan had to quit working and carry the plow home. At home the boy confessed to his ailing father, "The plow is broken. What am I going to do tomorrow?"

Lying on his mat on the floor, Wan gazed at his son's face with pity, but he did not say anything so as to avoid hurting the boy's feelings. Pan then went into the kitchen to eat lunch. Having eaten his fill, Pan tried to fix the plow himself. After a while he gave up and carried the broken plow to his neighbors. Pan walked from house to house until he found someone who could reattach the blade. By the end of the day Pan returned home with the plow repaired and ready to be used the next morning.

Pan struggled plowing and harrowing his parents' fields until all the work was done. He also sowed rice seeds in the nursery beds and later transplanted the seedlings into the rice paddies. Every morning Pan got up before dawn and ate his breakfast of sticky rice mixed with sugar. Then he walked to the paddy field and worked for half a day. Around 11 A.M. he walked home for lunch. After lunch Pan usually took the cattle out to graze. The cattle spent all afternoon grazing, and Pan walked them home in the evening.

When the paddy fields were green with young rice Pan had to find another place for the cattle to graze. There was a big pasture not far from the police station and the provincial government building. When Pan took his cattle to graze there he was confronted by a policeman who warned him, "If you bring your cattle here again I will arrest you." But since there was no other pasture nearby, Pan continued to take his cattle to graze near the station when the police were not around. It was a game of cat and mouse. Pan saw no good reason why he should not be allowed to bring his cattle to the pastures near the station. He was well aware that the life of a farmer was full enough of suffering. Luckily, Pan never got arrested. And the routine of his life continued: a boy with his cattle all day long.

As long as his father remained ill Pan was the head of the family. Not only did he perform his father's work, he also attended various social functions on behalf of his father. On one occasion Wan received an invitation to go to a wedding, and he asked his son to represent him. Pan was then fifteen years old. Siamese weddings are festive, and the custom in Phatthalung was for wedding guests to go first to the bride's parents' house for a feast. At this house Pan sat with his neighbors, all of whom were older. Pan enjoyed the good food, but he did not touch the rice whiskey. A neighbor who was fond of Pan said to the boy, "You are a grownup now. Why eat only rice? You should drink this with the meal." The man then handed Pan a glass of rice whiskey.

"No, I can't drink," Pan told his neighbor. "The last time I drank I threw up."

"You are a man of Muang Lung (Phatthalung)," Pan's neighbor insisted. "Real men must drink." Pan took the glass and drank it straight down. His neighbors laughed and loudly cheered the boy on, refilling his glass over and over. Pan's face turned redder as he drank every glass that came his way.

From the house of the bride's parents the guests walked to the house of the groom's parents, and there the feast continued. All the men encouraged Wan's son to drink. Wan was known for his generosity, and the neighbors wanted to turn his son into a real man. They certainly did not regard drunkenness as socially disgraceful. Pan had no choice but to comply with the local custom.[16] By the time Pan got home he was so sick that he threw up repeatedly. He realized that drinking caused suffering; it never brought happiness. Seeing his son kneeling on the porch and throwing up, Wan complained, "Why did you drink then? Drinking is bad. I, your own father, no longer drink."

Toward the end of the year Pan and his neighbors began to harvest the rice crop that they had planted. According to local custom, villagers took turns helping to harvest one another's fields. By December the harvesting was about finished. Then Pan and his neighbors started threshing, and when that work was completed they stored the rice in small granaries adjacent to their homes. This had been a good year for Pan. There was plenty of rice in the granary. The cattle were happy, too, as they no longer had to walk far to graze. They could feed on the grass that grew in the family's fields again.

Pan was sixteen when Luang Lung, the venerable uncle who took care of him when he was a temple boy, returned to his monastery in Phatthalung. Luang Lung had been invited to perform ceremonies at a Thai temple in Penang, a British colony in what is now Malaysia.

As soon as Khlai heard that Luang Lung had returned from Penang, she went to see him at Wat Khuha and told him that her son had quit the district school to work on their farm. Luang Lung was very concerned. He knew that in a remote province like Phatthalung, infamous for the buffalo rustlers who roamed in it, an intelligent, strong-willed boy like Pan might be drawn to mischief. Afraid that his young nephew might fall under the rustlers' influence, he asked Khlai to allow Pan to accompany him on another trip to Penang, and she consented.

Before the monk and his nephew embarked on their trip, Pan prostrated himself at the feet of his parents. Khlai asked her son to promise, "Wherever you are, no matter how far, when you reach the age of twenty you must return home to be ordained as a monk." Pan duly promised. He was sixteen when he left home. "I am a grownup now," he thought. "I should not depend on my parents financially. I must be self-reliant."

Luang Lung's aim was to enroll his nephew in an English-language school in Penang. But the proper documents and transcripts were lacking, so Pan was not accepted. The idea of further schooling for Pan was dropped.

Pan settled into a Thai monastery in Penang. As a temple boy his main duty was to cook breakfast and lunch and serve these meals to the monks (Thai monks do not eat after noontime). To take advantage of the opportunities that existed in this British colony, Luang Lung suggested that Pan acquire mechanical training and learn to drive. A few months later Pan became an apprentice to a mechanic in an automobile repair shop owned by a Malay. He learned how to take apart an engine and put it back together. As an apprentice Pan received free meals and a small amount of cash, enough to buy tea and coffee.

After he had been working for a month Pan's face suddenly became swollen. His hands and feet also swelled up, and in the end his whole body was swollen. Pan had to quit work temporarily and see a doctor. Fortunately, a Thai doctor in town was able to bring the swelling down, and Pan could resume his work at the garage. But soon his body grew swollen again, probably because he was allergic to engine oil or grease. Pan realized that being a car mechanic was not going to suit him.

22

BUFFALO BANDITS

I N THE SOUTHERN region there is an old saying: "A real man knows how to steal water buffaloes." According to custom in southern Siam, buffalo stealing was either a profession or a way for men to prove their manliness. As Ajahn Panya explains, "In the old days parents would not allow their daughter to marry a man who did not know how to steal a buffalo. The locals believed that a man without this knowledge would not be able to protect his own buffaloes." One can see a parallel with the English proverb "An old thief makes a good jailor."

When Pan was a child Phatthalung had a reputation for being home to many gangs of bandits. Each gang roamed free, unified by a common purpose and shared values. Bandit leaders bore names such as Cockcrow, Satin-Head Blackie, Red-Bearded Silver, Black-Bearded Inky, and Thunderbolt Lake.

Ajahn Panya recalled that when he was young "one village or another was raided almost every night, and buffaloes were taken from the fields. The bandits came, fired guns into the air, and rounded up all the buffaloes. As many as twenty might be taken away." This was a major economic blow to villagers, as they depended on the buffalo to plow and harrow their fields. The village in which Pan grew up was surrounded by high hills, wide pastures, and dense forests. Once they had stolen the buffaloes, the bandits simply disappeared into the forests with their plunder, and it was hard to track them down.

The most notorious bandit gang was led by Cockcrow, whose deputy was Satin-Head Blackie. Since Cockcrow came from Donsai, a subdistrict of Khuan Khanun district, he was known as Cockcrow Donsai by the police. Back then, people had no surnames. His deputy, Satin-Head Blackie, was so named because of his curly black hair and the satin cloth he liked to wrap around his head. Many bandits carried satin bandannas with them; in case of injury the thick strip of cloth could be tied around an arm or leg to stop bleeding.

Despite the frequent raids, Pan's parents' cattle and buffaloes were never stolen, regardless of whether the animals were being kept at home or left in the fields. Neighbors who lost cattle or buffaloes to the bandits sometimes got some of them back, thanks to Wan and Khlai. "For example," Ajahn Panya explains, "once when ten buffaloes were stolen, my parents were able to get back eight; the bandits had killed two buffaloes for food. This was not because my parents had power over the bandits or that the bandits felt obligated to my folks. It was due to the fact that my parents were kind to everybody. They willingly lent their buffaloes to anybody in need. It did not matter how many buffaloes or for how long. It was my parents' generosity that protected their buffaloes. Some of these bandits had been guests at our house at one time or another and might later have been lenient out of gratitude for the free food and shelter they once received."

These bandits—many of whom had been driven to banditry by poverty, corrupt officials, or excessive taxation—had their own principles and code of honor. Bandit Cockcrow, for example, forbade his gang members to hurt women or children, to harm people who did not resist them, to rob householders of their bare necessities, or to steal from people who had been hospitable.

Local taxes had become burdensome after the central government changed the tax system from payment in kind to payment in cash, even though most people were still living in a subsistence economy. In addition to paying a head tax of four baht per year and a household tax, people in southern Siam were also required to pay annual taxes on their farmland, fruit trees, farm animals, and produce. Products were taxed when brought to town for sale. The new tax system spelled great hardship for ordinary people. Men who could not afford to pay their taxes in cash were made to work for the local government, usually at hard labor, sometimes depriving their families of labor during peak agricultural periods.

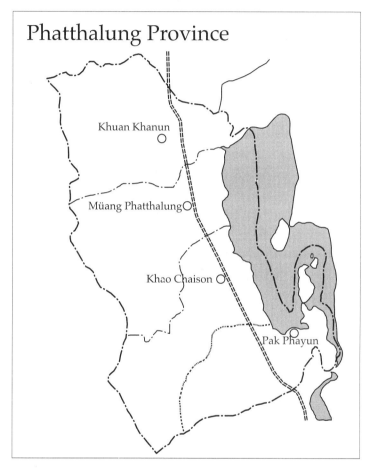

Phatthalung Province

Khuan Khanun

Müang Phatthalung

Khao Chaison

Pak Phayun

FIG. 20. PHATTHALUNG PROVINCE SHOWING DISTRICTS.

Understandably, heavily taxed villagers in distress looked for relief. Many revolted by aligning themselves with and even joining bandit gangs, whose leaders urged them not to pay taxes to the local officials and offered their protection to villagers.

In general, local people did not trust government officials. When asked to help locate bandits' hideouts, many locals refused. Finally the

district officer offered a pardon to any bandit who helped the government capture other bandits. Any bandit who turned over a bandit
leader to the local officials would be appointed a village headman.
Incentives like this created distrust among members of the bandit gangs.

One day Si, the Donsai subdistrict headman, asked In, the Khok-
wat village headman, to trick Cockcrow into coming near his village.
Chief In knew Cockcrow well and had often sent food supplies to the
bandit leader. So when the headman invited Cockcrow to have supper with him, the bandit leader did not suspect a thing. At the time they
were to meet, Chief In arrived in the company of three strongmen,
and Cockcrow arrived with his brother Chaeng. When the bandits let
down their guard while eating supper, the strongmen, armed with axes,
overpowered them, bound them with rope, and turned them over to
authorities.

After his brother died in the Nakhon prison, Cockcrow and a fellow prisoner named Sang broke out of jail. As soon as Cockcrow got
back to Phatthalung, he went straight to Donsai subdistrict and killed
Chief Si. Cockcrow then proclaimed himself leader of all the bandit
gangs. Members of quite a number of small bandit gangs, who had
heard the news of Cockcrow's daring, came out to join the bandit leader.

However, some villagers responded to the rewards offered for the
capture of bandits. Two villagers informed the police on Cockcrow
when he visited his wife in her village. He was killed by the police, who
tied his body to a palm tree in front of the local monastery, Wat Kuti,
as a warning to others. A local poet compared Cockcrow's death to a
golden bodhi tree that had fallen: both had provided shelter.

Blackie assumed control of the gang and murdered the male informer
but did not harm the female informer. Thereafter, three police suppression units were sent from Nakhon Si Thammarat to wipe out the bandits in Phatthalung. Injured in a shoot-out with the police, Blackie
escaped but hanged himself to rob the officials of their pleasure in capturing him alive. He was buried by his gang. The police found and dug
up his body and tied it to a palm tree in front of Wat Kuti. From then
on, hardly any villagers dared to walk past the palm tree at night, fear-
ing the bandit's ghost.

Pan was nine years old when Satin-Head Blackie died. With the death of the last bandit leader, the bandit gangs dissolved, and in 1920 the three suppression units were abolished. The three police sergeants who brought down Satin-Head Blackie were awarded gold medals by King Vajiravudh.

23

STORYTELLER IN A TIN MINE

WHILE PAN was living with his uncle, the monk he called Luang Lung, at a Thai monastery in Penang, he met a man who told him that there was plenty of work for young men in the tin mines of Phuket.[17] This was in the mid-1920s, and Phuket had not yet become the resort we know today. So Pan decided to go there to look for work. He asked one of his friends, Paan, to go with him. The boys went to consult Luang Lung, who gave them permission to make the trip. Before they left the monk gave each of the temple boys ten baht for their travel expenses.

Pan and Paan then accompanied the man from Phuket aboard a boat. Each boy was charged six baht for the fare. When the boat arrived at the harbor in Phuket, each passenger had to pay two more baht in order to get off. Pan and Paan now had only two baht left in their pockets, and Pan was disheartened. "Why did Luang Lung give us so little money?" he wondered. "How can we live with only two baht?" He then reasoned, "Certainly Luang Lung would not mean to starve us. He probably wanted to test our knowledge and perseverance. He was afraid that if he gave us a lot more money we might spend it on pleasures." Thinking thus, Pan felt more at ease. As the boys stood at the harbor, disoriented, not knowing where to go, the man from Phuket came up to them and asked, "Where do you want to go?"

"Why ask me? I have never been here before. I don't even have a single relative in this town," Pan replied.

"Calm down, brother. I will take you to one of my relatives," the Phuket man promised.

Good to his word, the man brought the boys to Choei, who took them in. Pan called his host Uncle Choei. Ever since Pan was a little boy he had always helped his parents with all kinds of household chores. When he became a temple boy, Pan performed a great many services, along with the other temple boys, for the monks at Wat Khuha. He had been taught that when you live with someone you should help out, so Pan helped the Phuket couple with their household tasks. Every day he got up early, cleaned the house, hauled water, and split firewood. Uncle Choei and his wife were pleased to have Pan live with them.

One morning Pan told Uncle Choei, "I came to Phuket to find a job. Would you please help me?" Uncle Choei was sympathetic. After they finished breakfast he took Pan to the Celestial Prince mine, one of several mines cut into the hillsides that, although expensive to operate, yielded more tin than the shallow, nearly depleted mines close to the coast. After introducing Pan to a foreman, Uncle Choei left. Pan fumbled, as he did not know quite what to do, having never worked in a mine before. Before the workday ended Pan was dismissed, and he returned to Uncle Choei's house feeling disheartened. Uncle Choei was kind; he told Pan to wait a while. Pan continued to do chores for Uncle Choei in return for room and board.

A week later Uncle Choei took Pan to the same mining company. This time he introduced the boy to a different foreman who was supervising men digging up the hillsides. Pan was hired. His job was to haul away the ore-bearing rock, soil, and clay dug from the hill. The rubble was put into two baskets that hung at either end of a bamboo pole. Carrying the pole over his shoulder, Pan followed the other haulers to a site about three hundred meters away where a dam was being built. The water from the dam was to be used to extract the crystals of ore from the rubble. Each worker got paid one baht and thirty satang per hour.

The first day of hauling rubble was difficult for Pan. When he got the baskets to the dam site he set them down on the ground before dumping out their contents. The foreman noticed this and told Pan it was more efficient to empty the baskets before putting them down. When Pan tried this, the pole pressed hard against his collarbone. It was a painful way to empty the baskets. Nevertheless, Pan persevered. After enduring the pain caused by the pole a few times, he figured out how to do it right. Now he could empty his baskets as fast as any of the experienced haulers.

The life of a full-time laborer is not easy. Working in the mine compelled Pan to realize that the haulers had to learn how to get along with the diggers; otherwise, the diggers could make life miserable. Pan was a newcomer, and the diggers knew it. One day a digger tested the boy by overloading his baskets with so much rubble that Pan could barely lift them. As Pan started walking the three hundred meters, he felt the bamboo pole pressing painfully into his shoulder with each step he took. He was in such agony that his vision became blurred, and his ears could hear no sound.

In his desire to get along with his coworkers, Pan figured out a way to make friends with them. As a child, Pan had gathered a rich store of ancient tales, told to him by his two grandmothers, that were now firmly embedded in his memory. By the time he enrolled in the district school he knew over a hundred of them. When he was in school Pan had loved reading all kinds of books, not just those required in the classroom. During lunch breaks he seldom ran around with other schoolchildren, preferring instead to spend his time reading. During the years he served as a temple boy Pan was exposed to even more folklore and religious stories.

The tin mine workers usually ate lunch together. After the meal they sat around in small groups talking among themselves. One day, after the men had finished their lunch, Pan began to entertain them. Whereas the workers normally talked about their villages, this time they listened to Pan tell them stories from ancient times. Every day Pan had a new story to tell his fellow workers, who were a mix of Buddhists, Muslims, and Chinese who practiced ancestor worship. Not only did Pan possess a retentive memory, he had a gift for vivid description. Before long the workers were hooked. The Muslim workers particularly loved a story about the prophet Mohammed that Pan had read as a young boy. They told Pan, "We like the way you explain the teachings of our prophet. They are easier to understand than the way our religious teacher explained them."

People in southern Siam respected hermits and other holy men, many of whom had been community advisors or founders of settlements. The number of these religious figures, and their relevance in local people's daily lives, ensured that Pan would never run out of stories to tell his fellow workers. Almost every village in the South had a legend about its sacred site or the founder of the community.

The diggers became so fond of Pan's stories that they began shoveling only small loads into Pan's baskets. His burden now felt so light that he could get to the dam site in no time at all. Pan learned that storytelling had the power to melt the heart of even a tough mine worker.

After their day's work the men went to the company dormitory to sleep. They could pick any spot on the floor on which to lie down. There were no radios, movies, or any other forms of organized entertainment. The dormitory was located in the forest where there were plenty of mosquitoes. Having no mosquito nets, the workers slept close by the fire, since the smoke helped to keep the mosquitoes away. Nevertheless, many workers were bitten by mosquitoes and came down with malaria.

The mining company provided their workers with plain cooked rice. The men could eat as many bowls of rice as they wanted, but they had to buy whatever other foods they wished to eat. Pan usually ate steamed rice with canned fish. Every day he spent fifteen satang to buy a can of fish for his meals. Since Pan neither smoked nor drank, he was able to live on fifteen satang a day.

FROM BROTHEL TO TEMPLE

THE MINING COMPANY that Pan worked for paid its workers every two weeks in cash. The first time young Pan received his pay and returned to the dormitory for the evening, he was surprised to see that only a few of his fellow workers were there.

"Where have all the men gone?" he asked.

"Why, don't you know?" they replied. "They went to open their eyes! We can't just live in the jungle all the time like monkeys and gibbons."

The seventeen-year-old Pan was puzzled. "Their eyes are already wide open," he mused. "Why do they need to open their eyes?"

Two weeks later the workers got paid again. After they received their pay, Pan begged an older worker, "Wait! Let me go with you. I too want to open my eyes."

His fellow workers took Pan to town on a minibus. The forest road was unpaved, so it was a bumpy ride. Slowly they crept toward the town. When the bus stopped, all the men got off, split up into small groups, and entered a narrow lane. The streetlights were bright, and it appeared to Pan that his fellow workers knew their way around very well. When they came to a particular house Pan saw several women sitting around. They were all wearing red lipstick and were dressed in beautiful clothes. It was a brothel. Pan learned that all the prostitutes were Chinese women from Penang.

Some of the mine workers were regular customers. They went straight to the woman in charge of the prostitutes and greeted her in a familiar way. Each man then claimed a young woman, and they all disappeared into private rooms. Pan turned to one of his companions, asking, "How much for one night?"

His friend replied, "Eight baht."

"I hate to spend the money. I had to work like a dog to earn eight baht. I don't want to spend it all in one night," Pan told his friend.

Actually, Pan was afraid of catching what the men called "the women's disease." Women who caught this disease called it "the men's disease." Whoever caught such a disease was looked down upon. Pan was indecisive, not knowing what to do with the situation. His friend urged, "Why stand there like a fool? Come on! All your buddies have already gone in." Not waiting for Pan, he too disappeared into a room.

For a while Pan stood in a daze. Then he decided to explore the lane. When he came to the end of the lane he walked further. After struggling along some minutes in the pitch dark he stumbled into a monastery called Wat Khachon. The sight of the monastery gladdened his heart. Pan knew that at least he could spend the night there free of charge. He entered the monastic compound and looked around. When he came to the ordination hall he stepped inside and saw a monk. The boy put his palms together and bowed to the monk. The monk was Venerable Thiap, a native of Nakhon Si Thammarat.

"Where are you from?" Ajahn Thiap asked the boy.

"Sir, I came from the tin mine," Pan replied.

"What brings you here?" the monk inquired.

"We came here to the brothel. All my friends picked their partners and went inside. I am the only one left," said Pan.

"Why didn't you go in?"

"I am afraid of disease," Pan confessed.

"Oh, you are a good boy," the monk replied.

The monk allowed Pan to sleep in the ordination hall. That night Pan felt happy and safe. In the morning he woke before dawn. While the monks went into town on alms round Pan swept the floor of the ordination hall clean. Then he went to haul water and filled all the earthenware jars in the monastery. After the monks finished their morning meal Pan ate whatever food was left. Then he cleaned the dining hall and washed all the dishes. Such service had always been Pan's way of showing gratitude to those who provided him with food and shelter. Pan had become a temple boy at the age of seven. He knew what needed to be done around a wat, and he felt comfortable serving the monks.

When he went to say good-bye and return to work at the mine, Ajahn Thiap told Pan, "Come again, son, and spend the night here." Putting his palms together respectfully, Pan replied softly, "Yes, sir." Then he took a minibus and headed back to the mine.

As it turned out the men who had gone to the brothel were now broke. Pan thought, "What a pity! They spent all their hard-earned money for a fleeting pleasure." Pan still had all his money in his pocket.

From the very first day Pan arrived in Phuket he always expressed his gratitude to anyone who offered him hospitality. By virtue of this, Pan always had a roof over his head. His father had been strict with Pan early on. To escape their miserable working conditions, the mine workers had sex with prostitutes, drank alcohol, smoked tobacco, and went to the cinema, all of which cost money. Pan did not completely reject these pleasures; occasionally he went to see a movie. In the town of Phuket a movie was shown for only three nights. When he did go to the cinema, Pan preferred going on the third night, when it was not so crowded.

Air conditioning did not exist in the 1920s, but there were fans in the cinema. There were three classes of tickets, priced at one, two, or three baht. Since Pan was frugal he always bought a one-baht ticket. Most of the movies shown in Phuket were Westerns from the United States. Pan and his fellow mine workers derived plenty of excitement from these shows.

In Pan's youth the most popular cowboy stars of the silent screen were William B. Hart and Tom Mix. Hart's Western hero was a tall, dark, silent loner. Tom Mix was called the King of the Cowboys in the 1920s. Mix's character lived by a code: no drinking, no smoking, no swearing, and no killing unless absolutely necessary.

The most popular comedians in the days of silent films were Buster

Keaton and Charlie Chaplin. In his films Keaton played a resourceful little man who struggles with modern machinery that goes wrong. Chaplin's films were full of comical incidents and unexpected encounters. His character was a sassy down-and-outer pitted against authorities like the police or against impersonal forces like machines. Young audiences of Pan's time found these characters more sympathetic than do the sophisticated audiences of today who have grown up with a new technology.

One of the most popular silent film stars who appealed especially to children was a German Shepherd named Rin Tin Tin, a dog that starred in more than forty films. Besides Westerns, other popular silents were swashbucklers like *The Prisoner of Zenda* and *Robin Hood*.

In addition to seeing American movies, Pan liked to go to the Chinese Club in the town of Phuket to read newspapers and magazines. Among the Thai newspapers that Pan read were *Thai Num* and *Si Krung*. When Pan decided to learn to speak English he ordered a set of books from Bangkok called *Conversations in English*, written by Phraya Worawitphisan, a Thai government official. The set consisted of five books, and Pan always carried one of the books with him. Whenever he had some free time Pan would read the book and memorize English terms.

In this regard Pan was different from his fellow laborers. Most young men who worked in the mine spent their wages on prostitutes and liquor, and some of them even went into debt. Young Pan knew how to spend money, where to go for entertainment, and how to choose good company. Although he worked as a manual laborer he found ways to improve the quality of his life.

25

HARD LABOR

EVENTUALLY Pan quit working at the mine. He stayed in Phuket, but he did not go back to live with Uncle Choei and his kind wife. Instead he returned to Wat Khachon, the monastery that he had stumbled into the first night he went into town. Here Pan did all kinds of chores in return for room and board. Every day he swept the ordination hall and the area around it, hauled water and filled the earthenware jars, cleaned the dining hall, and washed the dishes. After he finished his meal Pan would read whichever books he could find at the monastery, books such as the *Navakovada* (Instructions for Newly Ordained Monks and Novices), *The Life of the Buddha,* and the book of recitations for ordination. Consequently, Pan knew the recitations for ordination by heart long before he was ordained as a monk. If there was any time left, Pan went to the Chinese Club to read Thai newspapers and periodicals.

While living as a temple boy at Wat Khachon, Pan went to Phuket's Public Sanitation Department to apply for a job. One of the civil servants told Pan, "There are no job vacancies except that of garbage collector. Do you want it?"

Pan said, "Yes."

The civil servant replied, "You've got it. You can begin tomorrow."

When Pan returned to the monastery he saw a man looking for temple boys who wanted to find jobs. The man asked Pan, "Would you like to work on a rubber plantation?"

"I already have a job," Pan said. "I begin tomorrow."

"What kind of work and where?"

"Collecting garbage and putting it in a truck."

"Why do you want to collect garbage?" the man asked. "It is a dirty job. You'd do better to work on a rubber plantation pulling weeds. Weeds don't stink." Pan accepted without hesitation.

The next morning Pan said good-bye to Ajahn Thiap and went to the rubber plantation owned by a Thai government official. Pan was to be paid ninety satang a day. He had to buy his own food. Unlike those who ran the mining company, the rubber plantation owner did not provide his workers with cooked rice. The wage was low, but Pan needed a job.

His work was to cut grass and weeds. One day Pan cut down five young rubber plants by mistake. The young plants were only a few inches tall, and they looked like weeds to him. The plantation owner charged Pan one baht each for each of the five rubber shoots he had cut down. Pan thought, "I get paid only ninety satang a day. I was fined five baht. How am I going to pay him?" In the evening he quit his job and returned to Wat Khachon.

A few days later Pan went out to look for work again. This time he found a job as a coolie at a European-owned company in Phuket. The foreman was Chinese. As an unskilled laborer, Pan did whatever his boss told him to do. Every morning he was told to work at such and such a division, depending on whatever was needed. He was sent to haul rocks, dig up the ground, lay pipes, carry new machines to the factory, haul equipment and heavy sacks of rice, and more. Once he finished a task he could rest for awhile until another order came in. At first Pan felt utterly exhausted. Gradually he got used to coolie work, and he learned patience. After a few months his body grew strong.

According to an old Thai saying, "one who is diligent, has a strong will, does not give up easily, and is willing to face whatever comes will always progress." Pan was no exception. After working as a manual laborer in Phuket for two years he saw his life begin to improve. One day a monk named Ajahn Khong asked Pan, "Would you like to go to Ranong? Phra Khru needs to send a young teacher there."[18] "Phra Khru" was Phra Khru Phiphatsamachan, the Sangha head of Kratu district in

Phuket. Instead of calling him by his full ecclesiastical title, junior monks generally referred to him as Phra Khru, meaning Venerable Teacher.

Pan replied, "Yes, I'd like to go."

So Ajahn Khong took Pan to the monastery where Phra Khru was abbot. After the Ajahn had introduced Pan to Phra Khru, the abbot said to Pan, "I will be in Penang for seven days. Come and see me the day after I return."

It was well known among monks who served the Sangha chief that Phra Khru was very strict and hard to please. Junior monks who did not serve the chief well would be sent off with their ears ringing. Before Pan went to work for Phra Khru young monks warned him, "Watch out! Better not volunteer to serve him or you'll be sorry. You must get up very early and be very disciplined."

Pan replied, "That's easy. I will get up before he does. I will follow his instructions. If he still wants to dismiss me, so be it."

A week later Pan went to the monastery to keep his appointment. He arrived at Phra Khru's residence before dawn and sat on the porch waiting for Phra Khru to come out. When Phra Khru awoke he opened the door, and Pan prostrated himself at his feet. Even before he washed his face the abbot had assigned work to Pan. "Tomorrow we will have a blessing ceremony. Go sweep the kitchen, haul water, and set up lunch for forty." Pan set out to work. First he went to the well from which young monks usually drew water. Since the water level was very low, it took Pan quite a while to fill five huge earthenware jars. Then Pan went to sweep and mop the floor of the dining hall. Once he had cleaned the hall, Pan went to the storage room and took out forty sets of dinnerware and mats. He rinsed the dusty plates and bowls and set them out to dry in the sun. By the time Pan had finished his assignment the sun was setting.

Pan went to see Phra Khru at his kuti, "All the work is done, sir."

Phra Khru walked around to inspect the work. "Well done!" he said to Pan. "Where are you staying tonight?"

"I'll go back to Wat Khachon, sir."

"Come early tomorrow," the abbot insisted.

The next day Pan got up, washed his face, and went to Phra Khru's temple. He arrived before dawn and waited at the kuti as he had done the day before. When Phra Khru awoke he saw Pan sitting on the steps. The monk smiled kindly, "Oh, you're here early! Diligent boy! Good!"

Pan knew he had succeeded in what he intended when the abbot praised him. This was an important step in Pan's life. Any misstep and he would end up doing heavy labor again.

That day, from early morning on, Pan did all the work assigned to him. He laid out dishes and utensils in the dining hall. When the laypeople arrived at the monastery, they put their food on the plates and in the bowls. Then the lay folk offered the food to the monks. After the monks had finished their meal it was the laypeople's turn to eat. Pan brought dishes to serve the people. After they had eaten and left, Pan washed all the dishes, dried them in the sun, and put them back in the storage room. By this time it was almost evening. Pan then reported to the abbot, saying, "Everything is done, sir."

Phra Khru walked around inspecting. He spoke to Pan with kindness, saying, "Well done! Tomorrow we'll board the boat to Ranong."

26

JOURNEY TO MONKHOOD

W ANDERING ASCETICS preferred to go their way on foot, but given a choice, administrative monks chose to travel by sea. In the late 1920s when Pan and the district Sangha chief traveled to Ranong by ship, Phra Khru paid for Pan's boat fare. They left Phuket in May, at the beginning of the monsoon season. The wind was strong and the sea rough. Pan got so seasick he could not eat. He did not have the energy to come out and look at the beautiful scenery along the west coast. Pan continued to feel sick for several days, even after getting off the boat. He had come to Ranong to become a schoolteacher, but on arrival he found out that another man had applied for the job and had already been hired.

Phra Khru told Pan to stay with him at Wat Uppanan in Ranong. From then on the district Sangha chief always called Pan "Teacher." Whenever he asked Pan to do something, the monk would say, "Teacher, empty the spittoon. Teacher, mop the floor. Teacher, cut the grass." It was the Sangha chief who steered Pan away from working as a manual laborer to becoming a schoolteacher. All the monks at the wat called Pan "Teacher" even though he had no pupils to teach. In the meantime, Pan was doing the work of a janitor. He did not mind what kind of work he was doing as long as it was honest.

In 1929 Pan turned eighteen. On July 5 of that year, Phra Khru, having just finished his lunch, turned to Pan and asked, "Teacher, would you like to be ordained as a novice?"

Without hesitation Pan replied, "Yes, sir."

Immediately Phra Khru told Teacher Pan to get ready. "Go and shave your head." The monk managed to find two pieces of white cloth. One piece Pan was to wear as a lower garment; another piece was to be wrapped around his shoulders. A novice-to-be must change from his everyday clothing into white garments before the ordination ceremony. He is given a yellow robe to wear during the ceremony.

After Pan had put on the white garments a friend said to him, "Hey, your neck is bare. Here, take my amulet chain."

Pan replied, "Why do I need a chain? I am going to be ordained soon."

"I would like to see you wear this chain," Pan's friend insisted.

Pan complied with his friend's request. In all his eighteen years Pan had never paid much attention to his appearance. He never wore rings or gold chains. Sometimes, when he bought new clothes, he would put them away for special occasions, but by the time he had a chance to wear the garments, the fabric would have deteriorated. His lifestyle had always been simple.

When it was time for Pan to enter the ordination hall, he did not perform the customary circumambulation of the building three times. The novice-to-be was simply accompanied to the hall by an eighty-year-old nun and a young nun. Two monks took part in the ordination ceremony: Phra Khru Phiphat served as the preceptor; and Phra Palad In served as the ordination teacher.

Pan had often reflected on his days as a temple boy in other monasteries, but he had not thought of being ordained until now. Although there had been no time for preparation, the ceremony went smoothly. This was because Pan had already learned to recite the chants for ordination by heart while living at Wat Khachon. His preceptor was pleased.

After the ordination ceremony Novice Pan remained at Wat Uppanan and continued to serve his preceptor. Shortly after the rains retreat began, Teacher Sangat, who had obtained the teaching position that Pan had aspired to, resigned and returned to his hometown in Chumphon province. Novice Pan was appointed to replace him. The novice was to take charge of grades 1 through 3 in the one-room primary school.

Schoolteachers then, as now, were civil servants. In the 1920s it was not unusual for a person with a seventh-grade education to become an elementary school teacher in a remote town. In Novice Pan's case, he was the only teacher. He also served as school principal and head janitor. His salary was twenty-five baht per month. With the money he earned from teaching, Novice Pan indulged in buying books from Bangkok. He ordered books on a variety of topics written by well-known Thai intellectuals of the 1920s, some of whom were former monks.

The school where Pan taught looked more like a buffalo pen than a proper school. The structure had a thatched roof. A few wooden planks had been nailed along the sides to keep oxen from entering the long classroom. The students sat in three groups, representing each of the three grades. There were thirty-four students in all, mostly small children. While teaching, Pan would move from the first graders to the second and third graders. He would write simple arithmetic assignments on the blackboard for the first graders to work out. Then he would write some sentences on the board for the second graders to copy in their notebooks. Next he would walk over to the third graders to teach them science. Before returning to the second graders, Teacher Pan would leave some questions for the third graders to answer in their notebooks. Back with the second grade class, Pan would correct their writing. Then he went over the arithmetic with the first graders. Gradually, Teacher Pan was able to carry through the task he had set for himself.

As a new schoolmaster, Pan had little time to study the Nak-dham texts. In those days novices and young monks aspired to pass all three levels of the Dhamma studies exams. In a small town or village, a monk who had received a certificate of Dhamma studies had a better chance of being appointed abbot than one who had not. Furthermore, a novice who passed the first-level exam in Dhamma studies would be exempt from military conscription. All levels of Nak-dham examinations were given only once a year.

The first time Novice Pan took the exam he flunked. A year passed, and Pan gained more experience in teaching schoolchildren. Everything was now under control. Pan had more time to prepare himself for the Nak-dham examination.

The next time Pan took the Nak-dham exam he got the highest mark among all monastics who took the first-level exam in Monthon Phuket, which at that time included Ranong. The governor of Phuket made an offering of a set of robes and a clock to Novice Pan. Back then it was usually a monk, not a novice, who ranked first in the Dhamma exam. That was a proud moment in Pan's life.

In 1931 Novice Pan turned twenty. He remembered the promise he had made to his mother to return home and take higher ordination as a monk, so he took leave of his preceptor to return to Phatthalung. The trip home took two days by boat, bus, and train.

Once back in Phatthalung, Novice Pan went to stay with his uncle, Luang Lung, now at Wat Indrawat. Pan's parents and relatives came to visit him there. Luang Lung remarked to Pan's mother, "If I had been lenient with him, he might have turned into a bandit."

Pan had been away for four years. His family and friends had all missed him and were happy that he had turned out so well. When Pan left Phatthalung he was a boy, and his parents had worried about him. He returned home a grown man and a monastic. Pan did his parents proud. They thought that wearing the yellow robe suited their son well.

Novice Pan rested for five days before participating in the ordination ceremony that his parents sponsored for him. He took higher ordination as a monk on July 28, 1931, at Wat Nanglat, the monastery of his ancestors. Venerable Teacher Charunkorani was his preceptor. After his ordination the locals started calling him Phra Pan. For a time Phra Pan stayed at Wat Indrawat so that his parents could come to visit him. When Pan's cousin Paen, who had also been recently ordained, was about to set out for Nakhon Si Thammarat to study at the Nak-dham school there, Phra Pan decided to join him. By this time Pan had already resigned from his teaching position at the elementary school in Ranong.

On the first day that he arrived at Wat Boromthat, the oldest monastery in Nakhon Si Thammarat, Phra Pan made a vow to remain a monk for life. It was here that Phra Pan began training himself to preach. At that time there were several traditional pulpits or Dhamma seats located on the east side of the Boromthat stupa. Because each pulpit on which a monk sat while preaching was some distance from the next pulpit, young monks were provided with an ideal environment in which to study and practice the art of preaching. As Ajahn Panya recalled, "The pulpit for beginners was the farthest from the stupa. As the preacher gained more experience, he moved to a pulpit with a bigger audience. The pulpit right next to the stupa had the largest audience. On the first day I began preaching, my pulpit had only three people in the audience. At other pulpits there were five, ten, or twenty people in the audience. When I 'graduated' to the pulpit a short distance from the stupa, I had about fifty people listening to my sermon."

Back when there was no radio or television to provide distraction, there were always a number of people in a wat compound waiting to listen to a sermon from any monk who was willing to preach. Furthermore, monks who were good at preaching were often invited to the homes of laypeople. For example, during a rains retreat the governor's sister invited every available preacher to deliver sermons at her house. Each monk gave a sermon for three nights in a row. When Phra Pan received his invitation to preach, he prepared his talks in advance, but he delivered the sermons extemporaneously. The hostess greatly enjoyed Phra Pan's preaching style, and he was invited back often.

As Luang Lung had predicted, by the middle of the twentieth century his nephew had matured into a master preacher, unafraid of criticizing corrupt government officials or passive Sangha officials. In 1960 Ajahn Panya was invited to become abbot of a new monastery, Wat Chonprathan, in Nonthaburi province. At the new wat, Ajahn Panya established a meditation center to train urban youth in meditation practice. Luang Lung was especially happy when Ajahn Panya was given the power to ordain young men into the monkhood. Out of deep gratitude to his old teacher, Ajahn Panya invited Luang Lung, now an old man, to spend the rest of his life at the new monastery in Nonthaburi. Luang Lung died there in the 1960s, not long after Ajahn Panya had become abbot.

As a well-known preacher, Ajahn Panya credited his parents for forming his character and instilling in him a sense of social responsibility. "Although my family spent a lot of time helping neighbors, they never neglected their own children. In fact, the more love they had for their children, the more love and compassion they extended to other people."

FIG. 21. AJAHN PANYA, ABOUT 1940.

PART III

AJAHN JUMNIEN
(BOYHOOD NAME: JUMNIEN)

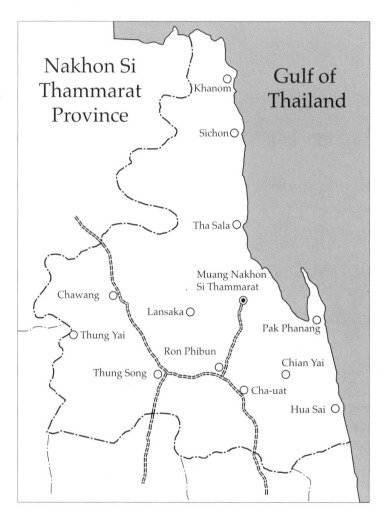

Nakhon Si Thammarat Province

Gulf of Thailand

Khanom

Sichon

Tha Sala

Muang Nakhon Si Thammarat

Chawang

Lansaka

Pak Phanang

Thung Yai

Ron Phibun

Chian Yai

Thung Song

Cha-uat

Hua Sai

FIG. 22. NAKHON SI THAMMARAT PROVINCE SHOWING DISTRICTS.

27

THE RESTORATION
OF A GREAT STUPA

AT WAT BOROMTHAT, where the two monks from Phatthalung, Phra Pan and Phra Paen, came to pursue Dhamma
studies, there was an ancient stupa called Boromthat. (In
1915 Bangkok authorities renamed it Wat Maha-
that,[19] but local people continued to call the wat by its old name.) The
stupa, containing relics of the Buddha, is the oldest in Nakhon Si Thammarat. Decades before the two Phatthalung monks arrived, the stupa
had undergone a major restoration due to the efforts of a wandering
monk named Paan.

As a native of Nakhon, Paan wished to see the stupa restored, but
he lacked the necessary resources and manpower. He had been ordained
as a monk in 1889 and later became a wandering ascetic. For four
years he wandered through the forests of the southern peninsula, receiving alms from people in many villages. Along the way Ajahn Paan
gained a large number of followers who had strong faith in him. On
one occasion he stayed near a hamlet called Ban Pa. After Ajahn Paan
told the villagers about his project to restore the Boromthat stupa, many
people volunteered to help him. They felled trees in the nearby forest
and floated the logs downstream to the town of Nakhon. Ajahn Paan
had obtained permission from the governor of Nakhon to restore the
monastery, in keeping with his means.

During the restoration, word spread around, and hundreds of people traveled from near and far to help. Not only Siamese but Chinese

and Malays too made pilgrimages to the stupa. People came from as far south as Phatthalung, Songkhla, Pattani, Nong Jik, and Saiburi and from towns north of Nakhon such as Kanchanadit, Chaiya, and Lang Suan. In Songkhla and Saiburi people raised enough money to buy two elephants to help the monks with the heavy construction work.

In just over a year as many as twenty thousand people showed up to donate their labor. Every day at least five hundred people were at work at the stupa. Some days as many as a thousand people came to work, many possessing a variety of much-needed special skills. Some men were over sixty or seventy years old, yet they were not afraid of working high up on the roof. Others helped by mixing cement, carrying bricks, or doing carpentry. Everybody was willing to contribute according to his means and abilities. Those who were well off donated money to buy materials. Those who lacked money went into nearby forests to cut trees or searched out food to feed the workers. The core work crew consisted of sixty men who delegated work to the others. Ajahn Paan gave the core workers black shirts and black pants to wear so they would stand out in the crowd. People who had no special skills offered to do heavy labor. Women took turns cooking breakfast and dinner for the workers. On holy days villagers brought sweets and fruits to feed workers as well.

Ajahn Paan, who supervised the restoration, lived in a hut that he built at the edge of the monastic compound. His assistant, a monk from Wat Pak Phanang, helped mobilize people to build the base of the stupa.

In addition to the stupa, Ajahn Paan restored twelve old buildings in the monastery. The Ajahn, together with fellow monks and novices, built a bridge and several public shelters along the road to the stupa. Every day at least fifty or sixty people volunteered their labor to help the monks and novices.

In those days the Siamese government was funding the creation of modern schools, not the restoration of royal monasteries, so it was up to individual abbots to find the financial resources for maintenance and repairs. But when King Chulalongkorn received word in Bangkok about Ajahn Paan's extraordinary work, he bestowed upon him the title

Phra Khru Thepmuni (Venerable Teacher Divine Sage). In his report to the king, the superintendent of the Nakhon Si Thammarat region stated his belief that Ajahn Paan was able to mobilize such great numbers of people because of their great faith in him.

FIG. 23. WAT BOROMTHAT, NAKHON SI THAMMARAT, 1896.

As a thudong monk Ajahn Paan was rooted in local culture. King Chulalongkorn noted in his diary that Ajahn Paan differed from the town monks belonging to the royal sect, who did not engage in manual labor. "Venerable Teacher Thepmuni (Paan) is the old kind of Dhammayut monk. The new breed of Dhammayut in Nakhon Si Thammarat do not consider him one of them. He has special gifts in his motivation to restore the stupa. It is a miracle that he could get people in every town throughout the peninsula to donate money. He received more than forty thousand baht in donations. Those who had no money worked for him without pay. All workers got free food—three meals a day. Phra Khru Paan never had to pay for food either, as it was given to him by his followers. He set up a kitchen capable of feeding over a thousand people a day—the monks as well as the laypeople who donated labor. It is amazing what Phra Khru has accomplished. No monk in Bangkok could have done what he did." Wat Boromthat in Nakhon Si Thammarat became known throughout the kingdom as a pilgrimage site.

About twelve kilometers from Wat Boromthat there was a fishing village called Ban Paknam. The village consisted of three hundred households. One of the inhabitants was a former monk named Phet, who was respected by the locals for his knowledge of herbal medicine and astrology. Phet was the son of an Indian father and a Siamese mother. His father's ancestors were Brahmin priests who had made their home in southern Siam. When he turned twenty Phet was ordained as a Buddhist monk. He lived with his preceptor for five years before becoming a wandering monk. In his wandering years Phet met many other thudong monks from whom he learned meditation methods and various kinds of knowledge including herbal medicine and astrology. Phet had the opportunity to learn even more about these subjects from his contacts with other peripatetics.

Phet had been a monk for almost twelve years when he disrobed. In time he met a young woman named Ta, whose father was Chinese and whose mother Siamese. They married and had six children. Their fifth child, whom they named Jumnien, grew up to be a meditation master and the founder of Tiger Cave Monastery in Krabi, a province south of Nakhon Si Thammarat.

28

KITES, DRUMS, AND MEDITATION

AJAHN JUMNIEN says that his father began teaching him to meditate before he was four years old. But as a child, the Ajahn says, "I was too lazy to practice meditation." He preferred to run around and fly kites rather than sit still and learn to meditate. But the boy did not have a choice. His father made him practice meditation and tried to convince him of its benefits: "When your mind is able to achieve total concentration, you will study well, remember things right, and think clearly. Whatever you do, you will get results quickly. And if you achieve higher levels of concentration, you will be able to display supernatural powers."

When Jumnien first heard that meditation could lead to the acquisition of magical powers, he got excited. "I wanted to go back in time," the Ajahn tells us, "to read people's minds, and to develop the divine eye and the divine ear. I thought it was going to be great to learn how to meditate."

Phet began by telling Jumnien to meditate on the mantra *Bud-dho*. When Jumnien asked what *bud* and *dho* meant, his father explained, "The word *bud* means to know, and the word *dho* means to be blissful. You have to have knowledge to be blissful. Do not be discouraged."

Both his father and mother forced him to practice meditation. "As I was sitting there concentrating on the mantra, 'Buddho, Buddho,' I would get antsy. I got tired and itchy and wanted to do anything other than sit there concentrating on my breath and the mantra."

On one occasion when Jumnien found it hard to concentrate on

Buddho he started thinking about how much fun it would be to go out and fly a kite. Then he heard his father, who had been watching him, saying, "Jumnien! Don't go thinking about flying a kite, or I'll slap your head! Just breathe in and concentrate on *bud*, breathe out and concentrate on *dho*. That's all you should be thinking about."

Wondering how his father could possibly have known that he was thinking about flying a kite, Jumnien decided to think about something else instead. He began thinking about climbing up to the highest branch of a tree near the pond and jumping off into the water. "At first, I will dive in headfirst," Jumnien mused, "and then I'll tuck my knees up to my stomach, make myself as round as a ball, and do a 'flying coconut.' That'll be so much fun."

Just then his father spoke up again. "Jumnien! Don't think about climbing up a tree and jumping into the water. You must concentrate on Buddho, Buddho."

"Yikes," Jumnien said to himself. "How does Father know what I am thinking, no matter where my mind goes? This is something worth learning. If I master this knowledge I can know what my friends are thinking. They won't be able to play tricks on me anymore."

These thoughts gave Jumnien an incentive to become proficient at meditation, but despite his desire, he was still too lazy to practice. His mind, the Ajahn tells us, began to wander again, and this time he started thinking about how much fun it would be to make a toy drum and bang on it. "Bang, Bang, Bang! Imagining this was a lot more fun than thinking, 'Buddho, Buddho.'"

But then, once again he heard his father's voice: "Don't you go thinking about beating a drum, or I will beat your head."

Afraid of his father's punishment, Jumnien returned to breathing in *bud* and breathing out *dho*.

Under his father's supervision Jumnien practiced meditation regularly. One day Phet told his wife that he would be gone for two days to look after some patients. When he was a young monk, Phet had learned a great deal about traditional medicine. He reminded his wife to make sure that Jumnien did his meditation practice without fail. "Be sure to watch over him. Don't let him think about other things."

"Well," Jumnien thought, "once Father leaves, I'll have it made. I am sure Mother won't be able to read my mind the way Father does."

On the first day his father left, around four o'clock in the afternoon, Jumnien's mother reminded him to meditate. "I sat down to meditate as she requested, musing, with a smile on my face, 'Mother has no idea what I am thinking when I meditate. Why bother with Buddho, Buddho?' Instead, I thought about building the biggest kite I have ever seen and flying it."

"Jumnien!" his mother shouted. "Your father told you to meditate, not to think about flying kites!"

"Hey," the boy thought, "Mother must know when I am thinking about kites! I'd better think about something else to trick her." Jumnien began thinking about making a toy cow out of a coconut leaf. "Once I finish it, I will drag the cow by its nose into the water in the canal."

"Jumnien!" his mother interrupted, "Don't think about making a toy cow to play with in the water. You'd better be thinking, 'Buddho, Buddho.' Otherwise you're going to get a slap on the head when your father comes home, because I'm not going to lie to him."

"Too bad," Jumnien thought. "It looks like Mother is just as good as Father at reading my thoughts."

"Mother probably knew best," the Ajahn later remembered thinking at the time. "Whatever I was thinking about Mother already knew it. I figured it was because Mother was already accomplished at meditation, so she probably knew what I was thinking as well as Father did."

Jumnien decided that if he couldn't think about other things, then meditation was not going to be any fun at all. "I was mad at my mother and father, so I decided to sit there and think about dying. I just sat there thinking, 'dying, dying, dying.' That was the only thing that I thought about."

After a while he heard his mother ask, "Son, what are you thinking about?"

The boy did not answer. Ajahn Jumnien recalled, "I just sat there thinking about dying. I did not think about playing, just about dying. My mother kept saying that she could not hear what I was thinking and kept asking me what was going through my mind. When my mother realized that she wasn't going to find out what I was thinking, she went around asking our neighbors and our relatives if they had secretly taught me this meditation."

When she couldn't get any answers, Jumnien's mother decided that she would have to wait for her husband to come home and have him figure out what their son was up to. Jumnien sat there in meditation until dawn.

When Phet returned early that morning to pick up more medicine for his patients. he saw his son sitting perfectly still. Phet asked his wife, "Ta, did Jumnien meditate all night long?"

"Yes," his wife replied. "He started sitting in the evening and kept at it past sunrise. I called him to come and eat, but he wouldn't get up."

Upon hearing that, Phet went over to Jumnien, sat down behind him and began gently patting Jumnien on the head. After a moment or two, he turned to his wife and asked, "Who came here and taught our child the *marana-sati*? Why has he kept doing marana-sati?"

"Marana-sati?" Ta asked incredulously.

Phet replied, "Yes! Marana-sati! Mindfulness of death."

As a former thudong monk, Phet had practiced marana-sati meditation.[20] Little Jumnien, however, had never heard of marana-sati and had no idea what it meant. The boy thought that he had finally fooled his father. "I was saying 'dying, dying, dying,' and he says I was saying 'marana-sati.' Before, my father and mother were always right at guessing what I was thinking. How come today they don't know what I am thinking?"

The more Jumnien thought about this, the more puzzling it became. "Was my father drunk? All night I simply thought, 'dying, dying.' Even though I was sore from sitting and I started to itch and got hungry, I kept thinking, 'dying, dying, dying.' There were a couple of moments when I noticed that my heart had skipped a beat or two. I thought that I might really be dying! I became frightened and thought if I did die at that moment I would go straight to hell. King Yama, the Lord of Death, would be waiting there to grab me and throw me into a pot of boiling water!"

The Ajahn recalled that when he was a child he had frequently stomped on crabs, crickets, ants, and beetles. "I had cut short the life of many living creatures. So the thought that I might die right then and there and go straight to hell really scared me. But I was also worried that if I did not die, then I would be forced by my parents to keep practicing meditation. I couldn't make up my mind. Was it better to die or not?"

Once again Jumnien went back to meditating on dying. "Even while mosquitoes bit me and I got hungry and got sore from sitting, I still kept thinking the same thing: 'dying, dying, dying.'"

There was a time toward dawn when Jumnien wanted to get up from meditating. But he also wanted to just keep sitting there. He decided to continue meditating. "If I run into King Yama at the gates of hell, then I'll stop the meditation and get up."

Around noon of that day, the Ajahn recalled. "My heart started racing and then skipping beats. I wanted to see if getting up would stop this, but then my mind became one-pointed. There was happiness, emptiness, and clarity. There was no me, there was no King Yama, no heavens, no male or female deities, nothing at all."

Jumnien was aware that his father and mother were talking, but he did not know what they were saying. "I couldn't hear anything clearly. I was only certain that my mind was clear and calm. A smile broke out across my face."

Ta called out to her husband, "What is wrong with our child? He's smiling! What do you suppose he is thinking about now?"

Phet came over to look at Jumnien and said, "He has entered his absorbed concentration. But this is not the path to nibbana."

"My father was right," the Ajahn tells us, "because after I stopped meditating, everything was just still and calm. But it wasn't the path to nibbana. How could it be? I did not see Lord Buddha or arahants or deities. There was just emptiness and a feeling of happiness."

Then his parents began pleading with Jumnien to get up. This, they knew, would break his absorbed concentration. "But I did not want to let go of the happiness," the Ajahn recalled. "I was afraid that if I got up, this happiness that I had discovered would disappear forever. I thought that it would be better to stay like this for a month or a year."

By now it was past the noontime meal. Jumnien's mother tried another tactic. In her sweetest voice she said, "Jumnien! Out of gratitude to your mother, please listen to me." When Jumnien heard the word gratitude he began to lose his resolve. "Since I love Mother very much and always have sympathy for her, what can I do?" Finally, Jumnien spoke to her. "If I open my eyes, and this happiness disappears, then what will I do?" he asked.

His mother replied, "You will be able to find that happiness again, son." Jumnien realized then that he was being stupid, and that if he wanted to he could meditate anytime. "I realized that in the future, whenever I finished my chores around the house, I could meditate to my heart's content."

So Jumnien opened his eyes. "It became apparent to me," the Ajahn later remarked, "that the happiness I felt was about halfway gone. I also started to feel a bit like my old self again. When we sat down to eat together, after taking the first bite of food, I started to feel warm and had a very heavy feeling. The happiness was all gone. My heart started to yearn for the bliss I had felt. I really missed that bliss now. It was a better feeling than anything I had ever experienced."

After that Jumnien felt the need to get away and meditate in solitude. He came up with a trick to ward off intruders: he went off to a cemetery to be alone. Unlike other people, Jumnien was not afraid of ghosts, since his father, an expert in herbal medicine, had often sent him to collect medicinal plants that grew near the forest cemetery. "I didn't want anybody to follow me, so I brought along a string and tied it to some branches. Whenever anyone came near I started yanking on the string, and the rustling of the branches scared off all visitors. But alas, Father was not afraid of ghosts. As he got closer and closer he noticed the string and followed it along until he reached the place where I was sitting. As soon as he discovered me, he started to slap me. I jumped up and ran back to the house."

Phet shouted after his son, "I don't want you to sit in the cemetery ever again!" To the former thudong monk, the boy was too young to practice mindfulness of death. Phet was afraid that once out of his parents' sight Jumnien would again take up the marana-sati meditation on his own.

"Father, please do not hit me," Jumnien pleaded, "I am only trying to get back to that feeling of bliss."

Phet's fear was not unfounded. By reciting "dying, dying, dying," Jumnien's mind had reached a very peaceful meditative state; he experienced a pure mind that was incredibly blissful. But bliss can be addictive, and the boy was determined to recover that peaceful state of mind. He had not understood what had happened to him. "It's funny," he thought, "I was just thinking about dying in a sarcastic sort of way, yet I was able to experience emptiness and peace. I knew that the happiness I had was something I would long for whenever I wasn't able to meditate."

Ever since that time, the Ajahn said, "I have tried to discipline myself to meditate. Usually I went back to the cemetery to meditate so that I wouldn't be bothered by anyone." Others ventured into the cemetery only when it was absolutely necessary. "When I was alone," the Ajahn said, "I had a profound experience that was rejuvenating, and happiness that could be compared only to the pure happiness that I felt from the love I had for my mother. I did not love my father, brothers, or sisters as much as I loved my mother."

As the days passed, it became part of Jumnien's routine to meditate as soon as he woke up. "Then in the afternoon, whenever I was free from doing chores, I would again practice meditating. I always looked for a way to go off and practice without being disturbed. I felt that if I could find that place of bliss again, I might never get up from my meditation. This was the result of my parents having forced me to practice meditation."

29

IN THE WATER WITH CROCODILES

J UMNIEN'S FATHER, following the local custom, taught his son to swim. A deep canal flowed near Paknam village, where Jumnien was born. Villagers felt that it was important for their children to learn how to swim at an early age. If a youngster should accidentally fall into the canal, the child would be able to swim to safety. "One day," Ajahn Jumnien tells us, "my father picked me up and threw me into the canal along with a coconut. Instinctively I grabbed hold of whatever was nearest to me and discovered that I could float as long as I held on to that coconut. After many training sessions like this I learned to swim even though I was only a little over one year old."

In the 1940s there were crocodiles in all of Siam's rivers. Local people who lived on riverbanks in Nakhon had long ago learned to coexist with crocodiles. And children learned to cope with real fear at an early age. Ajahn Jumnien recalled how Phet, his father, trained him to overcome his fear of crocodiles. "When I was just five years old my father taught me a *gatha* for warding off attacks by crocodiles: 'Metta Buddho, Metta Buddho, Metta Buddho.' He also told me the gatha would work against other deadly animals, and evil people as well, causing them to have feelings of kindness toward us instead of animosity."[21]

Not long after Phet taught Jumnien to recite the gatha, a villager went down to the canal to get water for his home. A crocodile attacked the villager. While the man was struggling, other crocodiles started to swarm around him. When Phet heard the commotion he went racing down to the water to try to help out. Jumnien and his older brother ran down too. As soon as Phet reached the canal he threw his ax into the water, then turned to his older son and said, "Go into the water and get my ax for me."

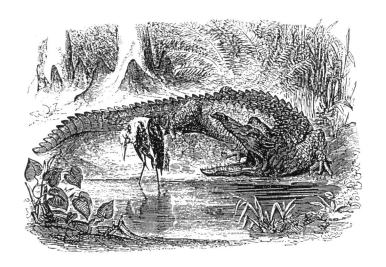

FIG. 24. CROCODILE AND CRANE.

As Ajahn Jumnien recalled, "My brother stood there with a look of utter horror on his face. He then told Father that he was too scared of being eaten by a crocodile. So Father turned to me and told me to get his ax out of the water. I was no braver than my brother, so I suggested that Father should get his ax himself." But Phet insisted that Jumnien go and get it. "Don't you remember the gatha I taught you for warding off dangerous animals?" Phet asked his son. "That gatha will work to ward off crocodiles too. Go down into the water and get my ax. I guarantee that the crocodiles won't attack you."

The way it looked to Jumnien was that if he did not do as his father said, he was certainly going to be punished. "So I closed my eyes," he said, "and raised my hands together in front of my chest and began the recitation. I roused as much courage as I could and then waded into the water. But the strangest thing happened! The crocodiles that were in the canal just stayed where they were, watching me."

Phet knew that crocodiles' behavior was predictable; splashing water around would trigger crocodiles to action. Besides the gatha, he taught Jumnien other techniques for warding off crocodiles, whether in the water or on dry land. "First, you try to be as brave as possible and avoid giving in to fear of death. And while you are in the water, you should try to stand as upright as possible, on both feet. If you are on land, you should also stand straight up, since crocodiles don't like to twist onto their side when attacking their prey. If you are swimming in the water rather than standing, it is easier for them to bite you because they don't have to turn onto their side."

Young Jumnien often wondered why it was that, when his father asked one of his older brothers to do something and the boy didn't do it, his father would just let it go. But if his father asked Jumnien to do something and he didn't, he was certain to get smacked. On one occasion Jumnien overheard his mother tell his father that he was pushing their son too hard. Jumnien first went out of the house to allow his parents to carry on their discussion freely, but then he sneaked back inside so he could hear what they were saying.

"You are making our son take too many dangerous risks," Ta complained to her husband. "If he makes a mistake when wrestling with a crocodile and gets eaten, what then?"

But his father, a former thudong monk, knew from his deep meditations (*jhana*) that his son's life was destined to be different from that of other children. "I have looked at his horoscope," Phet told his wife, "and I have seen his future in my meditative absorption. I am certain that whether he meets up with a wild animal or a dangerous criminal, nothing will ever harm him. I have seen that he will be a leader in the Buddhist community. He has accumulated spiritual perfections from his past life, and he will not be killed."

"But there will be danger," Phet added, "when our son is growing into manhood. If he associates with bad men he could grow up to be a bandit. If he should become a bandit leader, he will end up killing many people, and it would be extremely difficult for the authorities to suppress him. By then he will have attained a high level of concentration and have mastered many spells and incantations. Therefore, I have been forced to train our son ever since he was only three or four years old. I have to make him fear me more than he fears ghosts—more than he fears wild animals, more than he fears danger—if we want him to be good. And if we are able to lead him down a good path in this lifetime, he will attain a high level of Dhamma."

30

How to Become
Invulnerable

AJAHN JUMNIEN learned Thai massage when he was still a child. At home in Nakhon his father often called upon young Jumnien to massage his aching body in the evening. "It was often during these massage sessions that Father would tell me about various subjects, including traditional medicine and herbal remedies, Thai astrology, and sacred gathas. Once he taught me something, he never repeated the lesson. Instead he gave me a test later on, and if I flunked I would be slapped." Jumnien thus learned to be mindful as he listened carefully to every word that his father uttered.

Knowing there would be a penalty each time he failed to pass the test, Jumnien put extra effort into his study and came up with a memorization device. "Whenever I wanted to memorize something," the Ajahn recalled, "I would turn it into the lyrics for a song or into a verse. This made memorizing more fun and made what I had learned easier to recite."

By the time Jumnien was six years old he had memorized several recitations for blessings and protection including the Gatha of Thirty Perfections and the Gatha of Great Victory. "I recited them every day without fail. Sometimes I would recite them silently and sometimes aloud." Later on when Jumnien became a fisherman he recited protective gathas when heading out to sea.

Father Phet had mastered esoteric knowledge and passed it on to

Jumnien orally. "In the past," he told his son, "the masters did not always write down sacred texts. Masters who instructed their pupils in sacred gathas taught them verbally, forbidding the students to write the gathas down." As Ajahn Jumnien recalled, "My father used to say that studying different fields of knowledge would be of great benefit to me. He compared the benefits of study to the life of a master guru whose knowledge has been passed down through the ages." And he told Jumnien not to look down upon any kind of knowledge. "You should never think of any field of study as beneath you," he said, "as that would bring bad karma." Phet also told Jumnien that the Lord Buddha had taught verbally and that his followers throughout the ages had memorized the teachings. This way of teaching, his father said, is known as *mukpatha*, which means "from mouth to mouth."

Jumnien's father had the reputation of being invulnerable. On one occasion, when his father was relaxed during a massage and had let down his guard, the Ajahn recalled, "I reached for a brand new razor blade nearby. I wanted to see if there was any truth to the rumor being spread about my father: that he had impenetrable skin. So I tried to slice into it." Much to the boy's amazement the new blade was unable to pierce his father's skin; "it just slid off as if I were trying to cut through a plate or glass." Jumnien did not give up. Whenever an opportunity arose, he tried again. "There were other times when my father would just be sitting there, and I would sneak up behind his back trying to stab him, but the knife was unable to pierce through his flesh. Finally, I asked my father about this, and he said it was because he had regularly taken a medicine made from the roots of a *makham pom* tree."[22]

From his father Jumnien learned another benefit of the makham pom tree. To prepare the medicine that makes one invulnerable, his father said, "Locate a makham pom tree and then dig down to its roots. Place a small earthenware jar filled with alcohol at the bottom of the hole. Soak some of the roots in the alcohol. This will cause the roots to distribute the alcohol into the tree and in turn cause the toxins in the tree to go into the alcohol. You have to wait until all of the poisons have been drained out of the makham pom tree."

Jumnien's father went on to say, "Because of this transfer, the alcohol in the container will turn a deep green and the tree will die. It used to be believed that if you drank the entire jar of this alcohol, you would die because of the poisons in it. If you wish to develop thick skin you were advised to drink only some of the alcohol. Once the alcohol enters your body, you will become unconscious, as if dead. Then you must have a friend take your body outside and leave it in the open air so that it can absorb dewdrops overnight. In the morning you will come back to life. After you recover you must drink more of the alcohol and die again, at which point your friends must pummel the corpse that is your body along its entire length until you recover. Then you must drink the third and last portion of the alcohol and die yet again. This time the friends must build a large fire around your body. The person seeking invulnerability will show that they have recovered this final time by getting up on their own and stepping out of the fire pit."

Ajahn Jumnien explained, "In those days, people truly believed the person who drank the alcohol had actually died, but in reality he had just become unconscious. They also believed that anybody who had succeeded in drinking this medicine and recovering from this ordeal would develop magical powers. His skin would be impervious to weapons."

Phet also told Jumnien that when he was young, he and his boyhood friends were successful in making this medicine according to the prescription, but they did not have the courage to drink the full dose of alcohol. They were afraid that once they had "died" they would not recover. Instead, Phet and his friends tasted only a spoonful of the medicine. Ajahn Jumnien recounted, "Even though they only had a sip, the medicine was so strong that they all became intoxicated to the point of not knowing what they were doing. When they saw a pointed object, they grabbed it and stabbed themselves with it. If they saw something with a sharp edge, they tried to slice open their skin with it." The result, the Ajahn said, "was that their skin had truly become thick and hard to cut, and as for my father, his skin remained that way until he died."[23]

When Jumnien's father was young the monasteries were the repositories of knowledge. Monastic libraries contained palm-leaf texts on a great range of subjects, among them warfare, elephant training, herbal medicine, and astrology. Phatthalung was known for monasteries that specialized in training young men in the practice of *kamlang seua* (tiger strength). It was believed that whoever mastered this practice would gain physical strength far superior to that of ordinary people. In the days when fighting involved hand-to-hand combat, this kind of knowledge was most valued among warriors.

For several hundred years tiger strength was a practice that healthy young men in the southern kingdoms aspired to master. The elders tell us that men who wished to acquire this knowledge had to be skilled in concentration meditation. The realization of inner power through meditation would help them gain exceptional physical strength. Masters of the art would be able to lift objects that were far heavier than normal people could lift. Some of the monks who mastered tiger strength were Ajahn Maha Chuai of Wat Palelai and Ajahn Thong of Wat Khao O. Ajahn Chuai imparted this knowledge to his disciples so they could fight in the war against the Burmese. The elders recall that Ajahn Thong could haul boulders over a hill and line them up around the ordination hall.

31

THE KARMA
OF HARMING MOTHER

AT THE GOVERNMENT schools students studied modern geography and mathematics. At home children learned Thai cosmology from elderly relatives who told them stories about the Three Worlds—the human realm, hell, and heaven. The walls inside the ordination halls of local monasteries were alive with paintings illustrating heaven and hell. Scenes from the heavenly realms depicted the good people and their environment after the arrival on earth of the Buddha of Loving Kindness. Children of Jumnien's generation also learned about the Three Worlds from local preachers who recited, sang, and dramatized the story in verse of Phra Malai, an arahant known for his great compassion. Phra Malai's story imparted moral virtues and provided lessons in karma for children.

The story also taught children to understand the meaning of gratitude (*bunkhun*). According to Somdet Pun, abbot of Bodhi Monastery in Bangkok, the teachings of bunkhun represented "the wisdom that the elders planted in the mind of every child." Furthermore, Phra Malai's story taught children that the actions of body, speech, and mind make a difference in the end. According to Phra Malai, anyone who hits or harms a parent will be reborn as a hungry ghost. His or her hands will be as big as palm leaves. A person who talks back to his parents or insults those who raised him will be reborn as a hungry ghost with a mouth as tiny as the eye of a needle.

Since Jumnien's father was a stern disciplinarian, the boy felt much closer to his mother. When Jumnien was four years old he began to help his mother with household chores. As a child, Jumnien preferred being around his beautiful, gentle mother. "When my mother started cooking, I would help her clean and cook fish," the Ajahn recalled. "When she washed clothes, I helped her with the washing. I helped my mother because I loved being with her. Whatever she asked me to do, I would do it without fail. Even if she did not ask me, I would do chores for her anyway, because I wanted to lighten her load. My father always forced me to work, but my mother never did."

He looked forward to the time when his mother returned from the market, since she always brought home treats in her basket. "One day when I was about five years old," the Ajahn recalled, "I was busy playing when I saw my mother walking home. I was so happy anticipating the treat I knew she'd be bringing me that I ran up and tried to grab hold of her from behind and give her a big hug to show her how much I loved her. Unfortunately, she didn't see me, and I ended up butting her in the back with my head." Startled, Ta, unaware that it was her son who had thrown his arms around her, reached instinctively for the knife she kept in her basket and slashed blindly behind her. (A knife was an indispensable tool that every man and woman carried.) Luckily, Jumnien was able to duck out of the way. Utterly surprised, the little boy wondered, "Why is Mother trying to kill me?"

Ajahn Jumnien went on to say, "My mother was in shock from the pain my head caused her. She immediately began to feel tightness in her chest, and it became difficult for her to breathe. It turns out that when I ran into her, my head had struck a central nerve point in her back." (According to traditional Thai medicine, it is believed that if you are struck hard enough at that point, you could die on the spot.)

Jumnien's mother was angry with him once she realized that it was her own son who had hurt her. "Her face grew pale, and she was still having difficulty breathing. Mother's symptoms continued to worsen. She staggered over to the house to sit down, yet she was still unable to breathe normally, could only take rapid, shallow breaths." In those days villagers did not shut their doors during the daytime. "Our neighbors, once they heard about the state my mother was in, came running over to see what had happened, and quite a crowd developed. One of my older brothers started to beat me as punishment for running into her."

After a while Jumnien's mother began to breathe more easily. She then said to Jumnien, "Son, I almost chopped off your head. You struck me so hard and caused so much pain that I almost couldn't breathe." But the story ended happily, for, in the Ajahn's words, "with love in her heart, she picked me up and carried me off."

Some time after this incident Jumnien suddenly woke up in the middle of the night. When he realized he was having trouble breathing, he cried out, "Mother, I can't breathe!" His mother heard him and ran quickly to her son. She took a good look at him and said, "This is your karma for running into me and almost killing me. But I did not expect you to suffer like this." Then she blew on his head, "May your breathing become normal again." But as the Ajahn recalled, "I was not able to breathe normally right away. For a while I still was only able to take short breaths, and I felt like I was just about ready to die. It was really torture for me."

When Jumnien was about six years old, he went to his mother to seek forgiveness. "I was afraid that if there was something I had done in the past to hurt my mother or cause her to suffer, my life would be cursed, especially if she spoke unfavorably of me." The Ajahn explained that he had always been a deep believer in the power of his parents' words. Hence, he needed to ask for her forgiveness and beg her to give him a blessing.

With tenderness, his mother gently rubbed his head and gave Jumnien her blessing. "Whatever you do, may you experience success. When you become a monk, may you achieve the highest level of Dhamma and attain enlightenment."

For Ajahn Jumnien the word of a parent was sacrosanct, whether it was a blessing or a curse. "Parents," he says, "are like arahants. Killing one's parents is the same as killing an arahant. Receiving a blessing from a parent is like receiving a blessing from an arahant." The aging abbot said that he became "even more convinced of this belief later in life, and continuing until today, because the blessing my mother gave me that day turned into reality for me. As for an older brother of mine, my mother may have cursed him, because he was never successful. Although he became a monk and then an abbot at five different monasteries, not one of his endeavors was ever successful."

No matter where he was living, Ajahn Jumnien always experienced success. "I always had students and followers. Even when I moved into a cave that was a tiger den and was far away from everyone, over a hundred monks, nuns, and novices came to live in the area. A monastery was erected at this site. Now it has become something of a landmark for Krabi province."

As a preacher, Ajahn Jumnien always reminds laypeople, especially those who are parents, not to treat children too harshly or make dire threats or predictions, "like telling them they'll end up in jail or in hell." He explains that "if children live up to the harsh words of their parents, this will increase their karmic burden. And if the children follow a path of evil, then the parents will be tormented. Nobody will benefit. Instead, parents need to bless their children and encourage them to be good people and prosper. Once the children are well off, their parents may also benefit from their children's wealth or goodness. At the very least, the children probably won't grow up to become thieves or try to squeeze money out of their own parents."

32

COPING WITH FAMILY DISASTER

Jumnien lost his mother, Ta, when he was six and a half. Ta died only seven days after giving birth to her youngest son. In the days leading up to her death Phet had not been around. By the time he returned home, his wife was already in critical condition, and Phet was powerless to help her. When she died Jumnien was devastated.

During this time, Ajahn Jumnien recalled, "When I was distraught over my mother's recent death, my heart still would think about the feeling of emptiness and clarity that I had experienced in my first attempts at meditation. Since I had loved my mother so much, I became disillusioned with love. But I still had hope that in my lifetime I could at least regain that level of emptiness and clarity. I thought that I should become a monk for the rest of my life. I thought that was the only option I had."

Jumnien was the fifth child in his family. Though he was not yet seven years old when his mother died, he became an adult in many ways. "My father gave me many duties, and I had to be responsible for performing them. My work started in the early hours at dawn when I was held responsible for helping find food for my father, brothers, and sisters, and this work continued up until evening when I had to massage my father's achy body."

Phet was unable to cope with his wife's untimely death. As a traditional doctor, Phet might have saved her had he not been away helping sick people in another village. Ajahn Jumnien recalled, "My mother's death filled my father with such sadness that he found it hard to stay home, since home only reminded him of my mother. He went away frequently, trying to overcome his sadness. Sometimes he would look for odd jobs. Other times he would just go out drinking and playing cards. From that time on, I had to take over my mother's work: cooking, cleaning, all the household chores. It was work that was beyond my years."

While their father was absent, some of Jumnien's brothers and sisters went off to live with relatives. Jumnien, left on his own to care for his youngest brother, was having a difficult time. Whenever it came time to give the baby a bath, Jumnien tried to put him into a tub of water. Once the baby started squirming, Jumnien would immediately lift him out of the tub and say, "All right, bath time is over!" and try to feed him instead. When he tried to feed him some rice, his brother always cried. Jumnien kept asking the baby, "Why aren't you eating? Aren't you hungry?"

Jumnien was still too young to realize the baby was sick. He was unable to eat solid food because he had the disease call *sang*. According to traditional Thai medicine, *sang* caused sores in the mouth and on the tongue that made it difficult to eat or swallow. In the end his little brother died from the disease, simply because Jumnien had no idea how to care for him and also because his father was seldom home.

"When my father did come back home, he was so despondent over my mother's death that he began to ramble incoherently. You could say that he went crazy. At this time my father wasn't contributing to our welfare at all. He had really hit rock bottom and lost all his spirit. After my mother's death he felt burdened by the responsibility of looking after his children. Besides, he was unhappy with being a fisherman, knowing that killing animals violates the first precept."

Reflecting from the vantage point of old age, the Ajahn believes that his father was becoming "a man with two personalities." "One personality always longed for the life of a wandering ascetic who practiced Dhamma and was skilled in esoteric knowledge. But another personality was that of 'Father Phet,' the layman who had several children, whose wife had just died—a man who suffered mentally and physically.

"When my father was like this, his heart and mind were at odds within him. He sought release by going out drinking and gambling, and hanging out with friends. His longing for his old life as a monk was in direct conflict with his desire to go out drinking and having a good time. This caused him further sadness. The various shamanic practices that my father had studied came back to harm him, because he had broken so many of the vows he had taken in order to learn the sacred knowledge. There were times when he would act as if he didn't know what he was doing; at other times he acted like a crazy man. This behavior invited the sympathy of our relatives and neighbors."

Those who knew Phet as a healer were puzzled. Some people believed that he had been cursed, as a challenge, by a rival shaman. Others speculated that it was his karma catching up with him. Every person gave a different reason to explain why this odd behavior was going on.

As a child Jumnien had often wondered why his father seemed interested in training only him to be a traditional healer. Although Jumnien had four older siblings, his father showed no interest in teaching them. One day when Phet was home and seemed calm, Jumnien confronted him. "Why am I the only one who has to work so hard? How come at the end of the day I am the one who has to give you a massage? And on top of this, you expect me to find time for my meditation practice. It's late at night before I can go to bed, and early in the morning when I have to get up. Meanwhile, my brothers and sisters are all taking it easy. I don't see them doing anything."

Phet replied, "It is because I know that you are tougher than your brothers and sisters. On top of that you have a heart full of courage and a curious mind. You love to learn. Your hunger for knowledge makes you unlike other children. For these reasons, whenever I order you to do something, you should do it. Do not try to understand why. Do not feel resentment, because if you do as I say, when you are older you will definitely benefit."

Whenever he was home Phet continued to pass on his knowledge orally to Jumnien. Phet had not taught Jumnien how to read, because he considered it extremely important that his son learn by heart. "By the time I was eight years old," the Ajahn tells us, "I was able to take on many of his responsibilities as a traditional healer, and I gained quite a reputation in the surrounding villages. When I was only nine years old, I had an opportunity to perform a divination. The sacred gathas that I had learned from my father enabled me to earn enough money to help support the family."

33

FINDING A NEW WIFE
FOR FATHER

ONE DAY Phet came home and asked his son, "Jumnien, do you have any money? And have you started the rice yet?"

"I only have ten baht," Jumnien answered, "and I was just going out to buy some food."

"Give me five baht first," Phet said to the boy.

After he gave the money to his father, Jumnien asked him for a favor. "Please find a stepmother for me," the boy pleaded, "someone who can teach me. Make sure she knows how to read so that when I come home from work, she can teach me."

"Where am I going to find such a woman?" his father asked.

The boy then told his father about his plan. "I will borrow money from our relatives so that I can build a passenger boat. It will have a cabin and oars. When I finish it I will give it to you, Father. You can then ferry people back and forth across the river for a fee. Then if you meet a widow or an older single lady, you can ask about her."

"That is a good idea," Phet replied. "But how are we going to get this boat?"

"I will hire some people to build it. It will take about ten days to finish. Once our boat is finished you can take it out right away."

Eventually, Phet got his boat, and within a few days he met a woman named Heet, whose husband had died and left her with two daughters. After they became acquainted, Phet asked her, "Will you please become a mother for my children?" Heet replied that she would. So, right there in the boat, Phet and Heet agreed to marry.

When Heet first came to live with Phet and his children, she helped out with the cooking and other household chores. Jumnien still had to go to work away from home every day to earn money to help support his family.

When Heet met Phet, she had been working as a midwife. Whenever one of the women in the village was about to have a baby, she would come over to hire Heet. Since the midwife customarily stayed with the mother-to-be, Heet was often away from home for several days at a time.

Young Jumnien had always been curious about where babies came from. One day he heard that a woman in his village was about to give birth and that his stepmother was going there to lend her midwifery skills. Knowing that she would never allow him to watch her deliver a baby, Jumnien sneaked into the pregnant woman's house before his stepmother got there and hid himself in the wardrobe in the bedroom. Through a hole in the wardrobe Jumnien saw several women come into the room to help with the delivery. Then his stepmother arrived, and soon afterward the baby was born. Because Heet was a big woman, her back often blocked the view from the wardrobe. Nevertheless, Jumnien saw his stepmother pull the baby out with what he thought were intestines around its neck. He thought the mother must be dead. The baby was crying loudly. Seeing those intestines frightened the boy so badly that his trembling made the wardrobe shake. The sight of the wardrobe shaking made the women who were assisting the midwife think there was a ghost inside. As they fled the bedroom, Jumnien opened the door of the wardrobe, jumped out, and ran home as fast as he could. The midwife stayed with the mother and the newborn baby.

When his stepmother finally came home, she scolded Jumnien for scaring everybody.

"How is the baby? Did his mother die?" Jumnien asked his stepmother.

"The baby and the mother are all right."

"How can the mother still be alive when all her intestines came out?"

"What you saw was not intestines, it was the umbilical cord attached to the baby when he was born. We had to cut the cord, put it in a clay pot, and bury the pot." The midwife then explained the local custom.[24] Jumnien asked her where the cord was buried. When nobody was looking, he went to the spot under the tree where the pot had been buried. The boy dug it up to see what the umbilical cord looked like. Having satisfied his curiosity, he reburied the cord in the same spot.

LEARNING THE THREE R'S

WHILE HIS stepmother was away delivering babies Jumnien had to take responsibility for the cooking and other household chores. Whenever his stepmother was home, Jumnien asked her to teach him how to read and how to add and subtract. He wanted to be able to buy things at the market without making mistakes. Jumnien was determined to learn everything he could within a few weeks so he could use his knowledge right away. As the Ajahn recalled, "I did not want to have to work at it like the kids in state schools, who had to study for years."

When his stepmother was away, Jumnien asked students in the fourth grade to check his writing to see if he had misspelled any words. "But if instead they tried to teach me how to spell, I could never remember what they said. I had to do all the reading and writing myself first and then check with them whether I was wrong or not." Jumnien was his own disciplinarian. "My own personal method for remembering things was that I would pinch one of my fingers until it hurt if I made a mistake. That way I wouldn't forget."

Although Jumnien did manage to find opportunities to study with his stepmother, he was usually so tired from the physical work he had to do that his eyes would grow heavy. He had a special method for staying awake. "I kept a hot chili in my mouth, and whenever I found myself starting to feel drowsy, I would bite into it. As the pain kicked in and my eyes started to water, I became more alert and could concentrate on my studies again. Unfortunately, doing this too often caused my mouth to swell up. But I did learn quickly, especially arithmetic."

Jumnien found it easier to learn math than to write Thai words. "When I came across some loan words from Pali or Sanskrit, I would always misspell them. Because there are so many foreign words in Thai, I was always confused." Not only Jumnien but many children who were attending school regularly were also confused by the many Pali and Sanskrit words in the Thai language.[25]

One day Jumnien met a kind old man whom he later came to call Uncle Tat. In his younger days during the reign of King Vajiravudh, Uncle Tat had served in the cavalry. Jumnien noticed that Uncle Tat loved reading the Ramakian, the Thai version of the Ramayana, one of the classics of Indian literature. "Uncle Tat," the boy asked the old man, "I don't know how to read a lot of the words in the Ramakian. Please teach me how to read and understand the story." Uncle Tat let Jumnien borrow his book and assigned some sections from the Ramakian for the boy to read, pointing out, "There are a lot of words with deep meaning. These verses are hard to pronounce and difficult to understand. They are very poetic. If you do not understand them, you can always ask me."

As Ajahn Jumnien later recalled, "I found this method of study to be quite enjoyable, since I would do all the reading and Uncle Tat would just listen and wait, offering a correction whenever I misread a word. Later on Uncle Tat had me read some nineteenth-century works of Siamese literature, such as Prince Aphaimani and other novels written by the famous poet Sunthon Phu. These stories incorporated a lot of royal language. Sanskrit words were used exclusively when the authors were referring to members of the royal family or the nobility, or when they had these people talking to one another. Reading these stories really expanded my knowledge."

In his poems Sunthon Phu (1786–1855) often stressed the kinds of knowledge necessary to cope with life: knowledge of the essence of nature, particularly in the local environment; knowledge of the customs and traditions of the kingdom; and awareness of one's place in society. In his *nirat* (traveling) poems Phu, a former monk, often described

the environment, local people, their customs, and the difficulties people encountered while traveling to Buddhist pilgrimage sites such as
the Golden Mountain at Wat Saket in Bangkok and the great stupa in
Nakhon Prathom in the Central Plains. For young Jumnien these were
distant places that he hoped to visit some day.

Jumnien became a fast reader so that he could read a lot. "I began
to get addicted," the Ajahn admitted, "to all the nineteenth-century
works about kings and dynasties that belonged to Uncle Tat. I borrowed these books from him all the time. I read them whenever I was
waiting for the food to cook or was working on something else at
home."

The old man's various collections provided Jumnien with much
pleasure. "Uncle Tat had a lot of really good books that helped me learn
about a broad range of subjects. But he also had a lot of books that
left me puzzled, books that I really didn't understand at all. These were
highly regarded literary works, and even though I didn't understand
everything, I still found the poetic language interesting."

The Elementary Education Act of 1921 stipulated that every child
between the ages of seven and fourteen was required to attend a state
school. When he turned seven Jumnien enrolled in the local primary
school. On the day he arrived Jumnien told the teacher, "I've already
studied everything. What else do you want me to learn?"

The teacher gave Jumnien a book to read aloud and some arithmetic
problems to work out. Surprised to see that the boy already knew how
to read, add, subtract, and multiply, the teacher asked him, "When did
you study all this?"

Jumnien said that he had studied at home from the age of six. "I
had to learn it out of necessity," he said. "I had to go shopping at the
market every day. I didn't know how to add up money, and I didn't
know how much change I was supposed to get back. After I studied
with my stepmother it was easy for me to buy things at the market without making a mistake."

Jumnien also told the teacher that he had taught himself to read at
home and had been helped by Uncle Tat to read stories about kings
and their dynasties. The teacher, impressed by Jumnien's maturity and

intelligence, told him that he could go home, since his reading ability and comprehension were equivalent to those of a fourth-grade student. So Jumnien left school after the first grade and never went back.

35

A Gatha to Tame Cobras

IN THE LATE 1920S Frank Exell arrived in Thung Song, a
railway junction over four hundred miles south of Bangkok in Nakhon Si Thammarat. Before he left Bangkok,
Exell was told by his Thung Song predecessor that he was
about to begin living "in one of the most cobra-infested areas in the
world."

While living in the southern hinterland, Exell was puzzled by the
locals' attitudes toward illness and their lack of faith in the American
hospital. His admiration for the people came out, however, when Exell
spoke of snakes. "The attitude of the Siamese paddy farmers to snakes
was reassuring. They went about barefooted and took not the slightest notice of what might be underfoot. It could have been something
to do with Buddhist fatalism, but I don't think so. I think it was simply a case of familiarity breeding contempt. The only time I knew them
[to] get a bite was when they were harvesting the rice, but then it was
always a harmless water snake. In all the fourteen years I was in Siam,
I came across only two or three cases of venomous snake bite and two
of these were literally 'asked for.' Only one proved fatal and that was
an aged Siamese peasant who absolutely refused to have anything done
about it."

Living in snake territory compelled the locals to observe the reptiles'
habits and learn to coexist with them. Although farmers risked encoun-
tering snakes every day, they would never think of getting rid of the
snakes in the paddy fields. They knew that snakes were an important

part of their natural world. Big snakes could help save the farmers' crops. A single python, for example, can eat more than a hundred rats a year.

In Siam children learned from Buddhist monks or from their elders how to protect themselves from poisonous insects and reptiles. Young Jumnien learned from Grandfather On what to do when he encountered snakes. Grandfather On, who lived with Jumnien's family, was the father of the boy's stepmother. As Ajahn Jumnien later recalled, "Grandfather On was a man filled with kindness. In his younger days he had been a hunter, but in old age he became blind. Yet he was still so kind that it seemed remarkable to me."

One memorable event caused Jumnien to have deep faith in Grandfather On's abilities. As the abbot recalled, one day after a centipede had bitten someone it scurried into On's clothes. But the centipede did not bite him. Grandfather On grabbed the centipede and said to it, as he flung it far away from him, "Dear child, please be good and do not cause any harm." Considering that On was blind, Jumnien was really surprised that he could pluck the centipede from his body and give it a blessing.

Grandfather On's kindness also extended to cobras. Behind their house there was a cobra that had laid its eggs in the yard. This snake was very vicious, and whenever any of the children would come by to club it, Grandfather On would tell them not to hit the snake. When Jumnien asked Grandfather On what they should do about the cobra living behind the house, he replied, "I will go and call it out."

So the boy took Grandfather On by the hand and led the old man over to the cobra. "Once we got near the snake, as soon as Grandfather recited a gatha it retracted its hood and stopped acting threateningly, even after Grandfather had left the area. Eventually, the cobra slithered off, and we never saw it again." The astonished boy was curious as to how the old man had done this, so he asked him for his secret. "Grandpa, please teach me this holy gatha of loving kindness," Jumnien pleaded.

Grandfather On then told Jumnien that in the old days hunters had a code of conduct. "Back when I was a hunter, if I needed to kill a deer, a chicken, or a pig, I would not kill any other animal that day. I would kill only the animal that I needed to kill that day."

"In that case," Jumnien quipped, "you only have to kill one type of animal at a time until you kill them all."

"That's not it," Grandfather On explained. "You need to be truthful. No matter what you do, you must always be truthful."

When Jumnien again asked Grandfather On to teach him the gatha, the old man instructed the boy to have strong faith in the knowledge that he was about to receive. "I can teach you the gatha," he said, "but you will have to believe in its power. If you don't believe in the gatha, it will do you no good."

The boy gave his pledge, and Grandfather On began the instruction. "I will tell you how it goes. The first part is a girl's gatha because when a girl is born, she cries out *au-ae*. The second part is a boy's gatha because when a boy is born, he cries out *au-aa*. The third part is *Metta Buddho*." Grandfather On explained that *metta* meant "love for the whole world" and that *buddho* meant "one who is awakened." He told Jumnien, "This little gatha is for children as well as for Lord Buddha, because the Buddha was once a child too." Jumnien liked to practice saying, "Au-ae, au-aa, Metta Buddho," and he recited this gatha often.

The first time he tried it out was with Grandmother Chan, an elderly woman who made *khanom khrok* (a snack made of flour, sugar, and coconut cream) to sell at the market. Whenever Jumnien dashed by her stall, she was waiting there ready to swipe at him. She was afraid that the boy was going to get everything dirty. So on the day Jumnien tried out the gatha with Grandmother Chan, he started reciting, as he approached the market, "Au-ae, Au-aa, Metta Buddho." Mindfully the boy recited this gatha with each step he took.

"Grandma Chan," Jumnien pleaded, "please excuse me, I need to pass by."

She responded, "Today is a good day. I had already prepared a stick to hit you with, but since you are so well mannered and polite today, I feel sorry for you."

"Hey!" Jumnien thought to himself, "This gatha actually works.

Not only did I get past without getting a single swat, Grandma Chan also gave me some khanom khrok."

Recalling the event, the Ajahn remarked, "Since she had never given me any khanom before, I was convinced that the gatha was effective." Jumnien then rushed home to tell Grandfather On the good news.

"Grandpa, today someone who normally hates me ended up loving me," the boy said proudly.

Grandfather On told Jumnien that he should use this gatha to bless some food, then go out and give this food to the birds and other animals living near the house. "After I did this," the Ajahn recounted, "those animals that ate the food became much more friendly to me."

Ever since Jumnien learned the sacred gatha from Grandfather On, he continued to recite it for protection. "This gatha defended us against animals large and small, whether they were poisonous centipedes or venomous snakes. No animals dared to bite Grandfather On."

After he was ordained as a monk Ajahn Jumnien no longer needed the gatha.

36

THE PIG AND
THE STINGRAY TAIL

IN THE EARLY 1930S the bank manager Frank Exell was staying with an American missionary in Trang, a town on the west coast of southern Siam. One morning the Englishman decided to take a swim in the sea. "I took one look at the clear blue sunlit water," Exell wrote, "and made a dash for it. It was one of the most glorious things I have done in my life. There might have been sharks, there might have been poisonous jelly fish. I neither knew nor cared. It was just lovely. I swam out about thirty yards and then turned around to have a look at the shore. It was a perfect setting." There were no modern hotels for travelers in the South, and Exell often dreamed of having such a hotel built. "I was thinking of where a hotel might be sited when, from behind, came three terrific smacks. When I turned round there was nothing to see except the disturbed surface of the water. Then out into the sunlight leapt three enormous stingrays. They rose about six feet out of the water and, as they came down, brought their whiplike tails on to the surface with a crack. The head and fins formed a triangle which must have been ten feet long at the base. The long, thin tail was like a whiplash. Whether they were really dangerous I did not know, but they frightened the life out of me all the same, and I made for the beach where I could watch them doing their morning exercises in safety. It was lovely, no sandflies, no mosquitoes, no filthy smoke. Just a warm sunny morning without a cloud in the sky."

In Nakhon, northeast of Trang, Jumnien's family made a living by fishing. At their home, kept perhaps as a memento of a dangerous encounter, was the dried tail of a stingray. After his mother died Jumnien began growing vegetables to sell. This was in 1943, during World War II, when food was scarce. By maintaining his own vegetable garden Jumnien felt confident that he would always be able to feed the family.

One day a number of pigs wandered into Jumnien's garden and ate his vegetables. The sight of the pigs devouring the vegetables saddened the boy. He knew that these pigs belonged to the village headman, who let them roam throughout the village. With a heavy heart, Jumnien went over to the headman's house to ask him to keep his pigs in their pen and not let them come over to his house and eat from his garden. But the headman did not seem interested in listening to the boy. He continued to let the pigs roam freely.

The sight of the pigs feeding in his garden upset Jumnien so much that he decided to deal with the pigs on his own. One day he took the dried tail of the stingray to the garden and decided to use the ray's sharply pointed tail to stab at the pigs when they came around. "That way," he thought, "the pigs will have wounds on their skin when they go back home, and this might teach the village headman to keep his pigs in the pen where they belong, because if he lets them out again, he should certainly expect the pigs to be stabbed again."

But when it came time for Jumnien to stab the pigs, the boy instead started to feel sorry for the animals. "The pigs did not know what was going on," Ajahn Jumnien said as he recalled this incident from his youth. "They were just looking for something to eat and did not know anything about what belonged to whom. This caused me to hesitate as I tried to decide on the best place to stab them. I thought that if I stabbed them in the mouth, they would find it difficult to eat, and if I stabbed them in the leg, they might not be able to walk. If I stabbed them in the throat they might not be able to breathe. And if I stabbed them in the back, I was afraid they would not be able to lie down and sleep."

The boy spent a long time thinking about where the best place to stab the pigs might be. "In the end," the Ajahn recalled, "I decided that the best place to stab them would be in the hip where they were particularly fat. There is a lot of flesh in that area, and the wound probably would not hurt them too much. If I stabbed them in the hip, I thought, the pigs would probably just run back home. I didn't expect them to fall over and die in my garden. So I began by stabbing one in the hip."

"This turned into a big misfortune for me," Ajahn Jumnien continued, "I don't know what this pig was thinking. At first it started to back up and looked like it was going to run off. I had lost my grip on the tail of the stingray, and it had somehow pierced through the pig's back, only to exit out of the chest of the animal. The pig began to squeal out in pain, *eeed, eeed*, as loud as it could, and started running back home. Not long after the pig got back to the pen it lost its ability to walk. It just lay there in pain, wasting away, day after day. It was unable to eat anything because of the pain. Within a month the pig was dead."

The village headman performed an autopsy on the pig to figure out what had killed it. He was aware of the wound from the stingray tail that had entered the pig's back and exited out the front. The autopsy showed that a barb from the ray's tail had penetrated the pig's heart. The wound had become infected, causing great swelling and resulting in an extremely painful death for the pig.

Then the village headman remembered the threats Jumnien had made the day the boy came to tell him to keep the pigs away from his garden. Immediately, the headman knew that it was Jumnien who had stabbed his pig. Very upset, the headman cut out the swollen pig's heart with the barb still in it. He walked over to Jumnien's house and yelled right in the boy's face, "You damn brat! Your mother dies, and your own father has become a total mess, incapable of doing any good! And you have to go looking to cause bad karma by killing my pig! Just look at how this pig's heart was pierced by the barb from your stingray's tail! You take this pig's heart, and you eat it!" the headman ordered. "And you better not try and do anything bad to those pigs ever again! Remember that!" And he stomped off.

As a Buddhist, the boy knew perfectly well that he had violated the first of the five precepts, which forbids people from killing or doing any bodily harm to living beings. "I was really frightened by the fact that I had killed this pig without intending to," Ajahn Jumnien recalled. "I had just wanted to injure it a little. When I saw just how the pig had died, I was truly filled with remorse and felt so sorry for it that I began crying. I decided to take that pig's heart and throw it into the canal, since I was way too frightened to eat it."

One day, not long after this incident, young Jumnien started to feel spasms and a shooting pain in his heart. As the Ajahn recalled, "It would come and go and was an extremely intense pain. It felt as if I had a thorn stuck inside my heart. In the days that followed, the pain disappeared for a while but soon came back. This pain became something that I felt on a regular basis."

Thirteen years later, when Jumnien was ordained as a monk, he still had the pain. "There was a day," the Ajahn tells us, "when I was sitting in meditation and began to feel this pain in my heart again. This time it came on really strong and spread to my shoulders and down into the lower part of my arms. Even the base of my neck was in a lot of pain, and I broke out into a cold sweat." Intuitively, the Ajahn felt that he was getting a warning that this was karma for having stabbed the pig.

"But my mind was trying to tell me that this was not so," the Ajahn continued. "My mind was telling me not to believe this and not to cling to this view of karma; that my symptoms were simply those of someone with a heart ailment, and that anyone could suffer them."

The Ajahn then went on to say, "It was at this point that the pain became so intense that I could not tolerate it any longer, and I passed out, falling face down on the floor. At that very moment I saw a vision of myself stabbing that pig with the stingray's tail. It was a frightfully clear vision.

"When I regained consciousness, I meditated to overcome the pain. With a firmly established mind, I resolved to dedicate the merit of living a holy life, a life that is led according to the Noble Eightfold Path,[26] to the pig with whom I was karmically linked. I prayed that the pig would rejoice in my virtuous acts and begged it to please forgive me."

This suffering had strengthened his predilection for moral conduct and wisdom development. After he dedicated merit to the pig, Ajahn Jumnien noted, "I experienced a miracle. The pain I had been feeling disappeared, as if a thorn had been plucked from my heart. I was amazed. Before this I had tried to find a cure through both traditional medicine and Western medicine, all to no avail. I had even seen a heart specialist at a hospital, and he said that my heart was normal. He said that he could find nothing wrong with my heart, and he was just as confused as I was that I had this pain."

37

THE GOLDEN BOY AND BANDITS

I N THE EAST children mature sooner than their Western counterparts, the Swiss geologist Hans Morgenthaler observed. "A seven-year-old child in Siam can make himself more useful and find his way through life better than a student of twenty-five in Europe." Morgenthaler, who lived among the villagers of Nakhon Si Thammarat from 1917 to 1920, was once saved from drowning by a ten-year-old boy. While living in the southern region the Swiss geologist probably met many boys like Jumnien.

By the time he was eight Jumnien had become something of a prodigy in his village. Ajahn Jumnien recalled, "Since my father had mastered many esoteric practices during his lifetime, I gained a lot of knowledge by learning from him. I took on many of his responsibilities as a traditional doctor, and I gained quite a reputation in the surrounding villages."

Furthermore, whenever villagers got into an argument Jumnien was often the one who ended up helping them settle their dispute. Jumnien thought this was quite strange, since he was still a child, but people did seem to listen to him, whether it was a husband and wife with some dispute or others with a conflict of interest. On one occasion two villagers got into a fight because one of them could not pay the hundred baht he owed the other. Jumnien settled the argument by donating his own money to pay off the debt. Both men came to respect Jumnien for his willingness to help. No matter what the problem, Jumnien would work on it until it was resolved.

Not only was the boy a talented problem solver, he was also a remarkable astrologer. As Ajahn Jumnien tells us, "I had developed a reputation as an accurate forecaster. I attribute this to the fact that I was young and had a great memory that helped me make very accurate astrological calculations. Being skilled at meditation, which gave me a clear mind, increased the accuracy of my predictions."

One day some people in his village came to Jumnien and asked, "What do we have to do to prevent the bandits from bothering us?"

"Please do not worry about it," the eight-year-old boy replied. "I will take care of it myself."

"How?" the villagers asked the boy.

"I will come up with a strategy. Don't fret."

The boy's answer left the villagers confused, and some of them started to gossip that young Jumnien had somehow managed to capture and tame a spirit named Kuman Thong (Golden Boy). This curious spirit was called Phrai Kuman in the South, and Phi Noi (Little Spirit) in northeastern Thailand and Laos. Kuman Thong was created from the fetus torn from a pregnant woman who had died in childbirth. The fetus was first coated with indigo and various other herbs and then roasted. During this process magical incantations were chanted until Kuman Thong appeared to the spirit doctor. These locals speculated that Kuman Thong had hidden in Jumnien's body and could whisper to its master, warning him of impending disasters. Kuman Thong could also make its master invisible. "Combine this with the fact that people knew I was the son of a former thudong monk, and you can imagine why they showed me a lot of respect," Ajahn Jumnien said. "Of course, I did not raise Kuman Thong or any other spirits; it was the locals who spread these rumors. The only thing I had was my intellect and my wit, which I used in conjunction with some gathas that my father had taught me from an ancient text on warfare."

Knowing how much the villagers feared and worried about bandits, the boy came up with a plan that he had thought over very carefully. Ajahn Jumnien said this was how he usually thought things out. "Ever since I was about five or six years old, I tended to think carefully before doing things. I would never do anything immediately, opting instead to work out a plan first. Nobody taught me to do this. It came naturally."

When night fell Jumnien put his plan into action. The villagers usually sent a few men out to the road that led into their village; there they sat out the hours of darkness as security guards on the watch for bandits. On that night it was the boy who acted as a security guard. Jumnien had no weapons with him, and he was alone.

When a gang of bandits showed up in the middle of the night, the boy went out into the road to meet them and blocked their path.

"Please stop for a minute," Jumnien asked the bandits politely. "Uncles and elder brothers, I've got something I would like to say to you."

"Who do you think you are?" the bandit leader bellowed. "Get out of my way!"

"My name is Jumnien," the boy replied. "I am the son of Father Phet."

Once the bandits heard the names Jumnien and Phet, and knowing who the boy's father was, they started to mutter among themselves. Phet was particularly well known as an adept shaman. Nearly all of the bandits would have known of Father Phet by his excellent reputation.

One of the bandits stepped forward and shined a flashlight in the boy's face. "That is Jumnien!" the bandit shouted. "He is the kid who exorcised a ghost from my mother-in-law. She was crazy for years until the boy helped her. This kid has magical knowledge. He is a skillful healer and fortuneteller. He is a very good kid. A lot of people respect him."

As the bandit was talking, the boy silently recited the Gatha of Loving Kindness and blew a breath in their direction. Ajahn Jumnien explained, "This was a gatha that my father had me test out by having me get a cat to cuddle up next to a mouse instead of doing the usual cat thing. I also tried it out by having some baby chicks leave their mother's side to come over and play with me. The chicks completely ignored their mother."

The bandits then formed a circle around the boy and started a friendly conversation. Recalling the event, the Ajahn said, "They asked me how to read astrological signs, treat various diseases, and become invulnerable. I answered their questions until they were satisfied. After that I pleaded with them."

"Dear uncles and elder brothers," the boy addressed the bandits. "I beg you not to continue being bandits, because if you do you will only cause suffering for yourself and others. The only thing you will gain is bad karma. I respectfully request that you find legitimate work even though it might be difficult, and you might not make a lot of money. If you make little money, then spend little. If you make a lot, then spend a lot. Be content with what you have and you will not accumulate bad karma."

Empathizing with the bandits, the boy continued, "It is not like we are well educated. We are the children of farmers. Yet you want to have a big house and a car. You want to live a comfortable life like the governor or the owners of the rice mills. If you go out and steal or murder someone for money just so you can build up your position and possessions, this is called 'wrong thought, wrong action.' It is not only against the rule of law but against the rules of the Dhamma."

Jumnien warned, "If you are a bandit and you kill someone, you will have to spend your time hiding from the police. But there are policemen in every district and every province. The police will send news alerting others to be on the lookout for you. If you are caught, you will end up in jail. And if you are not caught, then you will have to spend all your time hiding. You will end up sleeping with one eye open, worrying about the day when the police will sneak up on you, arrest you, and put you away. This is the karma that will consume your heart and torture you."

"If you try to steal from someone who has a better weapon and decides to fight," the boy predicted, "then there is a chance you will be injured or killed. You will die far from home. Your wives and children will never see you again. If you try to fight the police you could also be killed—or injured, in which case they won't stop coming after you. It does not seem like there is much happiness in the life of a bandit. And what little happiness there is does not last long. But the suffering will continue, for the crimes you have committed will always follow you."

The boy noted that the bandits just stood there in complete silence, as if no one was breathing. Then the leader let out a sigh and said, "Little Jumnien, you talk like a monk; your teaching impresses me. But how do you think we are going to deal with finding another occupation? Our occupation is stealing. It will take us a long time to find some other kind of work." Turning to his gang, the bandit said, "Forget about it. Let's go find some other village to rob." And with that, they left by the way they had come.

From the vantage point of old age, Ajahn Jumnien remarked, "I myself found it surprising that the bandits would listen to a kid who was only eight years old. There were probably a lot of reasons why they listened so patiently to my advice—and left our village alone. Maybe it was because I was a traditional healer and fortuneteller for several subdistricts and had a good reputation. Or it might have been that they were afraid to anger me lest I put a curse on them."

38

HOW TO CAPTURE BANDITS

IN HIS CAPACITY as a manager of Siam Bank in Thung Song during the late 1920s, Frank Exell often traveled by train on business trips. "When in the South," Exell said, "I often had to carry quite large sums of cash from Thung Song to a large rice mill at Phatthalung. Since this had to be done at week-ends, it meant travelling for several hours by local train. There was no road. The Bank provided me with a very handy little Colt .38, but the local chief of police begged me not to carry it. He insisted that, whatever might happen to the cash, I should not be murdered. If it was known I carried a revolver, that alone would be a temptation. Such things were unprocurable by the 'bad hats' in the South. He was quite emphatic that the first thing the dacoits would do would be to kill me.... I took his advice. I was not the slightest use with a revolver anyway."

In his youth Jumnien made a good living as a fisherman, and he too had to find a way to keep his money safe while traveling from Nakhon to his village. Once he had sold his goods in town, Jumnien carried only a small amount of money on his person. He usually put most of the money he had earned in the bottom of a gunnysack containing shrimp paste. He then paid a boatman to transport the bags of shrimp paste to his village. It was a safe place to hide his money. When dacoits raided a boat, they usually took only money. Since they wanted to travel light, so that they could flee into the nearest jungle if the need arose, they would never steal a heavy sack of shrimp paste. The most Jumnien ever lost to thieves was pocket money. But other fishermen who carried large sums of money with them frequently lost it all.

By the time World War II ended in August 1945, many bandits had acquired rifles that they had stolen from military posts. One day Jumnien heard that a group of five bandits was planning to raid his village in Nakhon. The bandits figured that fishermen, who made good money, kept it in their houses. In accordance with bandit rules, they announced ahead of time that they planned to raid the village on a certain night. The bandits, who were led by a man named Plot, carried carbines—lightweight rifles with short barrels. The villagers only had knives with which to defend themselves.

On the day of the raid Jumnien prepared his weapon, using raw materials he found right at hand. He brought home a container full of the finest grains of sand from the beach. Next he raided an ants' nest in a tree. In his kitchen he ground dry chilies into powder, pounded the ants—with their formic acid—into the chili powder, and stirred this concoction into the fine sand. After adding water to the mixture, he ladled it into a length of bamboo, plugged the open end of the bamboo with a wad of cloth, and made a small hole in the node on the other end. With these preparations completed, Jumnien now had a rudimentary spray gun.

Jumnien then hid in a big tree at the entrance to his village that the five bandits would have to walk under. When night fell, Plot and the four men of his gang approached the village. It was pitch dark. When the bandits were well under the big tree, Jumnien aimed his spray gun. Hearing a sound above their heads, the bandits instinctively looked up. At that moment a spray of chili pepper, formic acid, and grit filled the air. The bandits screamed in pain as the stinging liquid went into their eyes. Unable to open their eyes, they could not see what was going on. Hearing screams, some village men came out of their houses carrying ropes and tied the bandits' hands. Others went to get the police, who ended up having to take the bandits to the health clinic. It took the doctors days to get all the fine sand out of the bandits' eyes. Once he could open his, Bandit Plot asked the police for the name of the man who had trapped him. The police told him it was Jumnien. The bandit leader then asked the police to take him to that man. When the bandit saw Jumnien, he was astounded that the "man" was only nine years old. Jumnien talked to the bandit leader and made him promise that the gang would stop raiding. Once the bandit leader gave his word, the police let the whole gang go.

Although Jumnien was able to convince one bandit gang not to raid his village, there were other robbers out there that he did not know or had not met. So young Jumnien found a way to use coconut shells to prevent robbers from entering his house.

In his village all the houses were built on pilings. After returning home from work, Jumnien would wash his feet with water from a jar at the foot of the stairs, and then go up and enter the house. One day, in anticipation of a raid upon his village, Jumnien cut a good number of coconut shells in half, stripped off the hairy fibers, and placed them, round side down, on each step, securing them in place with mud and clay. The boy then cut whole young coconuts in half and placed them, round side up, on the ground around the steps. He greased the smooth coconut skins with lard.

When the robbers came in the dark of night, unable to see what lay in store for them, they slipped on the shells or tripped over them and fell. One man broke a leg and cried out in pain, and another sprained an ankle. The noise alerted the villagers, who came out of their houses and overpowered them.

SLINGSHOT EXPERTS

T O HELP feed their families, sons of farmers learned to hunt birds and trap fish. If sons were not good at hunting or fishing, often their families would have to go without fish and fowl. Boys who were expert at using slingshots were greatly admired by their friends. Ajahn Jumnien recalled that of village boys his age he was the best shot. "I was very adept at using a slingshot. My friends admitted that I was better than they were. Every time I made bets with them about my skill, I always won—until my friends no longer dared to bet against me." For example, the Ajahn recounted, "We would bet that with four shots I could hit three birds. If I hit fewer than that, I'd lose the bet. And I had to hit the birds hard enough so that we could catch them after I'd knocked them down. If I hit a bird and it got up and flew away, it was considered a miss."

Ajahn Jumnien continued, "With those four shots I almost always hit four birds. The only thing was that some of them would be able to fly away because I had not hit them hard enough. In order to knock out a bird immediately you had to hit it in one of the death spots, on the head or at the base of the beak. I always aimed for these spots, which is why I always ended up scoring three or four birds with four shots."

When he was in his early teens, Jumnien was so good that he was able to hit a bird while sleepwalking. "Once in the middle of the night I got out of bed without waking up and grabbed my slingshot. I headed straight out the door, shot a bird, and then came back to my bedroom and went back to sleep. The next morning when I got up, my friends and neighbors had all gathered around trying to figure out what had happened. My feet were covered in mud, and there were muddy footprints all over the house and on my bed."

Looking back from his perspective as an elderly monk, Ajahn Jumnien admitted that "it was really a bizarre incident. I tried to figure out how I could have walked out of my house without waking up. It could not have been my friends who played a trick on me by covering my feet in mud. I had left muddy footprints all through the house."

Although the fields and forests of Siam were richly endowed with all kinds of birds, temple boys were not allowed to shoot them. Monks and novices living in monasteries in outlying areas usually received food on alms round. The temple boys normally shared the food that the monks received; but since they were still growing and ate a lot, they often had to supplement their diet with vegetables they found in the wild and cooked for themselves.

During the 1930s Krae and Chai were temple boys at a monastery outside Bangkok. Krae had a reputation for being one of the naughtiest boys. One day they went out and Krae killed a big bird with his slingshot. When the boys returned to the wat they built a small fire under the porch of their hut so that they could barbecue the bird.

As soon as he detected the smoke, the abbot left his kuti, and as he drew closer to the smell, he saw Krae plucking the feathers from the bird. The abbot then summoned all the temple boys who were at the monastery at the time to join him on the porch of his kuti (hut).

The abbot, who was holding a stick in his hand, asked Krae, "Why did you shoot the bird? What made you want to kill it?"

Krae sat in silence, his eyes downcast.

"What did the bird do to you?" The abbot had raised his voice. "Did the bird shit on your head? Is that why you shot it?"

"No, it did not," Krae replied.

"Killing an animal will earn you a demerit. Killing is not to be done for fun," the abbot said. "We must have empathy. We humans fear death and pain. Well, just like us, birds also do not want to die. You know you are stronger, so you took advantage of the bird. What if the bird could get hold of a gun and decide one day out of the blue to shoot you? What would you do?"

Krae remained silent and still except for the blinking of his eyes.

"All sentient beings treasure their lives," and as he said this the abbot whacked Krae with his stick. "Does this hurt?" he asked.

"Yes, sir," said Krae, rubbing his buttocks.

Pointing his finger at Krae, the monk said, sternly, "Remember this. You got only one whack, and you are still rubbing your bottom. Imagine how the bird felt when you shot him. Now throw your slingshot into the fire and burn it. From now on, whoever kills an animal will get a whipping on his backside."

To intentionally kill animals, no matter how small, is to break the first precept. Although temple boys were taught to observe the five precepts—to abstain from killing, from stealing, from illicit sexual activities, from lying, and from taking intoxicating drinks and drugs—they did not always follow the monks' teachings. On that day the temple boys learned to have compassion for animals. Buddhist monks usually teach that all sentient beings are our brothers and sisters in *samsara*—the cycle of birth, old age, sickness, and death.

THE CROCODILE HUNTER

A LARGE CROCODILE population once lived in the Chao Phraya River. "In Bangkok there are crocodile charmers," wrote Jean Pallegoix, a French priest who spent thirty years there during the nineteenth century. "When a man has been taken by one of these animals, the King gives the order to catch it. Then the charmer, accompanied by several boats with helpers armed with lances and ropes, comes to the place where he assumes the crocodile can be found. He recites superstitious formulae to make it surface from the water. As soon as it appears, he jumps on its back and while he sticks his fingers into its eyes, the helpers jump into the water, some tie up its mouth, others the legs and they pull the throbbing monster which appears to have lost all its power on land. They bring it to the mandarin who judges its case."

Jumnien was about ten years old when he began training with a crocodile master who lived in Nakhon Si Thammarat. Recalling his apprenticeship under the master, the Ajahn said, "The master had a pond where he raised crocodiles. When I poked at one of the vicious crocodiles with a long stick, it immediately bit the stick. I learned that crocodiles have a soft spot at the corners of their mouths. If you are able to straddle the back of a crocodile, you must quickly take hold of the corners of the croc's mouth with your fingers and use your thumbs to dig into its eyes. They will be less able to resist if you drag them along this way."

In addition to acquiring practical skills, crocodile hunters usually learned sacred gathas to aid in capturing crocodiles. Gathas like these Bishop Pallegoix called "superstitious formulae." Young Jumnien had both a gatha and an amulet for protection. The gatha that the boy recited had four syllables: *Ah eu leuk leu*. When he recited this gatha, Jumnien had to keep a small amulet in his closed mouth. He was instructed that if he opened his mouth even slightly, the crocodile would bite him immediately.

Crocodiles could lie still underwater for hours. Following the instructions, the Ajahn said, "When I entered the water I said *ah*, which means 'I.' This was followed by the word *eu*, meaning 'the crocodile.' Once I was actually in the water, then I said the word *leuk*, which means 'to control.' After I got to the word *leu*, the crocodiles would have scattered away. But if I did not recite the last word, then the crocs would just stay where they were. Sometimes, if I failed to recite the word *leu*, the crocs might stay there in the same place all day without moving. It was as if they were under some sort of spell." All Jumnien could figure out was that the crocodiles' behavior was subject to the four-syllable gatha. When Jumnien uttered the gatha *Ah eu leuk leu* without opening his mouth, he produced a sequence of sounds that were similar to a crocodile's growls, croaks, snorts, or snuffles. If a crocodile appeared, "then I would move in to catch it. You could not just stand there doing nothing."

Once Jumnien got on the back of a crocodile, he had to keep straddling the animal near its head. He was aware of the crocodile's powerful tail, which could sweep a person into the water. In order to survive as a crocodile hunter, Jumnien had to learn how to respond to a crocodile's habits. "Whenever I went into the water I tried to keep my body upright, since crocodiles don't like to eat their food if it's standing up. But if I got knocked down, the first thing I would do is curl up into a ball, and then go back to standing straight up again. The crocodiles had a more difficult time trying to bite me if I did this."

From the master, Jumnien learned how and why crocodiles did what they did. The Ajahn described how to get a crocodile up onto the bank of a canal or river. "If I were to bend down to grab it, I would be bitten immediately. Crocodiles are smart enough to wait until you are in a vulnerable position before attacking. So instead I had to drag the crocodile backward onto land. I think that when crocs realized I was willing to fight with them, they dared not bite me." But the main technique involved grabbing the crocodile by the corners of its mouth and pressing down on its eyes. "The crocodiles might still try to bite, but at the corners of their mouths there are no teeth."

When Jumnien grew brave enough to try catching larger crocodiles, he had a very difficult time grabbing them by the corners of the mouth. "And I didn't want to bring a knife along and kill a crocodile outright, because I was afraid of the bad karma that would follow me."

The Ajahn recounted one occasion when he and other boys his age failed to capture a large crocodile on their own. "I grabbed it by the head and started to press into the eyes, waiting for it to eventually raise its head out of the water. My plan was to wait until it ran out of strength from fighting and then bring it up onto the shore. But because this crocodile had such a large mouth and body, I was unable to grasp it firmly at the mouth. So I had to let go of it."

The sight of Jumnien struggling with the crocodile caused all of his close friends, who had come to help, to take off at a run. "Nobody ventured to help me hold on to the mouth of the croc, so I never succeeded in catching a large crocodile. At that time I was only about nine or ten years old, and was a lot smaller than some of the bigger crocodiles. But I was able to catch the small ones, and that made me happy. I really needed the money at that time to help support my family."

In the 1940s all crocodile hunters in the area were grown men— except for Jumnien. "Later on, after I had learned more about capturing crocodiles, I started to round them up and sell them in order to supplement my family's income. A large crocodile would sell for about four or five hundred baht, a small crocodile for two hundred. This was a lot of money. Back then ten baht could buy a bucket of rice. The owners of crocodile farms bought baby crocodiles and raised them so that the reptiles would become familiar with people. Once the crocodiles were mature, the farm owners bred them." One of the crocodile hunters, Yao, had also trained under the crocodile master who taught Jumnien. "I was just a small kid and could not compete with the older hunters like Yao," said the Ajahn. "But even though I was still a novice hunter and most of the crocs I caught were pretty small, I started to gain a good reputation among the local villagers." Yao was known for his ability to capture vicious crocodiles. Later in life he went on to work at the Crocodile Farm in Samut Prakan, a province next to Bangkok.

Jumnien never killed a single crocodile. He would just catch them and keep them alive. It was up to whoever bought them to actually kill the animals, or not. A village elder once told the boy, "Jumnien, do not kill crocodiles. There is an old saying that those who make a living by killing snakes will die from a snake. Crocodile hunters will die from a crocodile."

41

THE HEAD OF A MONKEY TROOP

VARIOUS MONKEY species inhabited the forests of Nakhon Si Thammarat. Local people would capture monkeys and train them to do work that men could not do easily. One day Jumnien heard that a company called Nakhon Phan was offering twenty-five baht (about one U.S. dollar) for every live monkey brought to them. This company, located in the provincial town of Nakhon, then exported the monkeys to Japan. Needing money to support his siblings, Jumnien decided to try his hand at capturing monkeys. "If I capture five or six monkeys a day," the boy figured, "I will earn about a hundred baht or so. Then I'll be able to save more money than I could doing any other kind of work."

To catch the monkeys Jumnien made a square cage and placed a barrel with some bananas in the middle. Once the monkeys had climbed down into the barrel to get the bananas, they would be unable to get out. "It will be real easy to catch them," Jumnien thought.

There was a troop of about a hundred monkeys with a troop leader who appeared to Jumnien to be almost as big as he was. "This troop leader is as smart as a human and will chase off the other monkeys before they fall into the trap," Jumnien observed. "And if he can't chase the monkeys away, this leader will simply pull them out of the trap."

The leader of this troop was so smart, nobody had been able to catch these monkeys. But after carefully observing the monkeys' behavior, Jumnien worked out a plan for dealing with this leader. He decided to train two dogs to help him. In his mind Jumnien came up with what he thought was a good strategy. "If the dogs chase this monkey up a small tree, I'll take an ax and start hacking down the tree. When the monkey falls down the dogs will start chasing after the monkey again. I will then sneak up behind the monkey and pounce on it. But I will have to pick just the right moment to pounce, and I will have to act quickly or I will get a nasty monkey bite." As it turned out, this would be no easy task for the two dogs, because monkeys are extremely agile and can put up a good fight.

One day when Jumnien was out trying to catch these monkeys, his two dogs suddenly took off after the leader of the pack. This monkey climbed up a fairly big tree. Jumnien started cutting down the tree with his ax while the two dogs circled around in anticipation.

When the tree fell, the dogs immediately moved in to attack the monkey chief. But this monkey was much stronger and fiercer than the others, so it lunged at and bit the dogs, which started yelping in pain.

It looked like the dogs were going to lose this battle, and Jumnien had to think fast. "If I kill this monkey first, it will make it easier to capture the other monkeys in this pack. Once this leader is dead, there probably won't be any other monkeys smart enough to prevent their friends from falling into my trap."

With this in mind, Jumnien sneaked up behind the big monkey while it was fighting off the two dogs. In the confusion, he found an opportunity to hit the monkey on the head with his ax as hard as he could. The blow knocked the monkey unconscious, and the dogs then killed the creature.

Jumnien cut the head off the monkey leader and took it around to show his friends. "You see this monkey?" he said to the other boys. "It caused me to miss out on earning any money for several days. It prevented me from catching other monkeys in his troop." And with that, he threw the monkey's head into a nearby canal. In the days that followed, Jumnien was able to trap the entire pack of monkeys.

Years later, long after he established Tiger Cave Monastery, Ajahn Jumnien recalled, "At that time I was still a child, and I did not understand that the leader of the troop loved the other monkeys. He was just trying to protect them from danger the way any father would protect his children."

As for the monkey's head that Jumnien had tossed into the canal, by the following day it had swollen grotesquely and came floating back in front of his house. Jumnien poked it with a stick so it would float away. When the tidewater in the canal started to ebb, the head floated out to the sea, about three kilometers away. But the next day, when the canal had filled with the rising tide, the monkey's head floated in and ended up right in front of Jumnien's house. Puzzled, the boy put the head into a plastic bag, went out on a fishing boat, and threw the head overboard when the boat was about ten kilometers from the shore.

But once again the monkey's head floated back up the channel and stopped right in front of his house. "This was really spooky," the Ajahn remarked. "It seemed like the monkey's head had become possessed by a spirit and had come back to seek vengeance. The really strange thing was that this time, when the water in the channel drained out to sea, the head would not float along with it. It just spun around in the water. I thought it might have gotten tangled in a branch or some waterweeds just under the surface." But when Jumnien went over to scoop out the head, he saw that it wasn't caught on anything.

Finally, in the middle of the day, Jumnien carried the head all the way to the seashore and threw it out once more. When he woke up the next morning the head had come back again and was waiting for him right in front of the house. "Maybe my friends are playing tricks on me," Jumnien thought. But he decided this was unlikely, since the head was now quite rotten and smelled putrid.

The boy next reasoned, "Maybe the head won't float along with the water draining out of the channel because the deities want me to become aware of the fact that I am earning bad karma." So in the end, Jumnien decided to dig a hole behind his house and bury the stinking head. He put the head in the hole, then covered up the head with dirt, which he packed down firmly. The boy was determined not to let this "miraculous" head rise up from the ground, no matter what.

After that day Jumnien started to get terrible headaches. He tried curing them with both traditional and Western medicines, but they would not go away. The headaches came and went by themselves, medicine or no medicine. "It turned out that these were migraines," the Ajahn said.

Later on in life, after he had become a monk, the Ajahn recalled, "There came a day when, sitting in meditation, I got a headache that made me feel like my head was going to explode. It was so painful it caused tears to run down my face. My body broke out into a sweat so heavy that it drenched my robes. I looked like I had been out in the rain. I was afraid that with a headache this bad, I was certain to have a stroke and die. I was convinced I was going to die that day.

"As the pain became more intense, I heard a loud cracking sound that made me think the roof was collapsing. At that time my body began to double over, and it looked like I was going to fall down, but before my head struck the ground I was able to straighten back up and resume sitting in meditation again. Immediately, I attained one-pointed concentration, and a vision appeared before me. I saw myself cutting down a tree and saw that monkey leader jumping out of the tree as it fell. The two dogs were attacking the monkey as it was running away. I saw myself sneaking up behind the monkey and clobbering it on the head. At this point the vision vanished."

Reflecting on this vision, Ajahn Jumnien understood that "the spirit of the monkey leader was still following me in order to seek revenge. This is because I had been so vicious in the way I killed that animal. Once I came to this realization, I put my mind in a state of concentrated calm and dedicated merit to the monkey leader. I prayed for the spirit of the monkey to be released from this world. I asked the monkey for his unending forgiveness from now on until I attain enlightenment."

The Ajahn recalled that after he dedicated merit to the spirit of the monkey, "the migraine headaches went away. This is a clear demonstration that future experiences in this life depend on whether the actions one performs are wholesome or unwholesome." As a Thai saying goes, the Ajahn concluded, "Good actions bring good results, bad actions bring bad results." This passage expresses the Buddha's teaching of karma:

> As the seed, so the fruit.
> Whoever does good, receives good,
> Whoever does evil, receives evil.

42

THE MONKEY LESSON

O NE DAY when he was about eighteen years old, Jumnien went into the forest to hunt monkeys. He was accompanied by his hunter friend, Kung, and a few other young men. They took a rifle with them, the kind that policemen used back then. Kung spotted a female monkey up in a tree holding its infant, and he shot it. The bullet entered the left side of the mother and exited the right. The hunters could see blood gushing from both holes.

Screaming in agony, the mother monkey still cradled her baby with one hand, while with the other hand she tore off some leaves and attempted to plug up the bullet holes to stop the bleeding. Jumnien and his friends watched in amazement. The Ajahn later recalled that "the way this monkey acted until the end demonstrated its intelligence and knowledge. We could see that she loved herself and feared death and that she loved her baby. We could see that she was suffering from her injuries."

The Ajahn, remembering the event that moved him so deeply, added, "She knew she was going to die. With tender love, she lifted the baby to her face and kissed it one last time. She then placed the little one on a branch as if she were teaching her baby to learn how to take care of itself, since in a few moments the baby would no longer have a mother."

The Ajahn recalled every second of the monkey's plight. "As the baby monkey had never been separated from its mother, once it was placed on the branch, it was unwilling to be by itself and climbed back to its mother. The mother knew that if the baby were to hold on to her when she fell to the ground after succumbing to her wounds, both of them would die. She cuddled her baby and kissed it repeatedly. I saw tears in her eyes as she let out a wail of anguish, knowing she would never see her offspring again. She kissed the baby monkey one last time, placed it once more on a safe branch, and then died. Her body plummeted to the ground, while her baby watched in safety, a blessing from the intelligence of the mother."

After this disturbing event, Kung, Jumnien, and their friends vowed that from that time on they would never shoot another mother monkey carrying its baby. They made a vow to stop creating karmic links with monkeys.

FIG. 25. MATERNAL CARE.

It was Jumnien's responsibility to climb the tree and retrieve the baby monkey. He took the orphan back home so he could raise it. Recalling the difficulty of raising a monkey, the Ajahn said, "It is the nature of monkeys to be mischievous, and baby monkeys are especially naughty. Many people don't understand that this is the nature of monkeys. Trying to train it, they will hit it again and again." Young Jumnien was one such person himself. "If the monkey was mischievous, I would strike it on the hand, making sure that it hurt. The monkey would learn not to do that again. But since it was a monkey and so childlike, it would get in trouble doing something else. If I hit it again, it would go find yet another way to get into trouble."

The last time this happened Jumnien hit the monkey's hand so hard that he split its littlest finger open. He had to put medicine on the wound and bandage it. The monkey hated this and gnawed through the bandage. Jumnien came up with a way to prevent this by coating the bandage with latex, which he had been using to repair his boat. The monkey disliked the smell of this and stopped gnawing on the bandage. But when the wound on the monkey's right hand finally healed, Jumnien discovered that the little finger had become disfigured and was now crippled.

Not long after that incident, the little finger on Jumnien's right hand became infected and started to swell. "I developed an abscess on that finger," the Ajahn recounted, "which remained with me until I was ordained as a monk. My finger was still bandaged, and the infection kept getting worse until the pain drove me to see a doctor. The doctor drained the infection, applied some medication, and rebandaged my finger. He told me to come back to see him every day for about five days."

The next day the young monk went to see the doctor as scheduled. "The doctor unwrapped the bandage and immediately a look of bewilderment appeared on his face. I looked down at my finger and was probably just as baffled by the sight as the doctor, since the infection that was so conspicuous the previous day had disappeared completely. We had no idea how in less than twenty-four hours the abscess could simply vanish."

The doctor said if this was the result of the medicine he had used, he would buy up the rights to produce it and sell it all over the world. He figured he would be one of the world's richest people in no time.

"As it turned out," the Ajahn recalled, "the medicine had dried up the infection and the flesh on my finger while it was bent. This meant that I wasn't able to straighten the finger when I tried to extend it. The doctor said I would need surgery if I wanted to regain the use of my finger."

On reflection Ajahn Jumnien realized, "This was karmic reckoning for the time that I wounded the hand of the baby monkey. Consequently, my finger was crippled just like the little finger of the monkey." Jumnien refused to have surgery, saying later, "I had to accept the karmic link and live it out. If I had had surgery to straighten my finger, in the future I would have injured some other part of my body, for I would not yet have mitigated my bad karma."

Recollecting this violation of the first precept, Ajahn Jumnien suggested that this story might serve as "a lesson to those who want to go hunting for fun, or those who like to buy baby monkeys and keep them as pets. It is imperative for you to understand that to get one baby monkey, as many as ten mothers have to be shot. A monkey mother sitting in a tree, if shot, is most likely to fall with her infant clinging to her. If the baby doesn't die from the fall, it will most likely be crippled in some way.

"When we did such things and forgot about them," Ajahn Jumnien continued, "we were surprised when the fruits of our karma affected us. 'Why is this be happening to me?' we wondered. We felt we had been cheated and complained that we had never taken a life and thus shouldn't have to suffer. But when our karma catches up to us, even though we are in pain and agony, we should admit that at least we are better off than the animals that suffered because of our actions. At least we have doctors and nurses to look after us. There will be medicine to ease our suffering, and our relatives will give us comfort and watch over us. And if we are incapable of eating on our own, there will be others to help feed us.

"As for the animals that are wounded by humans and run off to hide in the jungle, they have nothing at all. As thirsty as they might get, they will not have the strength to crawl out and find something to drink. They will lie there suffering from hunger, thirst, and pain. There is no ready-made medicine for them. Instead, the monkeys only have leaves and saliva to use as medicine as they lick their wounds. Their fate is infinitely worse than ours."

Monks and pious people who are well trained in moral virtue, mindfulness, and wisdom, the Ajahn tells us, "are willing to accept the truth when the results of their karma affect them. They do not become depressed to the point of going crazy. They do not lament the loss of a limb or an eye. They know that if they were to commit suicide to escape the agony of a disease, they would still not escape their karma. While in this life they may avoid their bad karma, in the next life they would certainly have to face it.

"Those on the path of practice, which leads to the cessation of karma, know that when their karma has caught up with them they should purify their heart. This may seem difficult, yet it is incredibly easy to do. All you have to do is just accept the truth."

43

COPING WITH ROUGH SEAS

YOUNG JUMNIEN learned to be an expert at fishing, a task he learned by necessity when his mother died in 1942. Jumnien was then about seven years old. It was then, too, that he started smoking local tobacco. "Fishermen believed that when you went out to sea, it was a good way to keep your body warm in the wind and cold."

Jumnien and his boyhood friends were the youngest fishermen from their village in Nakhon. Fishermen who lived along the east coast of the peninsula risked their lives every time they went out to sea. Whenever he went fishing Jumnien would recite the protective chants that he learned from his father. "I recited them every day without fail." To young fishermen in stormy weather the vibratory sounds of paritta chants were soothing and produced peace of mind. They were aware that while out on a sailboat, nothing was in their control; they were at the mercy of the winds and tides. But Jumnien believed that "if you plan things, they can be."

More than once, between the ages of ten and eighteen, Jumnien nearly lost his life at sea. Three times the boat he was on capsized. "The first time it happened," the Ajahn recalled, "I had a feeling ahead of time that the boat was going to sink. First, I noticed the ants and other insects on board were behaving strangely. The wind that day was strong, and I could tell by the waves that we could well capsize. When I first realized that the boat was going to sink that day, I warned my onboard friends. But because we had no radio, and thus no way to get weather reports, my friends refused to believe me. But since I was convinced we would capsize, I began roping together some bags of food and storage containers so that these items wouldn't scatter when we rolled over."

Jumnien's friends on the boat said, "We always thought you were braver than we were. Now you are more afraid than we are." Jumnien reminded them of his Safety First rule: "Nothing is in your control, but if you plan things they can be." He worked on securing the sail and other parts of the boat. "I prepared a buoy and flag too, so that we would be able to come back later and find our supplies and whatever equipment would have sunk."

When the wind began to blow harder and the waves got bigger, as young Jumnien had predicted, the boat indeed capsized. "I already had a rope prepared," the Ajahn recalled, "so as soon as the boat rolled onto its side, I tied myself and my friends to the capsized vessel. In the three times that I have been on capsized boats, no one on board ever died. The first time I was on a boat that capsized, we had to tread water for five hours before we were rescued by a passing boat. The second time we were able to right the boat ourselves, and the four of us bailed the water out of it. The third time we had to tread water in rough surf all night and half the next day, since we were caught in a storm. Finally, late in the second day a boat came along and helped us right our boat."

Ajahn Jumnien tells us, "I always believed in safety first because I have never been one to have blind faith in things. Accidents happen all the time, and this has caused me to always be on my guard." From the vantage point of old age the Ajahn admits, "I consider myself lucky still to be alive. I believe a big part of it is because of my awareness of the importance of safety."

As for the protective chants that his father taught him, the Ajahn said in 1995, "I have been reciting these gathas for almost fifty-five years from the time I was six. So I've been reciting for nearly twenty thousand days. It would be impossible to count the number of times I recited these gathas, because on any one day I would have recited each gatha many times."

44

Sharks and Sea Snakes

N THE 1940S the Gulf of Thailand was still teeming with
sharks. Fishermen had to contend with them each time their
boat capsized. When Jumnien was young, his father trained
him not to be afraid of sharks. One day as the father and
son were walking along the seashore, Phet told Jumnien to collect some
pieces of broken plates that were scattered around the beach. Although
puzzled by his father's instruction, Jumnien collected about half a bas-
ketful. "That's enough," his father said. "Let's get in the boat."

Phet sailed the boat out to sea until they arrived at an area where
three sharks were feeding. Then, Ajahn Jumnien recalled, his father told
him to throw the pieces of plate across the surface of the water so they
skipped a few times before sinking.

Jumnien wondered, "What does my father have planned this time?"
He asked his father why they were doing this, but Phet did not answer.
After Jumnien had skipped a few shards across the surface of the water,
the sharks began to dart after them. Ever alert to feeding opportunities, "the sharks had mistaken the plate fragments for fish," the Ajahn
recalled, "since the glinting pieces of white pottery looked like some
of the local fish. After a few moments I saw that there were a lot of
sharks swarming in the area, and I started to get a bit nervous."

Phet told his son, "These sharks can easily bite a person. But if you
stand straight then they will only be able to bite your hands or feet. So
if you're in the water near them, you should hold your hands and feet
close to your body. Then when a shark approaches it will have difficulty

biting, since its mouth is on the underside of its body, and it is not comfortable turning over onto its side to bite. However, if you are swimming along, a shark can bite you right in half.

"So if you are standing upright, sharks will have difficulty biting you.
First they come and bump against your leg and then swim off, only to
circle back to the same spot. Therefore, you should move a few steps
away from where you were, so when they come back they won't find
you and will just bite at the empty space where they thought you would
still be."

Once Phet finished telling Jumnien how to avoid being attacked by
sharks, he handed his son a spear, promptly pushed Jumnien over the
side into the water, and sailed away. "After they saw me bobbing up
and down in the water," Ajahn Jumnien recalled, "the sharks started
to come to investigate, and I got very frightened. But then my survival
instincts took over, and I remembered what my father had told me."
When one shark turned around too close to him, Jumnien put the spear
between them.

"Again and again the sharks came up to me," the Ajahn recalled,
"but once they realized I was a person and not a fish, they left."

By the time his father returned in the sailboat, the sharks had all
vanished. As soon as his father came near, Jumnien shouted, "Father!
Why did you push me out of the boat?"

"I am training you to become brave enough to swim with sharks,"
Phet replied. "I want you to overcome your fear."

"So that was it!" Jumnien thought. "Just being out here learning
how to be brave almost killed me!"

Fishermen knew that although sharks always cruised around on the
lookout for food, they were not motivated to eat until they detected
something edible. Sharks are not senseless killers; they prefer fish to
human flesh. They do not like hard objects; a tap on the mouth with
a hard stick will keep a shark away.

Jumnien also found that it helped to know what to say to an
approaching shark. "I am not going to harm you, so please do not bite
me," the boy said to each shark that came near him.

When Jumnien was out fishing he had little to fear from sharks. It was a sea snake that almost killed him. Sea snakes are poisonous snakes that live in salt water, and many species of them inhabit the waters of the Gulf of Siam. Some can reach a length of ten feet, although most adults are between four and five feet long. They swim by sweeping their paddle-like tails from side to side, keeping close to the surface of the water. Though sea snakes are able to submerge by closing the nostrils on the top of their snouts, they are air-breathing and must surface periodically or drown. All sea snakes have glands that release venom through cobra-like fangs at the front of the mouth.

"One day while my childhood friend Sombun and I were out on the water fishing," Ajahn Jumnien recalled, "I was bitten on the finger by a *phirang*. All the fishermen we ever knew or heard about who had been bitten by this type of sea snake died as a result. I was therefore really afraid that I would not survive. So I immediately tried to work out a deal with the Lord of Death."

As he lay in the fishing boat, Jumnien pleaded, "Please do not take me right now. Give me a chance to see my father first. My father is a great doctor. I know in my heart that he can work magic and has powerful medicine. If I can reach my father in time, then I will survive." Jumnien was then only seventeen, and he did not want to die.

Once he was able to get the boat ashore, Sombun quickly took Jumnien to see a traditional healer named Chaweng. "This particular doctor was an expert in treating sea snake bites," the Ajahn later recalled. "His knowledge came from what we called ghost instructions" (a mixture of obscure prescriptions and medical remedies).

The Ajahn described the treatment. "Doctor Chaweng had me crawl under a tree called *fa thalai chon* and collect some leaves and twigs with my mouth. He warned me that if my shadow were to fall upon the tree, the tree would no longer be sacred. If you collect the leaves and twigs of this tree in the middle of the night, then you don't have to crawl on your belly, since in the dark you won't cast a shadow." Fa thalai chon (*Andrographis paniculata Nees*) is known as the King of Bitterness, because every part of the tree is utterly bitter. Traditional healers usually prescribed it to bring down high fevers, cure malaria, and treat intestinal problems.

"After I had collected the leaves and twigs with my mouth," the Ajahn continued, "I brought them back to Doctor Chaweng, and after he ground them we mixed them with alcohol. I am happy to say that the doctor's medicine worked."

Ever since he was a young boy, Jumnien had known that his father was adept at treating snakebites with traditional medicines, bites not only from cobras but from all kinds of land snakes. Jumnien found out some time after he had been bitten by the sea snake that his father never dared to treat anyone bitten by such snakes. He had never had any experience with them.

45

LEARNING BY HEART

G ROWING UP in Nakhon Si Thammarat, the young Jumnien frequently heard people say that if you wanted to learn more about the Dhamma you should study at Wat Boromthat, the oldest monastery in Nakhon. The wat library contained many printed books, including a set of the books that young monks had to master in order to pass the Nak-dham examinations, such as the *Navakovada* (Instructions for Newly Ordained Monks and Novices), the *Buddhapavatti* (Life of the Buddha), the *Prathomsomphot* (First Step to Enlightenment), and the *Buddhasasana Suphasita* (Buddhist Proverbs), a book of five hundred Buddhist proverbs in Pali with Thai translations. These textbooks had been written by Prince Patriarch Wachirayan and other scholar monks in Bangkok.

"Back when I was eight," Ajahn Jumnien recalled, "I studied astrological, magical, and religious texts. Between the ages of eight and ten I studied everything I could for survival. I learned how to deal with thieves, dacoits, and bandits. When I was ten years old, I became interested in studying science." From the year 1946 on until he was ordained as a monk, Ajahn Jumnien says, he was determined to study the Tipitaka.

Jumnien's village was located about twelve kilometers from Wat Boromthat. Whenever Jumnien was not fishing at sea he would travel to the royal monastery by bus or boat and on foot. At times he would walk along the paddy fields all the way to the monastery. For several months the boy commuted to Wat Boromthat this way in order to read Buddhist texts.

Whenever Jumnien was unable to go to Wat Boromthat he went instead to Wat Naripradit, a monastery near his village. At this wat a copy of the entire set of the Tipitaka was kept in a cabinet. This was a traditional Dhamma cabinet made of wood, beautifully painted and decorated with gold leaf. The Tipitaka texts were written with a stylus on palm leaves and kept in bundles tied with cord. Although the king had sponsored the translation into Thai and the printing of the Tipitaka, and had sent copies to all royal monasteries, in rural areas monks still preserved the Pali texts on handwritten palm leaves.

Once Jumnien had learned to read the Nak-dham books, which focus on the commentaries, he became very curious about the original texts and wanted to study the Tipitaka. Whenever Jumnien went to Wat Naripradit, he always saw an elderly monk, whom he called Luang Ta (Venerable Grandfather), guarding the cabinet holding the Tipitaka. Jumnien often talked to Luang Ta and asked him questions. The monk told the boy that he had copied the words of the Buddha by hand into these palm-leaf books. The monk himself had not studied the Tipitaka; he hoped that in the next life he would accomplish a thorough study of the texts in Pali. In local Buddhism it was believed that one gains much merit by inscribing the Buddha's words on palm leaves, even if one does not entirely comprehend their meaning.

Luang Ta allowed Jumnien to take a bundle of the Tipitaka texts out of the cabinet and read them. On each visit Jumnien would sit there and read a portion. Before leaving the monastery Jumnien always donated money for the maintenance of the Tipitaka. The old monk was glad, for the money could be used to hire skilled calligraphers to help make new texts to replace old ones that had deteriorated.

Luang Ta also allowed the boy to read some of the books from his personal collection. Having read these Dhamma stories, Jumnien liked to relate what he had learned from them, not only to Luang Ta but to young monks at the wat as well. At one point Luang Ta remarked, "You are really smart. You must have attained spiritual perfection in a past life, so that you are now able to comprehend the Dhamma from every story that you read."

Jumnien replied, "I think the merit is from this lifetime, not a previous one. Before I came to this wat I studied many books on the Dhamma at another temple." Ajahn Jumnien later commented, "Although Luang Ta had copied the Tipitaka and maintained the texts well, he had not studied the words and had therefore gained little wisdom."

Sometimes, after the monks had finished their chants in Pali, Jumnien would translate the meaning of these chants into Thai for the lay folk who were present. Hearing Jumnien's accurate translations, the monks wondered how the young fisherman had become so interested in Dhamma. Jumnien told them that he had learned these chants by heart from his father long before he could read the book of chants.

From the training he received from his father, Jumnien had learned the benefit of concentration early on. "When I studied a subject, I thought only of that subject. By not thinking about anything else, I was able to make progress and see results quickly." After becoming a monk, Phra Jumnien had confidence in his Nak-dham studies because of his early training in meditation. As he later recalled, "I didn't attend any classes before taking the first-level Nak-dham exam. But when the day of the test neared, I did make an effort to study a bit."

The examination questions were posed orally. Phra Jumnien approached the exam using the Four Rules. "First, I listened to the story the teacher told. Second, I contemplated the meaning of the story. Third, I listened carefully to the questions the teacher asked about the story. Fourth, I wrote the answers down.

"Because I listened to the exam story with total concentration, I could tell what questions would follow. This allowed me to prepare the answers. Consequently, I finished answering all the questions before anybody else. I headed back to the monastery while other monks were still working on their exams.

"When you have absorbed concentration," the Ajahn concluded, "the knowledge you need to bring forward will appear in your heart."

46

THE DHAMMA
THAT LIFTS YOU UP

D URING THE FIRST HALF of the twentieth century, thudong monks from Peninsular Siam went on pilgrimages to the North or Northeast to practice meditation
in the forests, and thudong monks from the North
and Northeast went to the South. The Thai word *thudong* is derived
from the Pali *dhutanga*, which means a way of shaking off mental defilements. There are thirteen thudong practices. Monks vow to wear robes
made out of cast-off cloth; use only one set of (three) robes; go out
every day on alms round for food; visit every house, not omitting one,
no matter how poor the quality of the food offered; eat only one meal
a day but not before dawn or after the noon hour; eat only out of the
alms bowl; refuse to accept food presented after the alms round; dwell
in the wilderness; take shelter under a tree; stay in the open air; stay in
a cemetery; rest content with whatever shelter is provided; and refrain
from lying down. It was (and still is) up to each monk to decide how
many of these thudong practices to follow and how long to practice each
one. As one thudong master has explained, "These practices aid in the
cultivation of contentedness, renunciation, and energetic effort."

During the 1940s Jumnien often met wandering monks from the
Northeast or from southern provinces other than Nakhon who had
come to pay respect to the relics of the Buddha enshrined in the
Boromthat Stupa. Whenever a wandering monk came to his village,
Jumnien immediately went to visit him in the forest where he had

pitched his klot. The boy would ask questions about the life of wandering ascetics, how they practiced meditation, how they coped with living alone in the forest. Like many youths of his day, Jumnien asked the wandering monks about sacred amulets. Although his father was often away from home after his mother died, Jumnien had plenty of opportunities to learn from wandering monks. From them he learned the Dhamma as well as different methods of practicing.

For instance, when Jumnien was eight years old a wandering monk taught him the five principles of "the Dhamma that lifts you up and keeps you from falling":

> When others wrong you, keep your equanimity and let
> the wrongdoing go.
> Do not wrong others by improper speech or other forms
> of hostile expression, for others will want to retaliate.
> Accept the good regardless of the caste, religion, language,
> or nationality of the source.
> Be kind in speech and generous in material things as well
> as in hospitality, for as the Dhamma teaches, "When you
> do good you receive good."
> Keep your heart pure. It is easier to make a soiled cloth
> spotless than to cleanse one's heart.

The thudong monk explained to the boy, "When we follow these five points we will lift ourselves up and never fall. We will prosper because there are no obstacles in our hearts."

On another occasion Jumnien met a former monk named Ajahn Chu, who also taught him to watch the thought process. From Ajahn Chu, Jumnien learned that there were four ways to keep calm:

> Do not feel hurt or resent others. Such behavior is a waste of
> energy and an obstacle to success.
> Do not feel disappointed in yourself or in others. Resentment
> or disappointment can make one capable of murder or
> suicide. One might destroy everything one has.

Do not be angry with oneself or others. This can only
   bring harm.
Do not ridicule yourself or others. Ridicule will hinder you.

Whenever he had a chance Jumnien practiced these nine points he
learned from the wandering monk and the lay teacher.

DEATH OF A FATHER,
NEW LIFE FOR THE SON

T HE THUDONG PRACTICE was an integral part of local
Buddhism in southern Siam. In the early decades of the
twentieth century many village monks, including Father
Phet, still observed the peripatetic ascetic practice. As a
child, Jumnien enjoyed listening to his father tell him about his early
life as a wandering ascetic. Phet described for his son all the villages in
which he had preached and told the boy about the obstacles and chal-
lenges that he had faced, such as encounters with wild elephants or
tigers. There were times when Father Phet got lost in the jungle for as
many as five to ten days, never running into a single village, and so
getting nothing at all to eat.

Buddhist monks were not allowed to pick fruit or dig up roots to
eat. One of the thirteen rules of the thudong practice stipulates that
monks may receive food only during the alms round. Among the cap-
tivating stories Jumnien's father told him were those in which "my
father encountered horrible ghosts or helped cure people who were considered crazy, for, as a thudong monk, my father was also a healer. He
also told me that when he was a young man he would sometimes meditate nonstop for three or four days, sometimes even for seven days in
a row without taking a break."

After hearing all these stories about thudong monks, the little boy
thought to himself, "When I get a little older I will be ordained as a
monk and remain in the monastic life for my entire life. I want to

become a monk so that I can practice meditation without being disturbed. I will be so happy. And I want to be a healer and an astrologer so that I can help people." However, Jumnien was made to promise to wait before entering the monkhood until Phet had died. And before he died, Jumnien's father took patient care to teach his son all that he knew about herbal medicine and the medicinal properties of wild plants.

Toward the end of his life Phet was quite sick, suffering from several illnesses that normally afflict the elderly. The unusual thing was that, as Ajahn Jumnien tells us, "My father became more sane as his health deteriorated. He was able to maintain his mindfulness to the end when he faced death." His father passed away when Jumnien was nineteen years old.

The following year, in 1957, Jumnien turned twenty. He had to report to the district office for military conscription, but he was not drafted. Jumnien took this opportunity to be ordained as a monk. Having made up his mind to be a monk for life, Jumnien started giving away his money and worldly possessions. Since he derived his living from fishing, Jumnien owned two boats and had about twenty people working for him at this time. One of Jumnien's brothers asked for the two boats and got them.

Another brother, Ploy, went to live at a friend's house. Ajahn Jumnien recalled, "I thought at the time that if I let my brother stay at my house he would continue to accumulate bad karma from fishing. At the very least I wanted to completely stop whatever bad karma we had been accumulating as fishermen. I gathered my fishing nets together so that I could burn them. But while I was out buying some kerosene to build a fire, my brother gave the nets to his friends. He told them to take the nets quickly lest I burn them all."

Jumnien gave his house and everything inside it to the needy. By the day of his ordination, he had absolutely nothing left. He was ordained as a monk at Wat Naripradit, the name of which means the monastery established by women. Since the monastery was near his village, Jumnien was already acquainted with the resident monks. Venerable Teacher Kadoem of Wat Buranaram was his preceptor.

One thing that Jumnien had never owned was a pair of shoes. Like all rural youths of his generation, he went about barefoot. And as was typical of a rural monk, Jumnien continued to go barefoot. It was not until he had been in the monkhood for sixteen years that Ajahn Jumnien began, for the first time in his life, to wear sandals. By then he was thirty-six years old.

FIG. 26. AJAHN JUMNIEN AS A YOUNG MONK.

Reflecting on his father's life as a layman, Ajahn Jumnien says, "My father used to lament having to leave the monkhood. Sometimes he wished he had remained a monk. He missed the time when he was an ascetic and told me that the lives of the thudong monks were full of quiet happiness. Those were days with no hassles and no confrontations, no defilements or desire for competition of any kind."

As a young monk, Phra Jumnien served his teacher at Wat Naripradit for seven years. Then he went to practice vipassana meditation under the guidance of Ajahn Dhammaro, the abbot of Wat Chaina, located in the same province. By this time Ajahn Jumnien was almost thirty years old. "One day," the Ajahn recalled, "I had a frightening experience. While sitting in meditation, I started to feel chest pains, and it became difficult for me to breathe. It was as if I was about to die. I thought the reason I couldn't breathe was because I had some sort of lung disease." This was a reasonable supposition; after all, Jumnien had been smoking since he was seven years old.

"The pain kept getting worse until I fell face down onto the floor. I couldn't see a thing at that time; everything just went dark. Suddenly, I had a vision of my mother's face. This image was even clearer than the one I saw when my mother died. In this vision I saw the time when my mother tried to stab me with a knife after I had run into her back and almost caused her to die.

"After I regained consciousness and was able to sit up again, I just stayed where I was, feeling bewildered. With that image of my mother still fresh in my mind, I contemplated what it all meant. 'Aha!' I thought to myself, 'the reason that I couldn't breathe a moment ago was because of the karma I created when I nearly killed my mother that time when I ran into her.'"

Realizing this, the Ajahn said that he became quite sad and started to cry. "All day and all night I felt sorry for my mother. I thought that if she were still alive, I would rush back home and tell her, 'I have created so much karma with you, dear Mother, that I beg for your forgiveness. Please do not let me have this bad karma anymore.'"

But by this time his mother had already been dead for twenty-four years. "All I could do for her," the Ajahn concluded, was "to dedicate to her the merit that I gained from my ordination and devotion to practicing the Dhamma."

FIG. 27. VILLAGERS WELCOME AJAHN JUMNIEN HOME IN NAKHON SI THAMMARAT.

$\dagger$

IN THE UNITED STATES, one of the Thai master preachers inspired by Ajahn Buddhadasa and Ajahn Panya is Luang Ta Chi (Phramaha Surasak), the current abbot of Wat Thai in Washington, D.C. "Luang Ta" means Venerable Grandfather; "Chi" (pronounced "Chee") is the first syllable of his monastic name, Chiwanantho. As a young monk at the end of World War II, Luang Ta Chi traveled in 1945 from his village in northeastern Thailand to study Pali at Wat Mahathat, a prestigious monastery in Bangkok. It was during this period that Luang Ta Chi had the good fortune to meet both Ajahn Buddhadasa and Ajahn Panya, who had come to preach in Bangkok. As Luang Ta Chi recalled, "During the years between 1947 and 1950, Ajahn Panya began his first round of public teachings. I went to hear his Dhamma talks and was deeply impressed by his boldness. While in Bangkok, I also went to hear Ajahn Buddhadasa's Dhamma talks at the Buddhist Association and at Chulalongkorn University." Luang Ta Chi was profoundly influenced by both preachers' unconventional methods of teaching. Their moral courage and advocacy of social responsibility made a deep impression upon him. "From then on, their ways of teaching have guided me in my own teaching of Dhamma to other people."

In 1951, while Ajahn Panya was teaching in northern Thailand, Luang Ta Chi returned to teach in his hometown in the northeastern region. Four years later he succeeded his old teacher as abbot of Wat Phosikaeo and was also appointed Sangha head of Khamcha-ee district in Nakhon Phanom province. Under Luang Ta Chi's capable leadership, there was much improvement in communication and cooperation between the official Sangha and local people.

In keeping with Ajahn Buddhadasa's teachings, Luang Ta Chi believes that the physical world is inseparably intertwined with the spiritual. Following the local custom of monks initiating projects that benefit the whole community, Luang Ta Chi led fellow monks, novices, and laypeople in the construction of schools for village children in Khamcha-ee.

The construction of roads in Khamcha-ee, his home district, was also a communal undertaking in which Luang Ta Chi and his follow monks and novices worked alongside village folk. In the 1950s forested land was still available to anyone willing to clear it. Luang Ta Chi encouraged the villagers of Khamcha-ee to grow their own vegetables and other crops. The result was that the villagers were able to feed their families, sell their surplus, and obtain some income.

Less than a decade after Luang Ta Chi's return to Khamcha-ee, an increasing number of monks, novices, and laypeople had become devoted to practicing sila-dhamma. The abbot was able to awaken a large number of people and convince them to live their lives according to the Dhamma.

In September 1957, Field Marshall Sarit headed a coup that resulted in the overthrow of the government under Phibun. A year later Sarit abolished the constitution and put the country under martial law. The Sarit government held that the practice of meditation was unproductive, and monks who taught meditation were obstacles to material progress. All critics who resisted government efforts to restrain their activities were considered subversives and communists. The monks who were most at risk of being labeled communist were either those who criticized government officials and their activities or those who became socially engaged leaders of their communities. At that time both Ajahn Buddhadasa and Ajahn Panya fell within these categories.

Following Ajahn Panya's example, Luang Ta Chi was not afraid of taking a moral stand and criticizing officials who lacked sila-dhamma. Consequently, in 1960 Luang Ta Chi was accused of being a communist. The thirty-five-year-old abbot was sent to Bangkok and put into a jail cell already occupied by writers, journalists, lawyers, and activists. From the day Luang Ta Chi first entered prison, he maintained his monastic vows and continued to practice meditation. Prison brought him into close contact with many political activists, and Luang Ta Chi made the most of the situation.

His long sentence gave him the time to introspect. In jail he learned about people from all walks of life. The experience, he says, "deepened my understanding of the Dhamma. It confirmed my conviction in the principle of karma that says our actions do matter. I saw how political prisoners were treated. I saw how different ranks of the security police behaved."

Four years after his incarceration, Luang Ta Chi was found innocent of the charge that had been held against him. He was released in 1964.

Like his mentor Ajahn Panya, Luang Ta Chi had a knack for speaking directly to ordinary people. He showed them how to practice Dhamma in an increasingly complex society. At this time a whole generation of young people was struggling with uncertainty and looking for direction. As his reputation as a great preacher spread far and wide, Luang Ta Chi was invited to teach Dhamma at ceremonies outside the monastery, such as birthdays, the shaving of the topknot, ordinations, marriages, and funerals. Sometimes Luang Ta Chi gave Dhamma teachings at three different locations in a single day, so he seldom had much time for himself. Luang Ta Chi was either training lay folk in meditation or traveling around the province teaching Dhamma.

In 1975 Luang Ta Chi was invited to become abbot of Wat Thai in Washington, D.C., the second Thai temple built in the United States, now located in Silver Spring, Maryland. The abbot has written prolifically, using poetry, novels, and short stories to impart Dhamma to people who have grown up in modern society. With humor and in simple language, Luang Ta Chi shows his readers how to apply the Buddha's teachings to everyday life. Adults as well as children started calling him "Luang Ta Chi" affectionately after he began using this pen name in his writings. Every summer Luang Ta Chi has ordained a number of young men, both Thai and American. Although they ordained temporarily, these young monks had the opportunity to experience monastic life under Luang Ta Chi.

Like the three Buddhist masters in this book, Luang Ta Chi believes that children should be trained to practice meditation when they are quite young. "It is easy to teach children to meditate," the abbot tells us. "Children do not have a lot on their minds, and they have limited experience. They are able to concentrate their minds quickly. My experience has revealed that it is easier to teach children than it is to teach adults, including novices and monks. It is easier to teach village folk than teach monks or novices. It is easier to train novices than train monks. The more knowledgeable the monk is, the harder it is to teach him meditation. The older the monk, the harder he is to teach."

Luang Ta Chi, who turned eighty-one in 2006, welcomes all children, teenagers, and college students interested in Dhamma practice to visit Wat Thai, Washington, D.C.

FIG. 28. LUANG TA CHI AT WAT THAI.

ACKNOWLEDGMENTS

I AM DEEPLY GRATEFUL to the Buddhist masters in this book for their accounts of their upbringing and early life experiences. Luang Pho Panya kindly answered my questions and permitted me to translate his stories and use photographs from his books. Luang Ta Chi and Luang Pho Jumnien gave generously of their time and memories in interviews. I express my deep appreciation to Phra Pasanna-dhammo (now Pracha Hutanuwat) for his interviews with Ajahn Buddhadasa; to Metta Panich for permission to reproduce photographs from the Dhamma-dana Foundation; to Phramaha Chanya Suthiyano for his biography of Ajahn Panya; and to Ajahn Kasemsuk Khemsuko for writing down Ajahn Jumnien's oral recollections.

My sincere thanks go to John Badgley, Barbara Brown, Sister Dharmapali, Ajahn Khantipalo, Joel Fredell, and Erick White, who read an early draft and offered detailed comments and useful sugges-tions; to Patricia Connor, who edited a longer version of the manuscript with sensitivity and care; to Dolina Millar for checking my transla-tions and always lending a hand. For helping with library materials and field research I thank Ngampit Jagacinski, Jirawan Amornvech, Caverlee Cary, Supatra Yooto, Chanya Sethaput, Pitchamai Tiya-vanich, and Vissuda Nagadatta. Many thanks also to Ajahn Withoon Ajarasupho for facilitating my interviews with Ajahn Jumnien; to Mike Romeo for an early draft of his translation of Ajahn Jumnien's stories; to Peter Veil for translating the article "Muai Chaiya"; to Bayo Paul Omole at Cornell University's Southeast Asia Program Outreach Department for scanning all the illustrations; and to the librarians at Cornell's Kroch Asia Collections.

I will always be grateful to Professor David K. Wyatt for the consistent support he has given my work. He kindly made the maps for this book just months before he passed away. Professor Wyatt and his wife, Alene, have shown great kindness to me. Special thanks must also go to my siblings Kantima Virachsilp and Pitsanuwat Tiyavanich for supporting this project and to Trasvin Jittidecharak for her faith in my work.

Professor Stanley O'Connor, Professor Brian Karafin, and Ajahn Santikaro have my deepest thanks for their prompt and spontaneous contributions to the Foreword. I am also grateful to Wisdom Publications for publishing this book; to John LeRoy for his copyediting skills and computer expertise; to Julian Chase for initiating the contact for Wisdom; and to editor David Kittelstrom and production manager Tony Lulek, whose assistance has been invaluable.

Finally, I thank the students who took Asian Studies/Religious Studies 363 and AS/RS 364 with me for their interest and enthusiasm. This book is for all of you.

1   The Buddhist Association of Thailand was established by a group of lay Buddhists in 1933, the year Ven. Lokanatha was in Bangkok. Ajahn Karuna, who went to India with Lokanatha, wrote, "Its membership is open to both sexes, irrespective of class, creed, and color. The aim and object of the Buddhist Association of Thailand is to promote the study and practice of Buddhism and to propagate its message outside Siam. Besides arranging regular lectures and discussions on topics concerning the Dhamma, the Association also publishes a monthly journal in Thai language on the teachings of the Buddha."

2   In his poem "Work," Ajahn Buddhadasa states that work itself is essential to spiritual attainment.

> That work gives humanity its true value
> and is of the highest honor there's no doubt.
> If one enjoys work with a blossoming heart,
> soon knowledge of Dhamma deeply pervades.
>
> Because work is the very essence of Dhammic living,
> superbly bringing together wholesome virtues,
> By analogy, compare the intelligent sharpshooter
> who with a single shot bags a sack full of birds.
>
> Naturally, work is to be done mindfully,
> with calm focus, patience, and industry,
> with honesty, self-control, and intelligence,
> with faith and courage, truly love your work.
>
> The more one works, the more these dhammas flourish
> promoting the transcendent shore without pause;
> seeing the universal characteristics in everything,
> in a flash plunging into *vimutti* and freeing itself.

3   Many Thai sweets are also quite similar to those made by the Portuguese. This is not surprising considering that Portugal was the first European country to conclude a commercial treaty with the Kingdom of Siam. Duarte Fernandes, in the year 1511, was the first Portuguese envoy to visit Ayuthaya. Not long after, Roman Catholic priests from Portugal established a church and Christian community in Ayuthaya. Many Portuguese served as mercenary soldiers. After the fall of Ayuthaya in the eighteenth century, descendants of the Portuguese settled in Bangkok. Ajahn Buddhadasa speculated

that the Siamese probably took the different ingredients of a typical Portuguese cake and made them into *tongyip*, *tongyod*, and *foitong*, desserts made with sugar and egg yolks, which became favorite sweets of many children as well as adults.

4 The Great Birth festival was dedicated to the bodhisatta's fulfillment of the first of ten perfections (*parami*): generosity (*dana*). The practice of generosity, the most important of the ten perfections in local Buddhism, supports the cultivation of compassion and liberation. In the Great Birth story, Prince Vessantara accomplished dana parami in order to help sentient beings free themselves from samsara, the cycle of birth and death.

5 Until the abolition of the corvée, a lengthy process that took place in 1899–1905, all native men were required to work on government projects whenever summoned. For generations prior to 1905 the corvée meant that most men were away from home for a third or more of the year. Members of the royal family, the sons of the nobles, and all Chinese men were exempted from the corvée. However, the Chinese were subjected to a poll tax. When the practice of corvée labor was finally abolished, all men had to pay a poll tax.

6 In premodern Siam, Buddhist monks taught village boys to read and write local scripts; they also schooled them in Buddhist iconography, local history, astronomy, mathematics, herbal medicine, literature, law, and arts and crafts. After years of studying in the monastery, students either became masters of various arts or crafts, took posts as civil servants, or returned to their villages to take up farming. But during the last two decades of the nineteenth century, King Chulalongkorn set about constructing the modern kingdom of Siam. The king and his brothers, who held key government positions, used education reforms to unify regions of Siam where linguistic, religious, and cultural traditions differed from the national standard. One of their goals was to bring education to a level comparable to European—especially British—standards so that Siam's students would be able to acquire knowledge of key subjects taught routinely in the West.

In 1898, at the age of thirty-eight, Prince Wachirayan was assigned the task of reorganizing education in all provincial towns. To accomplish this task Wachirayan appointed senior abbots of royal monasteries as "education directors" charged with establishing secular education in the fourteen regions of Siam. In their new positions these senior monks, most of whom belonged to the Bangkok-based Dhammayut sect, visited rural monasteries. They endeavored to persuade the abbots to carry out the king's wish to modernize education by teaching from textbooks written and printed in Bangkok.

The Sangha officials got to witness firsthand how numerous and varied the Buddhist practices in Siam really were. The decentralized Sangha hierarchy was made up of sects based on teacher-disciple lineages, with no regard for geography. To correct this the king decreed the Sangha Act of 1902, a law that did away with the older Sangha hierarchy. The new law provided for the creation of a centralized ecclesiastical institution charged with developing a uniform, modern Buddhism by standardizing both the education and practices of all Buddhist monks.

In 1910 Vajiravudh, a son of King Chulalongkorn, ascended the throne of Siam. (As a child, Prince Vajiravudh was sent to Eton College in England. After completing his public school education, he studied at Oxford University and then attended Sandhurst Military Academy, England's equivalent of West Point.) The new king appointed his uncle, Wachirayan, as Sangharaja of the Buddhist religion in Siam. In 1921 the king decreed that primary education should be compulsory.

State Buddhism and modern education became the major vehicles through which the government was able to integrate and assimilate people of various ethnicities into the modern nation.

7 The Ramakian is the Thai version of an Indian epic, the Ramayana. Tosakan, the demon king, and Palee, the monkey king, are two of the main characters.

8 A local likay is popular theater similar to vaudeville that included stories told through songs and dialogues. A classical likay is a highly formalized dance drama preferred by the nobility. The word *manora* derives from the Jataka story of Prince Sudhana and a heavenly bird-woman named Manora.

9 *Soraida* and *The Thousand and One Days* were co-translated by two Thai scholars, Sathirakoses and Nagapradipa. *Soraida* was translated from the English novel *The Virgin of the Sun*, written by H. Rider Haggard (1856–1925), who served in the British civil service in Africa as a young man. The title of the Thai version, *Soraida*, came from the name of the female protagonist in the novel. *Soraida* is an adventure story about an Englishman who ventures into the hinterlands of Morocco and Algeria in the late nineteenth century. *The Thousand and One Days* was translated from the English version of the Persian original.

10 According to Ajahn Buddhadasa, "Mr. Kulap, through his books, was the voice of opposition at that time. But I think it was more like boasting in the face of the king that made him famous quickly; there weren't any principles in his work, and there was no basis to what he said." At sixty-eight, K.S.R. Kulap (1834–1921) was found guilty of falsifying texts, but he was pardoned because of his age.

11 *Nak-dham* (literally "Dhamma student") refers to the study materials created by Supreme Patriarch Wachirayan, who redefined Buddhism to fit with Western science. Abbots of town monasteries were required to use the Bangkok texts when teaching young monks and novices. Novices who passed the first level examination in Dhamma studies (*nak-dham tri*) were exempted from military conscription.

12 According to Phra Paisal, abbot of Sukhato Forest Monastery in Chaiyaphum province, one explanation for this failure is that rationalistic Buddhism lacks the sacred (*saksit*). This Thai word is derived from the Sanskrit *sakti* (status) and *siddhi* (power). As Phra Paisal explains it, "The sacred here refers to that which is beyond the five physical senses, and is inaccessible and unexplainable by mere rationality, but which, nonetheless, can be attained or realized by the mind. It has a quality or power that those who access it can receive and benefit from. It is a refuge or security for those who believe. Its dynamism is beyond social codes and is incomprehensible to the untrained mind. The ways to realize it are diverse, just as there are many ways of conceiving of it."

In his assessment of state Buddhism, whose beginnings reach back to the 1830s, Phra Paisal writes, "Once Buddhism was reformed to be more scientific, there were no tangible sacred things to take the place of deities, heaven, spirits, and the like. Even the Buddha was demystified to be made more human. Nibbana, or the ultimate, is in fact another form of the sacred, the unconditioned aspect (*asankhata*). Yet it, too, was removed from official Buddhism." As a result of stripping the sacred from the moral code of state Buddhism, Phra Paisal points out, "people are expected to practice morality through the sheer force of intellect and rationalization, but intellect alone is not effective enough to develop a moral life. Morality has to be deepened to the spiritual level. Faith or fear of sacred power, experience of inner peace, and connection with the ultimate through meditation are all necessary spiritual conditions for maintaining one's morality. With the absence of the sacred, the moral code of official Buddhism no longer has any spiritual support or meaning."

Referring to the *Navakovada*, Phra Paisal points out that the section describing the code of morality for laypeople "says nothing about the ultimate goal (*paramattha*). In discussing *attha* (goal or benefit), only temporal and mental goals are referred to. The Prince Patriarch considered nibbana unnecessary, not only for the laity, but also for the monks. This resulted in the phrase 'nibbana realization' being removed from the vow of candidacy in the ordination ceremony. In his teaching, the benefit of morality was emphasized only in temporal terms, without indicating any connection to the ultimate or spiritual goal. Meditation has also been ignored in the entirely bookish modern Sangha education system." Many monks today consider the Nak-dham texts to be only one scholar's interpretation and seek access to new texts.

13 The Milindapanha text was widely used by preachers in many monasteries both in the Central Plains and in southern Siam. This non-canonical text is a collection of dialogues between Milinda (Menander, the Greek king of Bactria) and the Buddhist sage Nagasena. Their dialogues, which included expositions of the Buddha's teachings on *anatta* (non-self), *nibbana* (enlightenment), and *kamma* (causes and results as rebirth), required two preachers occupying two different pulpits. One monk took the part of the king, and the other monk acted the part of the sage.

14 Po Tek Tung is a Chinese foundation that collects corpses and takes them to the morgue. The foundation, whose services have always been free, has recently come under criticism because it has been pressuring people for donations.

15 According to Ajahn Payutto, a scholar monk and the author of *Buddhadhamma*, a comprehensive text on Buddhism, the practice of sanghahavatthu is the external applications of the four *brahmaviharas*, or "sublime states": goodwill (*metta*), compassion (*karuna*), sympathetic joy (*mudita*), and equanimity (*upekkha*). In practical terms, Ajahn Payutto explains, the four sublime mental states manifest as the four conditions for social harmony. The *first* condition for harmony—generosity (*dana*), the gift of material things, knowledge, or labor—can be based on goodwill, on compassion, or on gladness when it is an offer of encouragement. The *second* condition for harmony—kindly speech (*piyavacca*)—may be based on all four sublime states: when based on goodwill, kindly speech is appropriate to everyday interactions; when based on compassion, it is appropriate to times of difficulty, as when one offers advice or condolence; when based on gladness, it expresses happiness or praise for someone's success; and when based on equanimity, kindly speech is an impartial and fair response to social problems. The *third* condition for harmony is helpful conduct (*atthacariya*), the offering of physical effort to help others. On ordinary occasions, help is based on goodwill; in times of difficulty, it is based on compassion; at the occasion of someone else's good fortune, it is based on one's joy or gladness for them. The *fourth* condition for harmony is making oneself accessible or equal (*samanattata*). It refers to cooperating and joining in, sharing with other people's pleasure and pains, remaining humble when helping others, and being fair when arbitrating in a dispute.

16 Frank Exell, who lived in the southern region between the late 1920s and early 1930s, commented on the farmers' drinking. "I hoped they would keep off the arak and turn up sober. Arak was terrible stuff distilled from fermented rice and very potent. The Siamese peasant class never drank as we did for pleasure or for the sake of the company. Their ambition seemed to be to get drunk quickly and they usually succeeded. As Buddhists they were not supposed to drink at all but then we, ourselves, do not always do what the Bible tells us."

17 Located off the west coast of southern Siam, the island of Phuket was in the late 1890s one of the most important tin-producing centers in the world. Hundreds and hundreds of workers had migrated from China to work in the mines, most of which were owned by Chinese, Australian, and European businessmen. "The whole island is a gigantic tin mine," observed a British geologist, H. Warrington Smyth, then the director of the Siamese Department of Mines. "The granite of the hills is full of tin, the soil of the valleys is heavy with it. There is tin under the inland forests, and tin beneath the sea. In search of tin the indefatigable Chinamen have transformed the scenery. The valleys have been turned inside out, the hills have been cut away, the sea has been undermined, and the harbour has disappeared. Leaving the ship a mile out in the bay, one crosses banks of silt derived entirely from the tin workings up the river.... [T]he banks of the river are heaps of tailings, quartz and hornblende crunch beneath one's feet, and the decomposing granite scents the air.... Inland, beyond the town, the open valleys lie cleared of jungle."

18 Today Ranong is a province north of Phuket.

19 This Wat Mahathat in Nakhon Si Thammarat should not be confused with the monastery in Bangkok that bears the same name.

20 Detailed instructions on the meditation on death can be found in the *Visuddhimagga* (*Path of Purification*). This meditation manual was written down in the fifth century by the great Buddhist commentator Venerable Buddhaghosa. According to Buddhaghosa, one can practice mindfulness of death in eight ways: by recollecting that death inevitably comes along with birth; death ruins all of life's successes; death spares no one, no matter how famous, wealthy, or wise; death can come as a result of many kinds of illnesses; life processes are frail and easily disturbed or disrupted; the length of life is unpredictable; life in any case is short; and ultimately, life lasts for only a single moment of consciousness.

21 A gatha is a verse or string of sacred words whose power lies both in the sounds made and in the person who utters it.

22 Makham pom trees grow in all regions of Thailand. According to George Bradley McFarland, a physician who once lived in old Siam, "makham pom (*Phyllanthus emblica*) is a tree of small or moderate size found in tropical southeastern Asia, and throughout Malaysia or Timor." McFarland mentions that the fruit of this tree has many uses, but he makes no mention of the magical quality that Ajahn Jumnien attests to.

23 In southern Siam, the knowledge of how to purify oneself and identify those medicinal plants that could render one invulnerable had been passed down for generations by the monks of Wat Khao O lineage in Phatthalung. This knowledge was very different from what Jumnien learned from his father. In Phatthalung the ritual required to obtain impenetrable skin was performed by a Buddhist master on the mountain ridge of Khao O and usually lasted from ten to fifteen days. To prepare for the ceremony the master, who was skilled in meditation, needed to pick 108 different medicinal plants from the forests and mountains of Phatthalung. The aspirant had to go through a process of purification, observe the five precepts most strictly, and recite gathas. During the ritual the aspirant had to bathe for seven days in water in which the medicinal plants had soaked. Before immersing himself, and throughout each of the seven days of bathing, the aspirant had to recite the sacred gathas continually. No other talk was allowed. It took tremendous patience for the aspirant to sit immersed up to his neck in the herbal bath and soak for seven full days. Even though he did not drink the bitter water, the aspirant could still taste the medicine,

which penetrated through his nose and the skin of his neck. The process was closely supervised by the master. If the bitter water got into the eyes or ears, the aspirant could become blind or deaf. However, soaking in the medicinal water could also heal many skin diseases as well as muscle and joint disorders.

24 A similar custom existed in Burma. During the first decade of the twentieth century an Englishwoman named Leslie Milne spent fifteen months in Namkham, a small town in a Shan state in northern Burma. Milne observed the Shans in many of their daily activities, and she was present at a birth. Milne wrote in her journal, "The mother, or a 'wise woman,' gives the necessary help at an infant's birth. If labour is slow and difficult, massage is used to assist delivery and drinks of hot water are given. The water is not heated on the fire in the usual way, but hot stones are dropped into it. This is never done unless the water is to be used for medicinal purposes." After a baby is born "the umbilical cord is severed by a piece of newly cut bamboo which had been sharpened." Milne tells us that "during the birth the husband does not remain in the room; he is, however, close at hand and the placenta and umbilical cord are given to him. He first washes them gently, then rolls them in a banana leaf, placing them with care in a deep hole, which he has dug under the steps of the house, covering them loosely with earth. It is believed that it is most important to the future health and happiness of the child that this ceremony should be carried out without any rough handling, as this would endanger the future well-being of the child. It is also important that the father should wear a smiling face while he is digging the hole and depositing the banana leaf with its contents. If he frowns the child will be cursed with a bad temper. Burying the afterbirth under the steps of the house is believed to bring more children to the family. If a child is born with the umbilical cord around its neck it is considered a sign of great good fortune."

25 For example, the Thai words *bodhisattva* and *Tripitaka* are from Sanskrit. The Thai terms *nibbana*, *katanyu katavedita*, and *hiriottapa* are from Pali. The word *karuna* is the same in Sanskrit, Pali, and Thai. In the 1970s Peter Skilling, a Canadian monk, was practicing meditation under Ajahn Jumnien in southern Thailand. Later, Skilling, who never studied Thai language formally, took a proficiency test in Thai. The Canadian guessed most of the Thai words on the exam and managed to pass with the help of his knowledge of Pali and Sanskrit.

26 In Buddhism, the Noble Eightfold Path is the last of the Four Noble Truths, the path that leads to the cessation of suffering. The Noble Eightfold Path requires one to observe and practice right view, right resolve, right speech, right action, right livelihood, right effort, right mindfulness, and right meditation. As the scholar monk Ajahn Payutto explains, "By practicing according to the Noble Eightfold Path, desire has no channel through which to function, and is eliminated. Greed, hatred and delusion do not arise. With no desire, greed, hatred or delusion, there is no kamma. With no kamma there are no kamma-results to bind the mind. With no kamma to bind the mind, there emerges a state of clarity which transcends suffering. The mind which was once a slave of desire becomes one that is guided by wisdom, directing actions independently of desire's influence."

ajahn. Teacher or master; often romanized as *achan* or *ajarn.* (Pali: *acariya*)

arahant. One who has attained enlightenment, whose mind is totally free of greed, anger, and delusion.

baht. Thai currency; one baht = 100 satang.

ban. Village or community.

bhikkhu. A Buddhist monk.

bodhisatta. One who strives, over many lives and through determined practice of the spiritual perfections (*parami*), to attain full awakening as a Buddha and thus benefit all beings. (Sanskrit: *bodhisattva*)

Buddha. The Fully Awakened One; the Enlightened One.

Dhamma. The truth of the way things are; the teachings of the Buddha that reveal that truth. (Sanskrit: *Dharma*)

Dhammayut. A reform monastic order founded by Prince Mongkut in the 1830s.

gatha. Sacred verse.

Jataka. Stories from the Buddha's previous lives.

kamma. The principle of cause and effect; intentional action by means of body, speech, or mind. (Sanskrit: *karma*)

klot. A large umbrella equipped with a mosquito net, used by wandering monks for shelter while meditating or when sleeping in wilderness areas.

kuti. The small, hut-like living quarters of a monk, made of wood and usually built on stilts, or a room assigned to a monk in a one-story building.

Luang Lung. Venerable Uncle.

Luang Pho. Venerable Father.

Luang Ta. Venerable Grandfather.

maha. Title given to monks or novices who have passed at least the third level of Pali examinations.

monthon. Largest administrative unit in Siam's provincial government comprising several provinces.

muang. Town, city, province, or principality.

Nak-dham. A collection of formal Dhamma courses created by Prince Wachirayan (1860–1921), head of the Dhammayut order.

nibbana. The ultimate goal of Buddhist practice; liberation from all greed, hatred, and delusion. (Sanskrit: *nirvana*)

Pali. The ancient language in which the scriptures of Theravada Buddhist teachings were first written down. In Bangkok, Pali texts are written and printed in Bangkok Thai script; local Buddhist texts were written in Khmer script.

panung. Sarong; unsewn strip of cloth that was wrapped around the body and tied in a knot at the navel.

phra. The honorific for monks, Buddha images, stupas, and relics.

Phra Khru. Venerable Teacher; the lowest title of monastic rank awarded through the national Sangha hierarchy.

saksit. The sacred; that which is beyond the five physical senses and is unexplainable by mere rationality. The power of saksit, according to local traditions, inheres in the landscape, in sacred objects, monks, and lay renouncers. The ultimate saksit is the attainment of nibbana.

sala. An open-sided pavilion mounted on posts used as a rest house, preaching hall, and meeting place.

Sangha. The monastic community; in official usage, the institution of Buddhist monks.

sangharaja. Administrative head of the Sangha.

satang. Thai coin; 100 satang = one baht.

Siam. Thailand before 1939.

Siamese. Ethnic Thai people concentrated in the Central Plains and Peninsular Siam.

sila-dhamma. Morality; the application of wisdom within a community that brings peace.

stupa. A monument used to house Buddhist relics, generally dome shaped and topped with a spire.

thudong. Ascetic or austere practice. A thudong monk is one who keeps some of the thirteen ascetic practices over and above the general monastic code of discipline. The word *thudong* in local terminology also means a pilgrimage made on foot by an ascetic monk. (Pali: *dhutanga*)

Tipitaka. The three baskets of Buddhist scriptures consisting of the Vinaya (the monastic code of discipline), the Sutta (discourses of the Buddha), and the Abhidhamma (psychological and philosophical analyses); called "baskets" after the containers which held the original manuscripts. (Sanskrit: *Tripitaka*)

wat. A place of residence for monastics; temple of worship; a community center for monastics and laypeople.

SOURCES

Introduction

The citation on votive tablets is from Pattaratorn Chirapravati, *Votive Tablets in Thailand: Origin, Styles, and Uses* (Kuala Lumpur: Oxford University Press, 1997), p. 1. For a discussion of Buddhist traditions in Peninsular Thailand, see Pattaratorn Chirapravati, "The Cult of Votive Tablets in Thailand (Sixth to Thirteenth Centuries)" (Ph.D. diss., Cornell University, 1994). For the impact of caves and high places on the religious imagination, see Stanley J. O'Connor, "Buddhist Votive Tablets and Caves in Peninsular Thailand," in *Art and Archaeology in Thailand* (Bangkok: The Fine Arts Department, 1964), pp. 67–84.

For the Dalai Lama's visit to Suan Mokkh, see *Phap chiwit 80 pi Buddhadasa Bhikkhu* [Pictorial Life of Buddhadasa Bhikkhu's 80 Years], edited by Phra Pracha Pasannadhammo and Santisuk Sophonsiri (Bangkok: Komol Kimtong Foundation, 1986), pp. 223–24.

The quotation about amulets is from Phra Paisal Visalo, "Buddhism for the Next Century: Toward Renewing a Moral Thai Society," in *Socially Engaged Buddhism for the New Millennium: Essays in Honor of Ven. Phra Dhammapitaka (Bhikkhu P. A. Payutto) on His 60th Birthday Anniversary* (Bangkok: Sathirakoses-Nagapradipa Foundation, 1999), pp. 238–39; for a detailed discussion of this topic, see Phra Paisal Visalo, *Buddhasasana thai nai anakhot: naeonom lae thangok chak wikrit* [The Future of Thai Buddhism: Crisis, Trends, and Solutions] (Bangkok: Sotsi-Saritwong Foundation, 2003), pp. 6–129, 212–44.

For information about Venerable Rattana as a preacher, see Daruni Bunphiban, "Phra Rattana Thatchamuni (Baen Khanathabharano)," in *Saranukrom Watthanatham Pak Tai* [Encyclopedia of Southern Thai Culture] (Songkhla: Southern Center for Cultural Studies, 1986), 6:2361–63; and Phra Dhammawaraporn (Abhakho), *Chao Khun Phra Rattana Thatchamuni (1884–1978)*, cremation volume (Nakhon Si Thammarat: Wat Mahathat, 1980), pp. 36–43.

Recollections about Ven. Lokanatha are from Chanya, *Chiwit lae ngan khong Than Panyanantha* [Venerable Panyanantha: His Life and Work] (Nonthaburi: Commemoration of Ajahn Panyanantha's 80th Birthday, 1991), pp. 63–88; and Karuna Kusalasaya, *Life without a Choice* (Bangkok: Sathirakoses-Nagapradipa Foundation, 1991), pp. 68–72.

For Ajahn Panya's first meeting with Ajahn Buddhadasa at Suan Mokkh, see *Panyanantha 80 (Nonthaburi: Commemoration of Ajahn Panyanantha's 80th Birthday, 1991)*, pp. 158–59.

For Ajahn Panya's preaching in southern Thailand, Chiang Mai, and Bangkok, see Phramaha Chanya Suthiyano, *Chiwit lae ngan khong Than Panyanantha* and *Panyanantha 80.*

The accoount of Buddhadasa's traveling in southern Thailand is from *Lao wai mua wai sonthaya* [As Told in the Twilight Years: The Memoirs of Venerable Buddhadasa] (Bangkok: Komol Kimthong Foundation, 1985; 2003), interviewed by Phra Pracha Pasanna-dhammo, edited by Aurasri Ngamwithayaphong, p. 248.

For Buddhadasa's lecture at Chulalongkorn University, see *Phap chiwit 80 pi Buddhadasa Bhikkhu,* p. 98.

The establishment of the Buddhist Association of Thailand is from Karuna Kusalasaya, *Buddhism in Thailand: Its Past and Its Present* (Kandy, Sri Lanka: Buddhist Publication Society, 1965), p. 28.

Ajahn Buddhadasa's teaching style is quoted from Sulak Sivaraksa, *Loyalty Demands Dissent* (Bangkok: Thai Inter-Religious Commission for Development; Berkeley: Parallax Press, 1998), pp. 88–89.

For the reaction to the lecture Ajahn Panya gave on the radio, see *75 pi Panyanantha Bhikkhu* (1911–1986) (Nonthaburi: Commemoration of Ajahn Panya's 75th Birthday, 1986), pp. 159–60.

Buddhadasa on work is quoted from Buddhadasa Bhikkhu, *Handbook for Mankind* (Bangkok: The Sublime Life Mission, 1984), p. 78.

The quotation from Ajahn Panya's talk to young monks is from Panyanantha Bhikkhu, "Khwam yurot khong phra phutthasatsana [Survival of Buddhism]," *Dhammapadip* 20 (May–June 1995): 12–13.

Buddhadasa's poem on work, translated by Santikaro, is from *Buddhadasa Bhikkhu's Ethical Poems* (Bangkok: Sukkhaphapchai, 2006), p. 45.

For a detailed discussion of TV Westerns, see Ralph Brauer, *The Horse, The Gun and The Piece of Property: Changing Images of the TV Western* (Bowling Green, Ohio: Popular Press, 1975).

For corruption in the police, see Pasuk Phongpaichit and Sungsidh Piriyarangsan, *Corruption & Democracy in Thailand* (Chiang Mai: Silkworm Books, 1994), pp. 108–30.

The quotation from Ajahn Buddhadasa's talk to students at Thammasat University is from Buddhadasa Bhikkhu, *Buddha-Dhamma for Students,* translated by Ariyananda Bhikkhu (Roderick S. Bucknell) (Bangkok: The Dhamma Study and Practice Group, 1988), pp. 71–72.

Ajahn Panya, abbot of Wat Chonprathan, interview by author, January 17, 2001.

For the interview of Ajahn Panya by a journalist, see Henry Fong, "A Champion of Religious Reform," *Bangkok Post,* June 12, 1983, sec. 2, p. 17.

Ajahn Jumnien, abbot of Tiger Cave Monastery, interview by author, June 16, 2004.

Ajahn Jumnien's words "The Dhamma is above politics ..." are cited in Jack Kornfield, *Living Dharma: Teachings of Twelve Buddhist Masters* (Kandy, Sri Lanka: Buddhist Publication Society, 1977; Boston: Shambhala, 1996), p. 283; for Ajahn Jumnien's teachings in English, see pp. 273–86.

For a discussion of Buddhadasa's reintegration of political and social issues within a Dhamma worldview, see Santikaro, "Buddhadasa Bhikkhu: Life and Society through the Natural Eyes of Voidness," in *Engaged Buddhism: Buddhist Liberation Movements in Asia,* edited by Christopher S. Queen and Sallie B. King (Albany: State University of New York Press, 1996), pp. 147–93.

Part I: Ajahn Buddhadasa

CHAPTER 1: A MERCHANT-POET FATHER

For a list of foreign officials in the Thai government in 1909, see Ross Prizzia, "King Chulalongkorn and the Reorganization of Thailand's Provincial Administration," in *Anuson Walter Vella* (Honolulu: Center for Asian and Pacific Studies, University of Hawaii at Manoa, 1986), p. 271.

H. Warrington Smyth, *Five Years in Siam, from 1891–96*, 2 vols. (New York: Charles Scribner's Sons, 1898), 2:70–75.

Buddhadasa, *Lao wai mua wai sonthaya*, pp. 10–12; translated by Santikaro.

The meaning of the name "Nguam" is from Poj Youngpholkan, *Mua rao yang dek* [When I Was Still a Child] (Bangkok: Sukhaphapchai, 2002), p. 61.

Vichak Panich, *Prawat khon bannok thammada: Damri Panich* [The Life Story of an Ordinary Provincial Man: Damri Panich], cremation volume (Bangkok: Damri Panich, 2004), pp. 1–4.

For information on mai takian, see George Bradley McFarland, *Thai-English Dictionary* (Palo Alto, Calif.: Stanford University Press, 1972), pp. 352.

CHAPTER 2: THE ART OF COOKING

W.A.R. Wood, *Consul in Paradise: Sixty-Eight Years in Siam* (London: Souvenir Press, 1965; Chiang Mai: Silkworm Books, 2003), p. 168.

Buddhadasa, *Lao wai mua wai sonthaya*, pp. 6–9.

The arrival of Portuguese in Ayuthaya is from David K. Wyatt, *Thailand: A Short History*, 2nd ed. (New Haven: Yale University Press, 2003), p. 74.

CHAPTER 3: TEACHERS OF FRUGALITY

Buddhadasa, *Lao wai mua wai sonthaya*, pp. 6–7.

For more details about Wachirayan as a spendthrift, see Prince Vajirananavarorasa (Wachirayan), *Autobiography: The Life of Prince-Patriarch Vajirana of Siam* (1860–1921), translated and edited by Craig J. Reynolds (Athens: Ohio University Press, 1979), pp. 19, 22–27.

CHAPTER 4: FIGHTING FISH

Arnold Wright and Oliver T. Breakspear, *Twentieth Century Impressions of Siam: Its History, People, Commerce, Industries, and Resources* (London: Lloyd's Greater Britain Publishing, 1908), p. 237.

W.A.R. Wood, *Consul in Paradise*, p. 77.

Buddhadasa, *Lao wai mua wai sonthaya*, pp. 25–26.

For raising exotic fish at Suan Mokkh, see Santikaro, "Buddhadasa Bhikkhu," p. 149.

"Chatting with the Fish" is translated by Santikaro in *Buddhadasa Bhikkhu's Ethical Poems*, p. 100.

CHAPTER 5: TEACHING TEMPLE BOYS

Buddhadasa, *Lao wai mua wai sonthaya*, pp. 18–19.

For the fruits of donating toilet facilities to the Sangha, see Chapana Pinngoen, "Anisong sang wit [Merit of building toilets]," *Panya: Official Journal of Mahamakut Buddhist University, Lan Na Campus* 9, no. 69 (April–June 2006): 27–30, citing the Apadana text from the Khuddaka Nikaya.

For a treatise on the ten perfections, see Bhikkhu Bodhi, trans., *The Discourse on the All-Embracing Net of Views: The Brahmajala Sutta and Its Commentaries* (Kandy: Buddhist Publication Society, 1992) pp. 243–317.
For examples of how Jataka stories illustrate the ten perfections, see I.B. Horner, *Ten Jataka Stories* (London: Luzac, 1957). For an English translation of the Vessantara Jataka, see Margaret Cone and Richard Gombrich, *Perfect Generosity of Prince Vessantara* (Oxford: Clarendon, 1977).
For more about the preachers of the Vessantara Jataka, see Kamala Tiyavanich, *Forest Recollections* (Honolulu: University of Hawaii Press, 1997), pp. 33–36; and *The Buddha in the Jungle* (Chiang Mai: Silkworm Books; Seattle: University of Washington Press, 2003), pp. 25–32.

CHAPTER 6: TRAINING STORYTELLERS
Buddhadasa, *Lao wai mua wai sonthaya*, pp. 19–20.
Poj, *Mua rao yang dek*, pp. 65–67.

CHAPTER 7: CHAIYA BOXERS
Thawi Chüaiam, "Muai Chaiya [Chaiya Boxing]," translated by Peter Vail, in *Saranukrom Watthanatham Pak Tai*, 7:2716–19.
For the abolition of corvée labor, see David K. Wyatt, *Studies in Thai History* (Chiang Mai: Silkworm Books, 1994), p. 240.
Buddhadasa, *Lao wai mua wai sonthaya*, pp. 15, 18–19.
For Chaiya boys and boxing, see Buddhadasa Bhikkhu, *Naeo sangkhep khong boran khadi rop ao Ban Don* [Fragments of Archaeology around the Bay of Ban Don] (Suratthani: Wat Boromthat, Chaiya, 1950), p. 62.
Dhammadasa Panich, *Prawatsat Chaiya Nakhon Si Thammarat* [A History of Chaiya and Nakhon Si Thammarat] (Suratthani: Dhammadana Foundation, 1998), pp. 164–67.

CHAPTER 8: FOLK REMEDIES
Buddhadasa, *Lao wai mua wai sonthaya*, pp. 12, 16–18.
F.K. Exell, *Siamese Tapestry* (London: Robert Hale, 1963), pp. 141–45.
For information on Sirirat Hospital, see *Medicinal Plants of Thailand: Past and Present* (Bangkok: National Identity Board, 1992).

CHAPTER 9: MODERN EDUCATION
For a discussion of how the Sangha Act of 1902 superseded the older hierarchy, see David K. Wyatt, *Politics of Reform in Thailand: Education in the Reign of King Chulalongkorn* (New Haven: Yale University Press, 1969), p. 247.
For information on the British teachers in the Education Department, see David K. Wyatt, "The Beginning of Modern Education in Thailand, 1868–1910" (Ph.D. diss., Cornell University, 1966), p. 565.
For the impact of modern state Buddhism on local monks, see Kamala, *Forest Recollections*, pp. 18–46, 152–86.
Buddhadasa, *Lao wai mua wai sonthaya*, pp. 21–23.
Poj, *Mua rao yang dek*, pp. 80, 117–18, 121.

Chapter 10: Finding Food

Buddhadasa, *Lao wai mua wai sonthaya*, pp. 23–25, 27.

Prathum Chumphengphan, "Amphoe Chaiya," in *Saranukrom Watthanatham Pak Tai*, 3:1079.

Chapter 11: Local Entertainment

Buddhadasa, *Lao wai mua wai sonthaya*, pp. 26–27, 30–31.

The quotation about Nguam and his bicycle is from Poj, *Mua rao yang dek*, p. 128.

For a discussion of three kinds of manora and nora lineages, see Lorraine M. Gesick, *In the Land of Lady White Blood: Southern Thailand and the Meaning of History* (Ithaca, N.Y.: Cornell Southeast Asia Program, 1995), pp. 66–70.

The information about nora and shadow masters is from an interview with Ajahn Panya, abbot of Wat Chonprathan, January 17, 2001.

Chapter 12: Dhamma Debates

Buddhadasa, *Lao wai mua wai sonthaya*, pp. 27–28, 48–49.

For the Thai version of *The Thousand and One Days* and *The Virgin of the Sun*, see *Phan Nung Thiwa* (Bangkok: Sathirakoses-Nagapradipa Foundation, 1988) and *Soraida* (Bangkok: Sathirakoses-Nagapradipa Foundation, 1990), translated by Sathirakoses and Nagapradipa.

For a brief biographical sketch of K.S.R. Kulap, see Chris Baker and Pasuk Phongpaichit, *A History of Thailand* (New York: Cambridge University Press, 2005), p. 283.

Phra Paisal Visalo's quotation in English is from his article "Buddhism for the Next Century: Toward Renewing a Moral Thai Society," in *Socially Engaged Buddhism for the New Millennium*, pp. 237–38; for a detailed discussion in Thai, see Phra Paisal Visalo, *Buddhasasana thai nai anakhot*, pp. 6–129, 212–44.

For the preaching of the Milindapanha text, see the education-directors' reports of Monthon Nakhon Sawan, Monthon Nakhon Chaisi, Monthon Ratburi, Monthon Chumphon, Monthon Phuket, *Ratchakijjanubeksa* [Royal Thai Government Gazette] (1899–1910). Monthon Chumphon included Luangsuan, Chaiya, and Kanchanadit. Monthon Phuket included Phuket, Krabi, Phang-nga, Ranong, Takuapa, and Trang.

The Questions of King Milinda, translated from the Pali by T.W. Rhys Davids, parts 1 & II (London: Oxford University Press, 1890; Delhi: Motilal Banarsidass, 1965).

Chapter 13: The Culture of Sila-Dhamma

Buddhadasa, *Lao wai mua wai sonthaya*, pp. 29–32, 43–45.

Buddhadasa, *Naeo sangkhep khong borankhadi*, pp. 90, 31.

For the lives of small farmers in the early twentieth century, see Baker and Phongpaichit, *History of Thailand*, pp. 85–89; for the growth of Thai economy, see pp. 140–67.

For a detailed discussion of the tonsure ceremony, see G.E. Gerini, *Chulakantamangala: The Tonsure Ceremony as Performed in Siam* (1893; repr., Bangkok: The Siam Society, 1976).

For a discussion of Buddhadasa's opinions over time, see Louis Gabaude, "Buddhadasa's Contributions: As a Human Being, as a Thai, and as a Buddhist," in *The Quest for a Just Society: The Legacy and Challenge of Buddhadasa Bhikkhu*, edited by Sulak Sivaraksa (Bangkok: Santi Pracha Dhamma Institute, 1994), pp. 71–106.

Part II: Ajahn Panya

CHAPTER 14: VILLAGE LIFE IN MUANG LUNG

Chanya, *Chiwit lae ngan khong Than Panyanantha*, pp. 1–3.

Panyanantha Bhikkhu, *Chiwit khong khapphajao* [My Life] (Bangkok: Commemoration of Ajahn Panyananatha's 72nd Birthday, 1983), pp. 3–4.

Ajahn Panyanantha, abbot of Wat Chonprathan, interview by author, January 17, 2001.

The four conditions for social welfare are excerpted from P.A. Payutto, *Good, Evil and Beyond: Kamma in the Buddha's Teaching*, translated by Bruce Evans (Bangkok: Buddhadhamma Foundation, 1996), pp. 69–71.

CHAPTER 15: LIFE WITH GRANDMOTHERS

Frank K. Exell, *In Siamese Service* (London: Cassell, 1967), p. 47.

Chanya, *Chiwit lae ngan khong Than Panyanantha*, pp. 5–6.

For a Phatthalung version of the tale of the Golden Swan, see Udom Nuthong, "Suwanahong," in *Saranukrom Watthanatham Pak Tai*, 10:3868–71.

CHAPTER 16: BUFFALO BOYS

P.A. Thompson, *Lotus Land: Being an Account of the Country and the People of Southern Siam* (Edinburgh: Riverside, 1906), p. 181.

Harold Fielding Hall, *The Soul of a People* (1898; repr., Bangkok: White Orchid, 1995), pp. 242–43.

Chanya, *Chiwit lae ngan khong than Panyanantha*, pp. 10–11.

Panyanantha, *Chiwit khong khapphajao*, pp. 4–5.

Luang Ta Chi, abbot of Wat Thai, Washington, D.C., interview by author, May 22, 1997.

CHAPTER 17: LEARNING THE FIRST LETTER

Panyanantha, *Chiwit khong khapphajao*, pp. 6–7.

Chanya, *Chiwit lae ngan khong Than Panyanantha*, pp. 7–8.

For a discussion of traditional learning as a religious act, see Wyatt, *Politics of Reform in Thailand*, pp. 5–7.

Charat Buakaeo, "Wat Nanglat," in *Saranukrom Watthanatham Pak Tai*, 5:1743–44.

CHAPTER 18: PASSION AND COMPASSION

Chanya, *Chiwit lae ngan khong Than Panyanantha*, pp. 12–17, 19–20.

S. G. McFarland, "The School of Siam," in *Siam and Laos: As Seen By Our Missionaries* (Philadelphia: Westcott & Thomson, 1884), pp. 207-88.

Panyanantha, *Chiwit khong khapphajao*, pp. 8–12, 18.

Panyanantha, interview.

CHAPTER 19: FOOD FOR BODY AND MIND

Panyanantha, *Chiwit khong khapphajao*, pp. 12–14.

Chanya, *Chiwit lae ngan khong Than Panyanantha*, pp. 20–24.

For the importance of krachut plants in southern Thailand, see Suphak Inthongkhong, "Krachut," in *Saranukrom Watthanatham Pak Tai*, 1:8–14; and McFarland, *Thai-English Dictionary*, p. 22.

CHAPTER 20: MOONSHINE

Chanya, *Chiwit lae ngan khong Than Panyanantha*, pp. 24–26.

Panyanantha, *Chiwit khong khapphajao*, pp. 14–16.

CHAPTER 21: BECOMING A MAN

Chanya, *Chiwit lae ngan khong than Panyanantha*, pp. 27–31.
Panyanantha, *Chiwit khong khapphajao*, pp. 16–19.
Exell, *Siamese Tapestry*, p. 151.
Panyanantha, interview.

CHAPTER 22: BUFFALO BANDITS

Panyanantha, *Chiwit khong khaphachao*, pp. 18–19.
Chanya, *Chiwit lae ngan khong Than Panyanantha*, pp. 3–4.
The story about the bandits is from Lom Phengkaeo, "Chum chon Ban Donsai: Rung Donsai and Dam Hua Phrae [The Community of Ban Donsai: Cockcrow Donsai and Satin-Head Blackie]," in *Saranukrom Watthanatham Pak Tai*, 3:987–92. Today Thale Noi district is called Khuan Khanun district; Wat Kuti has been renamed Wat Suwanwichai.
For the various taxes that the central government imposed on common people, see Sarasawadee Ongsakul, *History of Lanna*, translated by Chitraporn Tanratanakul (Chiang Mai: Silkworm Books, 2005), pp. 189–90. For thirty kinds of taxes the central government imposed on people in southern Siam, see Sangob Songmuang, "Phasi akon chak hua muang pak tai [Taxation in the South]," in *Saranukrom Watthanatham Pak Tai*, 7:2671–72.
Panyanantha, interview.

CHAPTER 23: STORYTELLER IN A TIN MINE

Smyth, *Five Years in Siam, from 1892–1896*, 1:316–21.
Chanya, *Chiwit lae ngan khong Than Panyanantha*, pp. 31–34.
Panyanantha, *Chiwit khong khapphajao*, pp. 20–22.
Panyanantha, interview.

CHAPTER 24: FROM BROTHEL TO TEMPLE

Chanya, *Chiwit lae ngan khong Than Panyanantha*, pp. 34–38.
Panyanantha, *Chiwit khong khapphajao*, pp. 22–23.
Ken Wlaschin, *The Illustrated Encyclopedia of the World's Great Movie Stars and Their Films* (London: Salamanda Books, 1979), pp. 8–35; Joel W. Finler, *The Movie Directors Story* (New York: Crescent Books, 1985), p. 21.
Panyanantha, interview.

CHAPTER 25: HARD LABOR

Panyanantha, *Chiwit khong khapphajao*, pp. 23–25.
Chanya, *Chiwit lae ngan khong Than Panyanantha*, pp. 38–41.

CHAPTER 26: JOURNEY TO MONKHOOD

Panyanantha, *Chiwit khong khapphajao*, pp. 25–27.
Chanya, *Chiwit lae ngan khong Than Panyanantha*, pp. 41–47, 59, 61; and *Panyanantha 80*, pp. 112–13; for the titles of books that Novice Pan read in the 1920s, see pp. 125–26.
Panyanantha, interview.

Part III: Ajahn Jumnien

CHAPTER 27: THE RESTORATION OF A GREAT STUPA

Suthiwong Phongpaibun, "Phra Khru Thepmuni (Paan)," in *Saranukrom Watthanatham Phak Thai*, 6:2231–32.

For the different kinds of Dhammayut monks during King Chulalongkorn's reign, see Kamala, *Forest Recollections*.

Ajahn Jumnien, abbot of Tiger Cave Monastery, interview by author, June 20, 2004.

CHAPTER 28: KITES, DRUMS, AND MEDITATION

Kasemsuk Khemsuko, *Luang Pho Chamnian Silasettho* (Bangkok, Commemoration of Ajahn Jumnien's 60TH Birthday, 1996), pp. 17–20.

Buddhaghosa, *The Path of Purification* (*Visuddhimagga*), translated from the Pali by Bhikkhu Nanamoli (Kandy: Buddhist Publication Society, 1975; Seattle: BPS Pariyatti Editions, 1999), chap. 8, paras. 1–41, pp. 225–35.

Jumnien, interview, June 11, 2004.

CHAPTER 29: IN THE WATER WITH CROCODILES

Kasemsuk, *Luang Pho Chamnian*, pp. 16, 24–25, 27.

Jumnien, interview, June 10, 2004.

CHAPTER 30: HOW TO BECOME INVULNERABLE

Kasemsuk, *Luang Pho Chamnian*, p. 31.

Jumnien, interview, June 10, 2004.

For the ritual of gaining invulnerability at Wat Khao O in Phatthalung, see Chaiyawat Piyakhun, "Chae Ya (Soaking in Medicinal Waters)," in *Saranukrom Watthanatham Phak Thai*, 3:1059–60.

The description of makham pom tree is from McFarland, *Thai-English Dictionary*, p. 632.

Charat Buakhwan, "Kamlang Sua [Tiger Strength]," in *Saranukrom Watthanatham Pak Tai*, 1:189.

CHAPTER 31: THE KARMA OF HARMING MOTHER

For a discussion of the coming of modern geography to Siam, see Thongchai Winichakul, *Siam Mapped: A History of the Geo-Body of a Nation* (Honolulu: University of Hawaii Press, 1994), pp. 37–61.

For a version of Phra Malai in English, see Bonnie Pacala Brereton, *Thai Telling of Phra Malai* (Tempe: Arizona State University, 1995).

Kasemsuk, *Luang Pho Chamnian*, pp. 33, 35.

Jumnien, interview, June 12, 2004.

CHAPTER 32: COPING WITH FAMILY DISASTER

Kasemsuk, *Luang Pho Chamnian*, pp. 36–37.

Jumnien, interview, June 14, 2004.

CHAPTER 33: FINDING A NEW WIFE FOR FATHER

Kasemsuk, *Luang Pho Chamnian*, pp. 49–51.

Jumnien, interview, June 15, 2004.

Leslie Milne, *Shans at Home: Burma's Shan States in the Early 1900s* (London: John Murray, 1910; Bangkok: White Lotus, 2001), pp. 181–82.

CHAPTER 34: LEARNING THE THREE R'S

Jumnien, interview, June 15, 2004.

Peter Skilling, personal communication, October 22, 2005.

For more about Sunthon Phu, see Klaus Wenk, *Thai Literature: An Introduction*, translated from the German by Eric W. Reinhold (Bangkok: White Lotus, 1995), pp. 32–51. For Sunthon Phu's poems in English, see "Lamentations (Ramphan Philap)," translated by Walter F. Vella, in *Anuson Walter Vella* (Honolulu: Center for Asian and Pacific Studies, University of Hawaii at Manoa, 1986), pp. 41–70.

CHAPTER 35: A GATHA TO TAME COBRAS

Exell, *In Siamese Service*, pp. 134–35.

Kasemsuk, *Luang Pho Chamnian*, pp. 45–46.

Jumnien, interview, June 16, 2004.

For stories about blind monks highly revered by local people, see Kamala Tiyavanich, "Venerable Father Dark Eyes," chap. 13 in *The Buddha in the Jungle*, pp. 79–86.

CHAPTER 36: THE PIG AND THE STINGRAY TAIL

Exell, *Siamese Tapestry*, pp. 151–52.

Kasemsuk, *Luang Pho Chamnian*, pp. 38–39.

Jumnien, interview, June 10, 2004.

Payutto, *Good, Evil and Beyond*, p. 78.

For a detailed discussion of the Eightfold Path in English, see Bhante Henepola Gunaratana, *Eight Mindful Steps to Happiness: Walking the Path of the Buddha* (Boston: Wisdom, 2001).

CHAPTER 37: THE GOLDEN BOY AND BANDITS

Hans Morgenthaler, *Matahari: Impressions of the Siamese-Malayan Jungle* (London: George Allen & Unwin, 1923), pp. 104, 46.

Kasemsuk, *Luang Pho Chamnian*, pp. 52–54.

For the making of *phi noi* in northeastern Thailand, see William J. Klausner, *Reflections on Thai Culture* (Bangkok: The Siam Society, 1983), p. 312; for the making of *phrai kuman* in the South, see Lom Phengkaeo, "Phrai Kuman," in *Saranukrom Watthanatham Phak Thai*, 6:2419–20.

Jumnien, interview, June 14, 2004.

CHAPTER 38: HOW TO CAPTURE BANDITS

Exell, *In Siamese Service*, pp. 113–15.

Jumnien, interview, June 14, 2004.

CHAPTER 39: SLINGSHOT EXPERTS

Kasemsuk, *Luang Pho Chamnian*, pp. 40, 60.

Jumnien, interview, June 12, 2004.

The story about Chai and Krae is from Chai Bangkok, *Chiwit chaoban* [Life of Village Folk] (Bangkok: Phrac Phitthaya, 1962), pp. 141–51.

CHAPTER 40: THE CROCODILE HUNTER

Jean-Baptiste Pallegoix, *Description of the Thai Kingdom or Siam: Thailand under King Mongkutt*, translated by Walter E.J. Tips (1854; repr., Bangkok: White Lotus, 2000), p. 89.

Kasemsuk, *Luang Pho Chamnian*, pp. 25–26.

Jumnien, interview, June 15, 2004.

CHAPTER 41: THE HEAD OF A MONKEY TROOP

Kasemsuk, *Luang Pho Chamnian*, pp. 41–43.
Jumnien, interview, June 15, 2004.

CHAPTER 42: THE MONKEY LESSON

Kasemsuk, *Luang Pho Chamnian*, pp. 62–64.
In the southern region the locals believe that if one harms a monkey, his karma will affect him in this life, see Chalieo Ruangdet, "Chai chat (Payback in This Life)," in *Saranukrom Watthanatham Phak Thai*, 3:1060.
Jumnien, interview, June 16, 2004.

CHAPTER 43: COPING WITH ROUGH SEAS

Kasemsuk, *Luang Pho Chamnian*, pp. 36, 59.
Jumnien, interview, June 15, 2004

CHAPTER 44: SHARKS AND SEA SNAKES

Kasemsuk, *Luang Pho Chamnian*, pp. 28–29, 61.
Jumnien, interview, June 15, 2004.
"Sea Snakes," *Encyclopaedia of Animals in Color* (London: Octopus books, 1972) edited by Dr. Maurice Burton, p. 253.

CHAPTER 45: LEARNING BY HEART

For a discussion of Nak-dham study courses, see Steven J. Zack, "Buddhist Education under Prince Wachirayan Warorot" (Ph.D. diss., Cornell University, 1977).
Kasemsuk, *Luang Pho Chamnian*, p. 58.
Jumnien, interview, June 12, 2004.

CHAPTER 46: THE DHAMMA THAT LIFTS YOU UP

The citation from the thudong master is from *Food for the Heart: The Collected Teachings of Ajahn Chah* (Boston: Wisdom, 2002), p. 398.
Kasemsuk, *Luang Pho Chamnian*, pp. 55–56.
Jumnien, interview, June 13, 2004.

CHAPTER 47: DEATH OF A FATHER, NEW LIFE FOR THE SON

Kasemsuk, *Luang Pho Chamnian*, pp. 65–67, 33–34.
Jumnien, interview, June 16, 2004.
For Ajahn Dhammadaro's teachings in English, see Kornfield, *Living Dharma*, pp. 257–70.

Epilogue

Interview with Luang Ta Chi, abbot of Wat Thai, Washington, D.C., May 17–20, 1997. Luang Ta Chi's brief biography was written by his brother, Surachai Sukri, and published in *Phramaha Surasak 72 pi* (Silver Spring, Md.: Wat Thai, Washington, D.C., 1997).

BUDDHADASA'S WORK IN ENGLISH

Buddhadasa Bhikkhu's Ethical Poems. Translated by Santikaro. Bangkok: Sukkha-phapchai, 2006

Dhammic Socialism. Edited by Donald Swearer. Bangkok: Komol Kimtong Foundation, 1986.

Evolution/Liberation. Periodical. Translated and edited by Santikaro. Chaiya: Suan Mokkh, 1988–.

The First Ten Years of Suan Mokkh. Translated by Mongkol Dejnakarintra. Bangkok: Dhamma Study and Practice Group, 1990.

Handbook for Mankind. Translated by Roderick Bucknell. Bangkok: Dhamma Study and Practice Group, 1989.

Heartwood of the Bodhi Tree: The Buddha's Teaching on Voidness. Edited by Santikaro. Translated by Dhammavicaro. Boston: Wisdom, 1994.

Key to Natural Truth. Translated by Santikaro and Roderick Bucknell. Bangkok: Dhamma Study and Practice Group, 1988.

Me and Mine: Selected Essays of Bhikkhu Buddhadasa. Edited by Donald Swearer. Albany: State University of New York Press, 1989.

Mindfulness with Breathing: A Manual for Serious Beginners. Translated by Santikaro. Boston: Wisdom, 1997.

No Religion. Translated by Bhikkhu Punno and Santikaro. Hinsdale, Ill.: Buddha-Dhamma Meditation Center, 1993.

Practical Dependent Origination. Translated by Steven Schmidt. Bangkok: Dhamma Study and Practice Group, 1992.

Toward the Truth. Edited by Donald K. Swearer. Philadelphia: Westminster Press, 1971.

ILLUSTRATION CREDITS

Cover photo: Wright and Breakspear, *Twentieth Century Impressions of Siam: Its History, People, Commerce, Industries, and Resources* (London: Lloyd's Greater Britain Publishing, 1908).

Figs. 1, 2, 7, 16, 20, 22. Maps by David K. Wyatt.

Figs. 3, 4, 8–15. Courtesy of Dhammadana Foundation.

Fig. 5. Courtesy of Wat Chonprathan.

Fig. 6, 26–27. Courtesy of Ajahn Kasemsuk.

Figs. 17, 19, 21. Phramaha Chanya Suthiyano, *Chiwit lae ngan khong Than Panyanantha* [*Venerable Panyanantha: His Life and Work*] (Nonthaburi: Commemoration of Ajahn Panyanantha's 80th Birthday, 1991). Fig. 19. drawing by Pranot.

Fig. 18. Drawing by At Otamphai (1935). Courtesy of Anake Nawikamun.

Fig. 23. H. Warrington Smyth, *Five Years in Siam, from 1891–96*, 2 vols. (New York: Charles Scribner's Sons, 1898).

Figs. 24, 25. Thomas W. Knox, *Adventures of Two Youths in a Journey to Siam and Java* (New York: Harper & Brothers, 1880).

Fig. 28. Courtesy of Wat Thai, Washington, D.C.

ABOUT WISDOM PUBLICATIONS

WISDOM PUBLICATIONS, a nonprofit publisher, is dedicated to making available authentic works relating to Buddhism for the benefit of all. We publish books by ancient and modern masters in all traditions of Buddhism, translations of important texts, and original scholarship. Additionally, we offer books that explore East-West themes unfolding as traditional Buddhism encounters our modern culture in all its aspects. Our titles are published with the appreciation of Buddhism as a living philosophy, and with the special commitment to preserve and transmit important works from Buddhism's many traditions.

To learn more about Wisdom, or to browse books online, visit our website at www.wisdompubs.org.

You may request a copy of our catalog online or by writing to this address:

Wisdom Publications
199 Elm Street
Somerville, Massachusetts 02144 USA
Telephone: 617-776-7416
Fax: 617-776-7841
Email: info@wisdompubs.org
www.wisdompubs.org

THE WISDOM TRUST

As a nonprofit publisher, Wisdom is dedicated to the publication of Dharma books for the benefit of all sentient beings and dependent upon the kindness and generosity of sponsors in order to do so. If you would like to make a donation to Wisdom, you may do so through our website or our Somerville office. If you would like to help sponsor the publication of a book, please write or email us at the address above.

Thank you.

Wisdom is a nonprofit, charitable 501(c)(3) organization affiliated with the Foundation for the Preservation of the Mahayana Tradition (FPMT).

Heartwood of the Bodhi Tree
The Buddha's Teachings on Voidness
Buddhadhasa Bhikkhu
176 pages, ISBN 0-86171-035-5, $15.95

"In this remarkable book, Ajahn Buddhadhasa teaches us beautifully, profoundly, and simply the meaning of sunnata, or voidness, which is a thread that links every great school of Buddhism. He teaches us the truth of this voidness with the same directness and simplicity with which he invites us into his forest."
—from the foreword by Jack Kornfield

"This beautiful book captures the spacious and profound teachings of the Thai forest tradition."—*Inquiring Mind*

"Clear, straightforward, and highly recommended. The reader feels just how possible and practical it is to lead a happy life."—Joseph Goldstein, author of *Insight Meditation: The Practice of Freedom*

Mindfulness With Breathing
A Manual for Serious Beginners
Ajahn Buddhadasa Bhikkhu
Foreword by Larry Rosenberg
160 pages, ISBN 0-86171-111-4, $14.95

"In this book, Ajahn Buddhadhasa will take you by the hand and lead you, as he did me, all the way from the first attempt to observe the in-breaths and out-breaths, to the kinds of insight that have the power to liberate. You will begin with merely a set of instructions, but then you must take these clear words of teaching and put them into practice. If you do, you will not be disappointed. You have in your hands a precious yogic manual."—Larry Rosenberg, Guiding Teacher, Cambridge Insight Meditation Center and author of *Breath by Breath*, from his foreword

In the Buddha's Words
An Anthology of Discourses
from the Pali Canon
Edited and introduced by Bhikkhu Bodhi
Foreword by the Dalai Lama
496 pages, ISBN 0-86171-491-1, $18.95

This landmark collection is the definitive introduction to the Buddha's teachings—in his own words. The American scholar-monk Bhikkhu Bodhi, whose voluminous translations have won widespread acclaim, here presents selected discourses of the Buddha from the Pali Canon, the earliest record of what the Buddha taught. Divided into ten thematic chapters, *In the Buddha's Words* reveals the full scope of the Buddha's discourses, from family life and marriage to renunciation and the path of insight. A concise, informative introduction precedes each chapter, guiding the reader toward a deeper understanding of the texts that follow.

In the Buddha's Words allows even readers unacquainted with Buddhism to grasp the significance of the Buddha's contributions to our world heritage. Taken as a whole, these texts bear eloquent testimony to the breadth and intelligence of the Buddha's teachings, and point the way to an ancient yet ever-vital path. Students and seekers alike will find this systematic presentation indispensable.

"Any amount of study or practice that helps to deepen wisdom and assist us to emerge from layers of delusion is precious. This book could contribute to this enterprise more than almost anything else in print."—Andrew Olendzki, Executive Director of the Barre Center of Buddhist Studies, in *Buddhadharma: The Practitioner's Quarterly*

Great Disciples of the Buddha
Their Lives, Their Works, Their Legacy
Nyanaponika Thera and Hellmuth Hecker
Edited by Bhikkhu Bodhi
412 pp, ISBN 0-86171-381-8, $18.95

In this inspiring book, twenty-four of the Buddha's most distinguished disciples, including eight women, are brought to life in ten chapters of rich narration. Drawn from a wide range of authentic Pali sources, the material in these stories has never before been assembled in a single volume. Through these engaging tales, we meet all manner of human beings—rich, poor, male, female, young, old—whose unique stories are told with an eye to the details of ordinary human concerns. If read with careful attention, these stories can sharpen our understanding of the Buddhist path by allowing us to contemplate the living portraits of the people who fulfilled the early Buddhist ideals of human perfection.

"A truly unique and excellent addition to the literature from the Pali texts. *Great Disciples* is a rich sourcebook, offering lucid stories and translations and brilliant scholarship, all visibly crafted with a love of the Dhamma."—Jack Kornfield, author of *A Path with Heart*

"I recommend it to friends and students alike."—Thich Nhat Hanh, author of *Living Buddha, Living Christ*